Withdrawn

Made in America
Our Best Chefs Reinvent Comfort Food

Lucy Lean

Introduction by Joseph Bastianich

welcome
BOOKS

NEW YORK

To Didier, Minty and Rémy
and the
Plucky Housewives of 2011,
Who Master Their Work Instead of Allowing it to Master Them,
This Book is Dedicated

Published in 2011 by Welcome Books®
An imprint of Welcome Enterprises, Inc.
6 West 18th Street, New York, NY, 10011
(212) 989-3200; fax (212) 989-3205
www.welcomebooks.com

Publisher: Lena Tabori
President: H. Clark Wakabayashi
Editor: Katrina Fried
Designer: Gregory Wakabayashi
Editorial Assistant: Emily Green

ISBN: 978-1-59962-101-2

Library of Congress Cataloging-in-Publication Data on file

First Edition
10 9 8 7 6 5 4 3 2 1

PRINTED IN CHINA

For further information about this book please visit online:
www.madeinamericacookbook.com

Contents

Preface

Lucy Lean

"CAN YOU COOK?" HE ASKED.

"No, but I know you can," I replied.

These were the first words my father-in-law, Jean-Jacques Rachou, and I ever exchanged when we met in Cannes, France, back in the summer of 1996. I had met his son, Didier, two nights earlier in a nightclub of all places, and he invited me to dine with his father. Wanting to do a little background check about this famous chef, I called our family friend Annabel, who lives in New York City, to ask about Rachou's restaurant, La Côte Basque. "I don't have anything fancy enough to wear to dine there," she said, in that self deprecating way English people living in America never lose.

Three months later I packed up my life in London and moved to America and so began my love affair not only with my husband but also with the kitchen.

There's nothing quite like the excitement of restaurant kitchens: so much activity, so many people focused on their piece of a well-oiled machine, so many delicious smells from steaming pots on stoves. The atmosphere is hot and highly charged; working the line is not for the faint-hearted. At the center of it all is "Chef"—checking plates, tasting sauces, giving orders, and running the show.

I am lucky enough to call a lot of the top chefs in America my friends. They welcome me into their restaurants and when I'm really lucky I'm invited back to the kitchen. Many times I've eaten an exquisite restaurant dish and then tried to recreate it at home, with varying degrees of success. I've learned that the easiest way to get the best results is to simply ask the chef for the recipe. Chefs are incredibly generous, they love to share and inspire. To be a great chef perhaps you have to be generous. How else can they give of themselves day and night so the diners have the best possible experience?

I love cooking from recipe books—it's like magic when you follow the instructions and everyone tucks into your creations with gusto. I am particularly fond of looking back through history and exploring early regional American recipe books. I love the short, direct instructions, Twitter's 140 characters would have been a piece of cake for these accomplished cooks. It's amazing that from these brief sentences, often without fixed quantities, anyone could have cooked anything consistent, let alone edible. It's pure alchemy. How could they possibly work without a great deal of prior knowledge? It seems like the cooks in the nineteenth century were much better home cooks than we are today and knew how to fill in the gaps, the recipes being there just as a basic guide.

I needed to learn how to be a better cook and who better to teach me than our country's best chefs? Asking today's chefs for their interpretations of these nineteenth century recipes was not only a way of journeying back through time but also a fun way to explore the culinary landscape of America in the twenty-first century.

Most American food originated somewhere else in the world, was brought here and then adapted and adopted. America is, in the case of food, the true melting pot of many cuisines and cultures. Whether it's spaghetti and meatballs from Italy, apple pie from England, hamburgers and hot dogs from Germany, or fried chicken from African-American slaves and Scottish immigrants—all these dishes and more have come to America and then been made into truly American food. As I traveled from New England to Hawaii and from Chicago to Miami, crisscrossing the country many times, it was refreshing to see how much Americans love their regionally specific cuisine. From truffles in Oregon to Gulf shrimp in Louisiana, the local produce was celebrated and honored by the chefs, as they took pride in the classic American dishes they were reinventing and revisiting.

I not only traveled great distances geographically by plane, train, and automobile, but I also traveled back in time to those early colonial days as I tried to imagine what it was like to cook in America long before gas stoves, refrigerators and electric stand mixers. Early American cooks would have had an open fire with a spit for roasting, later they would have had a wood fired range with no temperature gauge and very limited refrigeration. Yet even with these limitations they somehow managed to make ice cream. What they didn't have in electric gadgets they made up for in utensils, there is a vast "List of Utensils, Needed in Every Well-to-do Family of Six Persons or More" in *How We Cook in Los Angeles* (1894) and Mrs. Lincoln

writes pages and pages on utensils and the care of them in her *Boston Cook Book* (1884).

The good news is that home cooks today have access to a far greater variety of produce than anyone cooking in the nineteenth century. Mario Batali wisely says to buy less but shop more often—there's nothing like fresh, local ingredients to elevate any dish. At the Santa Monica Farmers' Market chefs can be seen navigating the crowds with flats of peaches, pluots or potatoes. Here you can buy the exact same tomato or butternut squash that a two-star Michelin chef is selecting for his menu. Most of these chefs shop at their local farmers' market because the food tastes better for it and in a number of cases around the country they are cultivating the land themselves.

Throughout this delicious journey, I cooked every dish in the book, and collaborated with the chefs to make sure their recipes work for the home cook, in some cases I had to reduce the yield and in others I simply pared the recipe back so that it wasn't off putting by its sheer complexity. I have tried to keep the more challenging aspects of the recipes as an optional item—a fancy garnish or side—rather than the heart of the dish. I hope that in some small way these recipes feel like you have invited America's chefs into your kitchen to cook with you.

I've included as many chef's tips as possible—things that they take for granted but will really help you to get the best results. My mantra was always, "If I can cook it, anyone can." The best part about learning from a professional is in the details of their technique, which can make the difference between a good dish and a great dish. Alain Ducasse was kind enough to share his tips for cutting onions with me, going straight to the underpinnings of most cooking—the knife. "The fumes that cause your eyes to water are released when the petals are crushed," says Ducasse, "a common issue when slicing with a dull knife. Minimize the tears by using a properly sharpened blade that will cut the vegetable cleanly." Valuable advice to follow when making his French onion soup and for any recipe that requires chopped onion—I think of Ducasse every time my eyes tear up in the kitchen. So sharpen your knives and let the cooking begin.

Introduction

Joseph Bastianich

FOOD IS THE LIFEBLOOD OF THIS COUN-
try, in all its glorious variety. It tells our story, the story of
America. Immigrants arrived in this country often with
little but culinary know-how. They adapted their life to
their lot, their recipes to their situation, and American
cuisine with all its wonderful diversity was born.

My own history as an Italian American is inextrica-
bly linked to what we eat. Growing up in Queens, New
York, the son of Italian immigrants who forged ahead
making a living as restaurateurs, food is what made it
possible for my family to survive here, and shaped the
man I was to become. It defines me as it defines a Chinese American, or a German American or Japanese
American.

So when Lucy Lean told me about her project, I
was beyond excited. Here was an English woman, married to an American, with a French father-in-law, setting off on a culinary journey across the United States.
Armed with a camera, a laptop, and her historical research, she invited top chefs to reinterpret recipes from
years gone by. Her itinerary was astonishing. She is so
obviously passionate about food that people just open up
and seem happy to share their wisdom and their time
with her. Gaining privileged behind-the-scenes access
to the kitchens of America's greatest chefs, she watched,
she listened, and she learned.

Lucy is a fierce advocate for sourcing local, seasonal, and sustainable ingredients and so are the chefs she's
profiled in this book. Across America, professional cooks
take pride in their local produce and their relationships
with farmers and artisans. Restaurant menus trumpet
the origins of meat, cheese, fruit and vegetables. This,
for me, is real progress. In a country so vast, we are finally accepting the importance of our own small plot
of land. This was particularly evident to me during my

experience as a judge on *MasterChef*. Home cooks from
every state proudly brought forth dishes they grew up
making, passed down from their parents and grandparents, all examples of local ingredients and techniques.

I feel privileged to be a part of this inspiring time in
America's restaurant scene. In every city, in every town,
there are gems to be found, and local brilliance shines
out. Never has there been such a stellar and passionate
group of chefs whose culinary innovations break new
boundaries every day. Who better to rework our staple
dishes? The results are nothing short of mind blowing.
A classic Reuben sandwich in the hands of Marc Vetri
becomes a delicious Italian American treasure, and the
iconic hot dog gets new life from the Swiss born Daniel
Humm—it doesn't get any more American than that.

Very much like food itself, Lucy has a knack for
bringing people together, and has found a way to present these recipes in a way that makes them accessible to
everyone, no matter what your level of culinary prowess
may be. She shares our top chefs' reinterpretations of
classic American recipes so that you, in turn, can create
and enjoy them in your own kitchen.

Made in America is a seminal book for all home
cooks. By putting a new twist on our beloved traditions,
these recipes showcase American cookery at its best,
while maintaining a sense a reverence for the original.
It is a vast project spanning time and geography, a huge
undertaking that only the tenacious Lucy Lean could
have pulled off. She has taken the pulse of America's
kitchens and I am very happy to say that from shore to
shore, we are in very good health.

This masterful anthology will inspire and inform
you. Lucy has distilled the very best of what this country has to offer. One hundred chefs, one hundred great
recipes: *Made in America*.

Breakfast & Brunch

Grandma's Fines Herbes French Omelet

ALAIN GIRAUD [Maison Giraud, *Los Angeles, California*]

"MY MATERNAL GRANDMOTHER LIVED IN A FARMHOUSE IN Corrèze, the green department of France," says Alain Giraud. "This undiscovered part of France is one of the best places on earth, and where I spent my childhood, before moving to Provence. My grandmother used to cook this type of omelet for dinner, served with a very vinegary salad on the side. The potatoes came from the garden and the eggs from the chicken coop. She kept dozens of hens and we always had lots of fresh eggs—perfect for omelets. During the winter she used to cook it on top of the fireplace. The lightly smoky taste is still in my mouth, and my heart."

So simple, and yet so easy to do wrong. Who better to ask how to make an omelet than a Frenchman—and one who has been cooking in the top restaurants of Los Angeles (Citrus, Bastide and Anisette) for twenty years? In French kitchens, making an omelet is often the first test given to a new cook. Like all things, perfection is often hard to attain, but practice does make perfect. In the late 1800s, the art of making a good omelet was also much discussed. "Failures come from beating the eggs until they are too light, or having the butter too hot, or cooking the omelet too long," warns Mrs. S. T. Rorer in *Many Ways for Cooking Eggs* (1907). And in *Miss Parloa's New Cook Book* (1882), the author writes, "There is no better form in which to serve egg. So few people make a good omelet that it is one of the last things the inexperienced housekeeper or cook will attempt."

Giraud and I meet at the Santa Monica Farmers' Market on a sunny Wednesday morning to shop for omelet ingredients. Spending any time with Giraud is always fun, flirtatious, and undeniably French. Our first stop is the Weiser Family Farms stand to chat with owner Alex Weiser, and to pick out a few French pink potatoes. Giraud is a regular at the market—he pauses frequently to shake hands with a friend or greet a farmer, and he knows which stall is best for every ingredient. "The best strawberries are Harry's," he says, as we pass Harry's Berries. "But sixteen dollars a basket is a lot." I ask him if it's worth the price, and he's adamant. "It's like a wine, you pay three hundred dollars for a Burgundy against a shit-cheap wine, it makes a difference. Buy a cheap strawberry at the supermarket and you compare it to a Gaviota or a Seascape from Harry's Berries and there is no doubt: night and day. The texture, flavor, it tastes like a strawberry, and you can remember why it is that you fell in love with it so much." At the Schaner Farms table Giraud greets Peter Schaner, the owner, who is sorting boxes in his truck. "Peter has the best eggs. In France they have a saying, *On ne fait pas d'omelette sans casser des oeufs* [You can't make an omelet without breaking eggs]."

When asked to describe his dream restaurant he becomes very animated. "Not high-end, but not bistro—and spontaneous: today I buy this and tonight I want to cook that. To approach it from the ingredients. I want to have the luxury to buy those Harry's Berries strawberries." Giraud's dream will soon be a reality. He is opening Maison Giraud in the Pacific Palisades, a neighborhood restaurant that will serve breakfast, lunch, and dinner. No doubt a version of his grandmother's French omelet will be on the menu, with a bright frisée salad and perhaps a glass of rosé.

Grandma's Fines Herbes French Omelet

This is a large omelet, made for sharing, and contains the best of the farmers' market. If you need to feed four, make two 6-egg omelets rather than one that's double the size. Using the freshest possible herbs will transform a simple dish like this into something spectacular. The single best bit of advice I can give a home cook is to plant an herb garden—you can always start small with just a couple of containers.

2 medium red French fingerling potatoes, unpeeled

6 farm eggs

1½ tablespoons crème fraîche

Salt and freshly ground pepper

1½ tablespoons fresh fines herbes (parsley, chives, chervil, and tarragon, picked very, very fine)

2 teaspoons corn oil

3 slices thick-cut, applewood bacon, diced

½ a scallion, peeled and finely sliced

1 shallot, finely sliced

1 tablespoon unsalted butter

MAKES 1 OMELET, LARGE ENOUGH TO SERVE 2

1. Bring a small pot of water to a boil and add the potatoes (skin on). Cook the potatoes until tender. Peel while still warm, cut into ½-inch dice, and reserve.

2. Break the eggs into a large bowl and beat them well; add the crème fraîche and the herbs. Season lightly with salt and pepper.

3. In a large skillet, heat the corn oil and butter on medium-low heat. Add the bacon and cook until crisp. Add the spring onion and shallots and cook until tender. Add the potatoes.

4. Increase the temperature to medium-high and pour in the beaten eggs. Shake the pan vigorously until the eggs start to thicken, then stop as the mixture browns. When the omelet is almost cooked through, carefully fold one half over onto the other half and transfer it to a large platter, preferably warmed.

5. Serve immediately with country bread and a seasonal salad with a French vinaigrette.

Chef Giraud's Tips

"The bacon will add salt, so be careful not to oversalt when you season."

"The herbs are not chopped, they are hand picked—and they are put in the omelet, not sprinkled on the top as a garnish."

Soft-Boiled Duck Eggs with Nettle Pesto, Porcini, and Parmigiano-Reggiano

ETHAN STOWELL [Staple & Fancy Mercantile, *Seattle, Washington*]

WITH FOUR SUCCESSFUL RESTAURANTS IN SEATTLE, ALL WITH different menus that often change daily depending on what's in season, Ethan Stowell is a very busy man. At Staple & Fancy Mercantile, Stowell is in the kitchen—he's the chef. He prefers that his diners put the meal planning into his hands so that he can create the most well-balanced, memorable progression of dishes. The menu states: "If you would like to avoid the trouble of ordering altogether, please feel free to hand your menu back to your server and let the kitchen prepare you a family style supper served in four courses . . . We would also like to inform you that you really should do this."

The technique of boiling eggs goes far back into history— early settlers ate a lot of eggs because chickens were easy to bring over with them on the ships and would provide breakfast, lunch, or dinner. Early American cookbooks are full of amusing opinions such as the importance of cleaning the eggs before boiling, because "a dirty egg is vulgar."

Stowell's recipe for duck eggs reflects his Italian style of cooking and showcases foraged ingredients like nettles and porcini. Duck eggs are beautiful soft boiled—they have a bigger yolk-to-white ratio than chicken eggs so it's easier to get the right balance of soft-boiled yolk and cooked-through white.

Porcini are found in the Northwest in the early summer with other varieties harvested later in the year. Named after their resemblance to "little pigs," porcini are also known as "the poor man's steak" because of their meaty flavor. For his recipe, Stowell marinates paper-thin slices of foraged button porcini with lemon juice. Make sure you know what you are looking for before you set out to forage for wild food—mushrooms can be poisonous. (If in France, you can take wild mushrooms to the pharmacist and he will identify them for you.) You might also get lucky and find wild mushrooms at the local market. In New York City at the Union Square Greenmarket, I recently found a hen of the woods—the whole mushroom would have cost nearly one hundred dollars, but luckily a little goes a long way. A few choice pieces cooked up in a little olive oil with salt and pepper were enough to feed four of us for brunch.

Freshly picked nettles are also called for in this dish—I "foraged" a nice bunch at the farmers' market, along with a half-dozen fresh, farm duck eggs. Be careful—they aren't called stinging nettles for nothing, and I learned the hard way. If you aren't able to find nettles—either in the countryside or at the market—Stowell suggests substituting the more traditional basil or parsley pesto. However, try to forage—there's nothing more satisfying than being a hunter (of little piggies) and a gatherer (of beastly stinging nettles).

6 fresh duck eggs

1/4 cup white vinegar

1/4 pound button-size fresh porcini mushrooms

1/2 lemon

1/4 pound fresh nettles, stems removed

3 cloves garlic

3/4 cup toasted pine nuts

1 cup extra-virgin olive oil

1 cup grated Parmigiano-Reggiano cheese, plus a small chunk for shaving as a garnish

Salt and freshly ground pepper

SERVES 4

1. Bring a medium pot of water to a soft boil and add the vinegar. Carefully place the duck eggs in the pot and cook at a slow boil for 7 to 8 minutes.

2. Using a slotted spoon, immediately transfer the eggs to a large bowl of ice water to stop the cooking process. When the eggs are cold, remove them from the ice water and carefully remove the shell. Place in the refrigerator until ready to serve.

3. Bring a pot of salted water to a boil and prepare an ice bath. Add the nettles to the boiling water and cook for 3 minutes, then immediately plunge them into the ice bath to stop the cooking process. Remove the nettles, squeeze dry, and chop finely.

4. Combine the nettles, garlic, pine nuts, and a pinch of salt in a food processor. Purée, adding the olive oil in a steady stream, until you have a thick, uniform paste. Transfer to a bowl and fold in the grated cheese. Taste and adjust the seasoning with salt and pepper, and set the pesto aside at room temperature until needed.

5. Slice the mushrooms paper thin using a mandoline and lay out flat on a large plate. Sprinkle with salt, pepper, a little olive oil, and a few drops of lemon juice. Marinate for 5 minutes.

6. Cut the duck eggs in half lengthwise and season with salt and pepper. Place a dollop of nettle pesto on top of each egg half, then a few slices of marinated porcini mushrooms, and finally, using a vegetable peeler, shave a few strips of Parmigiano-Reggiano over the top. Serve 3 halves per plate.

Chef Stowell's Tip

"When the porcini mushrooms are not in season, you can just clean any wild mushrooms, give them a quick sauté in olive oil and salt, then cool them down and add as a component to the dish."

Scrambled Eggs, Smoked Salmon Threads, and Crushed Bagel Chips

WYLIE DUFRESNE [wd-50, *New York, New York*]

THE MAD SCIENTIST, THE KITCHEN GADGET GEEK, THE BRIL-
liant chef, Wylie Dufresne, is doing such exciting things in his kitchen at wd-50 in New
York City's Lower East Side, particularly with eggs. This is a man who takes yolks, covers them in a plastic "sausage skin," and slow-cooks them with precision in an immersion
circulator. The result is a thick yellow custard. He cuts off a tiny cylinder and offers it to
me to try on the end of the knife. It's dense, with the consistency of soft fudge—almost
chewy. There are other "top-secret" cooking techniques that he's working on in the kitch-
en, which he asks me not to disclose. No security leaks here, my lips are sealed.

With the intensity of the obsessive that he is, he grills me about the concept of the
book, why I'm doing it, what he can bring to it, and more. "What's the point of having
chefs cook comfort food?" he asks. Despite the tough questions, I enjoy this probing discussion, refreshingly in-depth and intellectual. He gets so inside his subject that you can
see why he's not agreeing to commit so easily—he has to really believe in something to do
it, there are no half-measures here.

"I have a personal connection to eggs, and think I can make something really fun
with them," Dufresne says. He settles on using the traditional New York bagel with
cream cheese and lox as his inspiration for scrambled eggs. "To make the best scrambled
eggs you've ever had, here's my first tip: include cream cheese—it gives a nice texture.
The great thing about cream cheese is it doesn't break down when it melts, the oil doesn't
separate out. It's also very American and everyone knows what it is and loves it."

Dufresne disappears into the kitchen and reappears a moment later with a little
container of pale pink "powdered" smoked salmon. By cooking the salmon for a very long
time with constant stirring, it turns into dry, light, and airy threads (like saffron almost).
"It's lovely with scrambled eggs. It's an old Japanese technique. I was inspired by the
seasoned salmon flakes in the book *Washoku: Recipes from a Japanese Home Kitchen* by

Elizabeth Andoh and we modified it slightly." It's very
easy to make, can be done in advance, and can be stored
for up to a month. "This would be lovely scattered on
top with some chopped chives and some bagel chips for
texture." In the restaurant Dufresne would freeze a bagel and then use the industrial deli slicer to make perfect
thin slices. For the home cook he has a solution: "Buy
bagel chips, put them in a sandwich bag, and just give
them a whack with a rolling pin. Sprinkle them on top.
No shame in store-bought." He suggests mixing it up
by using differently flavored bagel chips but warns, "If
you use cinnamon raisin it's going to be kinda gross—
the eggs with the sweet bagel chip is okay, but with the
fish?" He makes a face and then adds, "But, hey, we're
not judging, right? Whatever floats your boat."

Scrambled Eggs, Smoked Salmon Threads, and Crushed Bagel Chips

Dufresne elevates a breakfast staple with his unique combination of textures and flavors—creamy yellow eggs with crunchy crushed bagel chips, and soft, salty, smoked salmon threads. The secret to the scrambled eggs is the cream cheese, which Dufresne likes for its melting properties and richness. Once you've tasted Dufresne's scrambled eggs, you'll never make them any other way again.

Smoked Salmon Threads

1 boneless, skinless salmon fillet (about 4 1/2 ounces)

1 piece kombu (about 3 1/2 ounces)

3 tablespoons sake

2 teaspoons soy sauce

1 to 2 drops liquid smoke

Scrambled Eggs

7 large eggs

2 tablespoons (1/4 stick) unsalted butter

3 ounces cream cheese

Salt

Cayenne pepper

1 tablespoon chopped fresh chives

4 tablespoons Smoked Salmon Threads

1 small bag bagel chips

SERVES 4

To Make the Smoked Salmon Threads

1. Place the salmon and kombu in a small pot and cover with cold water. Bring to a simmer and cook for 5 minutes, or until the salmon is cooked through. Drain and discard the water and kombu. Rinse the fish under cold running water to cool.

2. Once cool, using your hands, shred the salmon as finely as possible. Place into a nonstick pan and add the sake. Cook over medium heat, stirring constantly with a silicone or plastic spatula. As the salmon dries, it will become light and fluffy, 5 to 7 minutes. Add the soy sauce and continue cooking for 5 more minutes. Stir in the liquid smoke and let cool. (This can be stored for up to 1 month in an airtight container.)

To Make the Scrambled Eggs

1. In a bowl, whisk the eggs. Heat a medium saucepan over medium heat, add the butter, and once it begins to foam, add the eggs. Using a sauce whisk, stir vigorously and constantly for 2 minutes, or until soft, loose curds form.

2. Add the cream cheese and cook 2 to 3 minutes more, being careful not to overcook the eggs. Season with salt and cayenne and divide the egg mixture among four bowls. Top with chopped chives, smoked salmon threads, and crushed bagel chips. Serve immediately.

Chef Dufresne's Tip

"If you don't have liquid smoke, you can incorporate a small amount of smoked salmon into the regular salmon to give a smoky flavor."

Coddled Sea Island Farm Egg with Stone Crab, Parsnip Cream, English Peas, and Country Ham

Mike Lata [FIG, *Charleston, South Carolina*]

SO MANY CHEFS TELL ME THE SAME thing: always prepare your ingredients ahead of time (known as *mise en place* in restaurant kitchens). Mike Lata is no different when I ask him how to get the best results from his recipe. "This is definitely one of those dishes that has to be 'mise en placed,'" Lata says. "Take the time to read and reread the recipe. Get all the ingredients in front of you before you start, and then proceed with focus and confidence. Visualize your guests enjoying the dish. Take that inspiration and babysit the egg from oven to table."

Lata's restaurant FIG: Food Is Good, is all about the food. "We have a passion for pure flavor, quality ingredients, and for creating an atmosphere that is convivial, approachable, and a haven for people who simply love food." Lata has been sourcing his ingredients locally and encouraging others to do the same in Charleston since he moved there in 1998. Time spent cooking in France also influences Lata's ever-changing seasonal menu at FIG, which has garnered many awards, not the least being a James Beard Award for the chef.

In *Many Ways For Cooking Eggs* (1907), a recipe for "Eggs en Cocotte" calls for a mixture of onions, mushrooms, and parsley in the base of the cup, and then instructs: "Break into each cup one egg. Pour over remaining mixture. Stand the cups in a pan of hot water and bake in a moderate oven about five minutes."

Coddling eggs is a good technique to master because you can be creative and serve them with so many ingredients, depending on what looks best at your local market. Here we have it with stone crabmeat, English peas, and a parsnip cream, but if those ingredients aren't readily available, use what is. "We change the topping of the egg—as well as the purée—seasonally," says Lata. "In the early summer, we might do a potato purée and garnish with corn, peppers, and basil. Let the seasons inspire the composition. Just be sure to use an ingredient that produces a luxurious texture."

2 cups parsnips, peeled and diced

1 small leek, white part only, diced

3/4 cup whole milk

1/2 cup heavy cream

Fresh bay leaf

1 teaspoon sea salt, plus extra for topping

8 farm eggs

3 tablespoons unsalted butter

1 pound picked fresh stone crabmeat (or lump crab)

1 cup English peas, blanched

4 thin slices of country ham or prosciutto, julienned

1 tablespoon fresh snipped chives

1 loaf brioche

SERVES 8

1. Combine the parsnips, leek, milk, cream, bay leaf, and a teaspoon of sea salt; simmer very lightly until the vegetables are tender. Remove the bay leaf and reserve 1/4 cup of the cooking liquid. Purée in a blender, adding in the reserved cooking liquid as needed, until the consistency is silky smooth. Place the parsnip mixture in a small pan and cover with plastic wrap. Keep warm.

2. Heat the oven to 325°F.

3. Place eight 8-ounce ramekins in a deep casserole dish and quarter fill each ramekin with parsnip cream, about 4 tablespoons each. Crack an egg into a coffee cup and slide it onto the parsnip cream. Repeat for the other ramekins. When all the eggs are in, place the casserole in the oven and fill with hot water until it reaches halfway up the sides of the ramekins. Bake for 8 to 10 minutes, until the whites are firm and the yolks are still runny. It is important not to leave the kitchen during this time, since the eggs can go from perfect to overdone in seconds.

4. In the meantime, melt the butter in a small sauté pan. Swirl it around over medium heat until it begins to foam up and brown. Add the crab, peas, and ham. Warm through, season with salt, and finish with the chives. Slice and toast the brioche.

5. When the eggs are done, divide the stone crab mixture among the tops of the ramekins and sprinkle with a touch of sea salt. Serve the with toasted brioche.

Paniolo Breakfast Skillet Roast Beef Hash with Fried Eggs and Crispy Onions

JAMES BABIAN [Pahu i`a, Hualālai Four Seasons Resort, *Hawaii*]

THE HUALALAI FOUR SEASONS RESORT SITS IN THE ANCIENT land division known as Ka'ūpūlehu, once a thriving fishing village, and the cooks in James Babian's kitchen still fish the local waters during their free time. Babian enjoys the bounty and variety of produce from the Big Island and works closely with his local farmers to get the best ingredients—fresh lobster and baby abalone, artisan honey and goat cheese, Kona coffee and avocados. He is particularly proud of the beef on the menu, sourced from the local Kahua Ranch in North Kohala on the northern tip of the Big Island.

Here we have Babian's *paniolo* beef hash cooked up in a cast-iron skillet—no campfire needed. The *paniolos* [Hawaiian cowboys] are part of a rich tradition and history on the islands—they taught the Hawaiians their ranching skills, and presumably their outdoor cooking techniques, too.

Crispy Onions

1 large Spanish onion, sliced very thinly on a mandoline

2 cups whole milk

2 tablespoons Cajun seasoning

2 cups all-purpose flour

1 quart canola oil

Roast Beef Hash

2 cups Yukon Gold potatoes, peeled, cut into 1/4-inch dice

3 tablespoons sea salt

1/4 cup olive oil

1 medium Spanish onion, diced

1/2 small green bell pepper, cut into small dice

1/2 small red bell pepper, cut into small dice

2 cups cooked roast beef, cut into 1/2-inch dice

2 cloves garlic, minced

1 sprig thyme, leaves picked

3 tablespoons chopped fresh flat-leaf parsley

1 tablespoon Worcestershire sauce

Salt and freshly ground pepper

1 pinch cayenne pepper or paprika

Beef broth, if desired

6 large eggs, fried

6 slices sourdough bread, toasted

SERVES 6

To Make the Crispy Onions

1. Soak the sliced onion in the milk for 30 minutes, then drain well.

2. Mix the Cajun seasoning into the flour and dust the onion rings in the seasoned flour.

3. Pour the canola oil into a deep, heavy-bottomed pot. Heat the oil to 350°F over medium-high heat. Line a large plate with paper towels. Carefully lower the floured onion slices into the hot oil, a few at a time, and fry for about 2 minutes, or until golden and crispy. Remove from the oil with a slotted spoon and transfer to the paper towels to drain off excess oil. Continue frying until all the onions are cooked. Set them aside.

To Make the Roast Beef Hash

1. In a medium saucepan, bring 3 quarts of water to a boil, and add 3 tablespoons of sea salt. Reduce to a simmer, add the potatoes, and cook for 3 minutes, or until they just start to become tender. Drain and spread on a small sheet pan. Refrigerate for a few minutes to stop the cooking.

2. In a large nonstick skillet, heat the olive oil over medium heat. Add the potatoes and cook until they just start to brown. Add the diced onion and bell peppers and cook another 3 to 4 minutes, stirring or tossing often. Add the beef and toss well. Add the garlic, 2 tablespoons of fresh thyme leaves, and 1 tablespoon of the chopped parsley and toss well. Cook until the potatoes are golden brown.

3. Add the Worcestershire sauce and season with salt and pepper to taste. Continue to toss until the hash begins to caramelize but not burn. You can add beef broth to keep the hash moist, if desired. The chef prefers his a bit crispy and caramelized. You can also add a bit more olive oil, if desired.

4. Fry the eggs. Divide the hash evenly among six plates and top with the fried eggs. Top the eggs with the remaining tablespoon of chopped parsley, a pinch of cayenne or paprika, and some crispy onions.

5. Serve with sourdough toast.

Chef Babian's Tips

"If you do not have a deep-fry thermometer, heat the canola oil until a small piece of bread dropped in rises quickly to the surface and starts to brown."

"This recipe a great way to use up leftover roasts, it can also be done with short ribs, prime rib, pot roast, and turkey."

"You can also add beef gravy to the hash at the end of the cooking, or drizzle some on top of the eggs and hash after plating."

Truffled Egg Toast

JASON DENTON ['ino, *New York, New York*]

A recipe for "Birds' Nests" from Many Ways for Cooking Eggs *by Mrs. S. T. Rorer, published in 1907.*

LONG BEFORE PANINI-PRESSED SAND-wiches were everywhere, Jason Denton experienced a life-changing moment over bruschetta at a little café in Liguria, Italy, with his wife, who said, "We can do this." She wrote out the menu for 'ino, a small panini shop in the West Village that serves wine and small plates, and Denton executed the plan. *Ino* in Italian is a suffix meaning "smallness," and the place is exactly that (the tiny open kitchen at the back of the restaurant is probably the smallest I visited in my travels around America). The flavors created here, however, are not.

Jason Denton grew up in Kimberly, a town near the city of Twin Falls, Idaho. His grandfather had subscriptions to the *New York Times* and *Gourmet*, and he remembers eagerly reading each issue, gathering as much information as he could about food and entertaining. Following a trip around Europe and North Africa at the age of twenty-four, he ended up in London, from where he was promptly deported. Back in the States he worked for Mario Batali at Pó in New York before branching out on his own.

Denton's recipe for Truffled Egg Toast calls for yolks cooked in the centers of hollowed-out toast slices served with melted cheese, truffle oil, asparagus, and lots of salt and pepper. It has been on the menu since 'ino opened, back in 1998.

In Mrs. S. T. Rorer's book *Many Ways for Cooking Eggs* (1907), there is a recipe for "Birds' Nests." Rorer separates the eggs and beats the whites to create a frothy nest for the yolks to sit in. "This is one of the most sightly of all egg dishes," says Rorer. Denton makes it easy, using carved-out bread for his nests, and suggests using the egg whites for an omelet. You can also get creative and give the nests a more modern look by using a large cookie cutter to shape the bread into circles.

Birds' Nests

Separate the eggs, allowing one to each person. Beat the whites to a stiff froth. Heap them into individual dishes, make a nest, or hole, in the center. Drop into this a whole yolk. Stand the dish in a pan of water, cover, and cook in the oven about two or three minutes. Dust lightly with salt and pepper, put a tiny bit of butter in the center of each, and send at once to the table. This is one of the most sightly of all egg dishes

2 asparagus spears, woody
  stems removed

4 slices white bread,
  1 inch thick

8 thin slices of Fontina cheese
  (about 6 ounces)

8 large egg yolks

3 tablespoons truffle-
  infused oil

1/2 teaspoon coarse sea salt

Freshly ground pepper

SERVES 4

1. Preheat the oven to 350°F.

2. Using a panini grill, an outdoor grill, or a griddle pan, grill the asparagus spears for 2 minutes, or until they appear roasted but are still crunchy. Transfer them to a cutting board and slice thinly on the diagonal. Set aside.

3. Lightly toast the bread. Using a serrated knife, score a 2-inch square in the center of each slice; then use the handle end of the knife to press the squares down, creating indentations to contain the eggs.

4. Place the toast on a sheet pan and arrange the Fontina slices to form borders around the indented centers, with no cheese overhanging.

5. Place 2 yolks into the center of each slice of bread and place the sheet pan in the oven. Heat until the cheese has melted and begins to bubble, about 3 minutes. For those who prefer a fully cooked egg, bake the toast for an additional 2 minutes, or until the yellows have set.

6. Transfer the toast to four small serving plates. Stir the runny yolks with the tip of a knife and garnish with the asparagus slices. Drizzle a generous amount of truffle oil over each and sprinkle with salt and pepper. Serve immediately.

Our Daily Bread Eggs à la Benedictus

JEFF MICHAUD [Osteria, *Philadelphia, Pennsylvania*]

TAKING A WELL-KNOWN AMERICAN FAVORITE, EGGS BENEDICT, and switching it up is a risky thing to do, but Jeff Michaud is up for the challenge. In fact, he serves a version of this dish at his restaurant Osteria in Philadelphia. "The *zabaione* is almost like a hollandaise and is our Italian twist on eggs Benedict," says Michaud. In 2010, Michaud won the James Beard Award for Best Mid-Atlantic Chef, and his restaurant was nominated as a Best New Restaurant. Not bad for someone who started cooking at the age of thirteen at a pizza shop in New Hampshire. After graduating from the Culinary Institute of America, he decided to move to Italy for three years to really get inside the cuisine and hone his skills. In addition to cooking in restaurants, he worked in a butcher's shop, where he learned all about making salami and sausage, as well as how to break down an animal.

There are several stories about the origins of eggs Benedict—all surrounding late-nineteenth-century New York. According to one, Charles Ranhofer created "Eggs à la Benedick" for his customer Mrs. LeGrand Benedict, and there is a recipe for it in his book *The Epicurean* (1894). In the story of the Waldorf's claim to the dish—which was written up in *The New Yorker* decades later—Mr. Benedict, a wealthy stockbroker, asked for toast topped with bacon, poached eggs, and hollandaise to cure his hangover. Two people, both named Benedict, had the same idea for a poached-egg sandwich and they definitely weren't the only ones. Mary Lincoln in the 1896 edition of her book *Mrs. Lincoln's Boston Cook Book* includes a recipe for "Dropped or Poached Eggs on Toast." She cuts the toast with a round cutter, and suggests making a thin cream sauce to pour around them. She goes on to recommend using muffin rings to give the poached eggs a better shape and includes an option to "serve poached eggs on thin slices of broiled or fried ham."

Eggs Benedict did not start appearing on restaurant menus until quite a bit later, with an English muffin substituted for the toast, and bacon replaced by ham. Michaud uses the original bread option like Mrs. Lincoln, with a thin zabaione sauce and fried mortadella—he also includes the recipe for the bread used in his delicious sandwich.

Mrs. S. T. Rorer in the *Philadelphia Cook Book* (1886), writes, "Bread heads the list of foods for man. It is said a slave of an archon at Athens first made leaven bread by accident." (He apparently discovered some old dough that was sour, and rather than throw it away he mixed it with fresh dough.) "Of course the bread this produced was delicious." Her "Milk Bread" is a basic everyday bread similar to Michaud's American sandwich bread.

Michaud's wonderfully simple bread recipe reads much like one from the nineteenth century. He lists the ingredients and then two lines of instruction—that's it: mix, proof, and bake! I have adapted it slightly and added a few more details to the steps, but here it is—a very accessible bread recipe. Use it for sandwiches, including Michaud's Italian version of eggs Benedict.

American Sandwich Bread

1 pound bread flour, sifted

1 envelope (¼ ounce) active dry yeast

1½ tablespoons sugar

¾ cup milk, warmed to 120°F

1 teaspoon salt

4 tablespoons (½ stick) unsalted butter, melted

Makes 1 loaf

Savory Zabaione

8 large egg yolks

2 whole large eggs

Freshly squeezed juice of 1 lemon

½ cup white wine

1 cup olive oil

Salt

Eggs Benedict

8 slices mortadella (have deli slice it on 1½ setting)

8 slices American sandwich bread

1 tablespoon white vinegar

8 large eggs

1 ounce finely grated Parmesan cheese

1 tablespoon finely chopped fresh chives

1 tablespoon finely chopped fresh flat-leaf parsley

Sea salt and freshly ground pepper

MAKES 4 SANDWICHES

To Make the Bread

1. In the bowl of a stand mixer fitted with hook attachment, combine the flour, yeast, and sugar. Heat ¾ cup of water to 120°F and add it to the dry ingredients along with the warmed milk. Knead for 2 minutes. If dough is too dry or too wet, add more flour or water accordingly. Add the salt and the butter, and knead 3 minutes longer, to form a soft, smooth, elastic dough. Cover and let rise for 30 minutes. The dough should double in size.

2. Gently turn out the dough into a buttered loaf pan, pressing it gently into the corners of the pan so as not to deflate it. Cover it with a cloth and let it rise again for 1 hour in a warm place.

3. Preheat the oven to 375°F.

4. Bake the bread for 40 minutes until light golden brown. Remove the loaf from the pan and test for doneness by tapping on the bottom; it should make a hollow sound. Transfer the bread to a wire rack and let cool completely before slicing.

To Make Zabaione

1. Heat the egg yolks and whole eggs in the top of a double boiler; whip until thick ribbons form.

2. Add the lemon juice, wine, and olive oil, a little at a time, until the mixture reaches the desired thickness. Season with salt and reserve at room temperature.

To Make the Eggs Benedict

1. Cut the mortadella slices in half and fry on a cast-iron griddle until golden brown and crispy. Remove from griddle, set aside, and reserve the fat.

2. Using a 3½-inch cutter or knife, cut 8 bread slices into circles. Toast them in the fat from the mortadella.

3. Add the vinegar to a pan of boiling water and reduce to a low simmer; a few tiny bubbles should be breaking the surface. Crack 2 of the eggs into a cup. Add the eggs to the water using the vortex method: swirl the water using a whisk and gently slide the eggs in from just above the surface. Repeat for each two eggs, cooking them for 4 minutes.

4. Meanwhile, place the toasted bread on plates and cover with slices of fried mortadella. Remove the poached eggs from the water, drain on a paper towel, trim if needed, and place 2 of them on top of the mortadella on each plate. Top the eggs with room-temperature zabaione sauce, Parmesan cheese, and mixed herbs. Finish with salt and pepper.

Lemon Ricotta Pancakes

LINDA RODRIGUEZ [Pahu i`a, Hualālai Four Seasons Resort, *Hawaii*]

WITH MORE THAN THIRTY YEARS OF INTERNATIONAL EXPERI-ence, pastry chef Linda Rodriguez is a seasoned veteran. A California native, and graduate of the Culinary Institute of America, Rodriguez is responsible for all breads, pastries, and desserts served at the Hualālai Four Seasons Resort. "I love creating the first and last thing our guests eat at a meal," she says.

Mixing up a batter of eggs, milk, and flour, and cooking up small cakes on a griddle is an ancient cooking technique and can be seen in various forms around the world: French crepes, Russian blini, British drop scones, Ethiopian *injera*, and Indian *poori*—a happy global family of pancakes. In America, the variety is vast—Native American *nokehick*, Dutch *pannekoeken*, buckwheat cakes and hoecakes, Johnnycakes and journey cakes, flapjacks and slapjacks, flippers and flapcakes (flap means to toss), griddle cakes, batter cakes, and plain old pancakes. Growing up in England, large pan-size pancakes appeared only once a year for Shrove Tuesday, topped with lemon juice and sugar, and rolled up—a huge treat. My children would eat pancakes for breakfast every day if they could—as it is, I whip up some batter at least once a week.

Rodriguez uses ricotta in her zesty lemon pancakes, which gives them a fluffy texture. "Careful not to overmix the batter," she says, "the cakes won't be as tender and delicate."

6 large eggs, separated

Scant cup all-purpose flour

1/2 cup granulated sugar

Finely grated zest of
  1 1/2 lemons

Freshly squeezed juice of
  3 lemons

3/4 pound whole milk
  ricotta cheese

8 tablespoons (1 stick)
  unsalted butter, clarified,
  plus more for cooking

Pinch of salt

Confectioners' sugar

Seasonal berries

Good-quality maple syrup

SERVES 4

1. In a large bowl, mix together the flour and sugar. Add the lemon zest, lemon juice, and egg yolks and mix just until the batter comes together.

2. Add the ricotta but do not overmix. Slowly mix in the clarified butter (again, do not overmix).

3. Whip the egg whites with a pinch of salt until they form stiff peaks. Just before cooking, gently fold the whites into the batter.

4. In a preheated nonstick pan or griddle over medium heat, add some clarified butter and about 1 1/2 ounces of batter per cake; each pancake will be about 5 inches in diameter and the batter will make approximately 12 cakes.

5. Cook the pancakes until they are golden brown and the edges have started to brown. Flip and cook through.

6. Place 3 pancakes on each of four serving plates, sprinkle with confectioners' sugar, garnish with seasonal berries, and drizzle with good-quality maple syrup.

Chef Rodriguez's Tip

"Because of the ricotta, these pancakes do not bubble like normal pancakes, so you need to watch their color for doneness."

Pain Perdu—Crème Brûlée French Toast

David Myers [Comme Ça, *Los Angeles, California*]

"THIS RECIPE WAS INSPIRED BY MY GOOD FRIEND BETSY, AN incredible home cook," says David Myers. "It's a light creamy texture—almost like a custard with the crisp golden crust of the caramel."

Myers' latest obsession is Japan, and in particular the breads that he has found there. He scrolls through photo after photo on his iPhone, showing me food photography

from his travels. He has a pastry shop and a café in Tokyo. Before Myers traveled the globe gathering flavors, techniques, and photos, he honed his craft in some of the best restaurants of America. Charlie Trotter's was followed by a stint in France, after which he returned to New York to work at Daniel. Finally he was ready for his own creativity to be on the plate, and he opened his first restaurant, Sona. Next came Comme Ça in Los Angeles and now Las Vegas. His artisanal storefront Boulé—a personal favorite of mine for the fleur de sel caramels—came and went, and now he's focused on unveiling plans for a new and improved Sona, in a new location in the heart of Hollywood. For someone who has no French heritage, he's certainly adopted the cuisine and culture as his. His black-and-white bistro, Comme Ça, is packed from morning to night with young Angelenos getting a taste of Paris—think mussels, steak frites, and burgers, washed down with pretty cocktails.

French toast, an American adaptation of *pain perdu*—literally translated as "lost bread"—consists of a sweet custard poured over stale bread that is then fried into crisp golden pillows. More a dessert in France than the brunch classic it has become in America, and yet still a tried-and-true favorite—why not have dessert for breakfast? Crème Brûlée French Toast is on the brunch menu at Comme Ça.

In 1885's *La Cuisine Creole*, Lafcadio Hearn's recipe for "*Pain Perdu*" simply calls for soaking slices of bread for a few minutes in a basic mixture of sweetened milk and eggs, and then pan-frying them in butter. Myers' recipe is a little more complicated and a lot more decadent, with double the eggs and cream, plus you have to plan ahead. If the bread isn't stale you make it so, and then you soak it in the custard overnight so the rich, sweet caramel is fully absorbed and forms the brûlée when fried. The great thing about doing all the work the night before is that in the morning it's ready to go, straight from the refrigerator into the pan, making it a great go-to brunch dish when you have guests.

I find the caramel gives it enough sweetness and it needs neither maple syrup nor powdered sugar. I like to serve it with a pile of fresh berries from the farmers' market and some thick-cut strips of salty bacon to cut through the sweetness.

- 2 Tahitian vanilla beans, scraped clean (the better quality beans you use, the better the mixture)
- 4 large eggs
- 1/2 cup whole milk
- 1/2 cup heavy cream
- Six 1-inch-thick slices of stale brioche left uncovered for one day with crusts removed
- 1/2 cup packed light brown sugar
- 8 tablespoons (1 stick) unsalted butter, plus 1 tablespoon for browning bread
- Pure Vermont maple syrup and confectioners' sugar for topping

SERVES 4

1. In a medium bowl, combine the vanilla, eggs, milk, and cream. Lay the bread slices out in a shallow dish and pour the mixture over them. Refrigerate until cold.

2. Remove the bread from the mixture and set aside.

3. In a small saucepan, heat the sugar over medium heat until it caramelizes and forms a soft ball, 240°F on a candy thermometer. Turn off the heat and add the 8 tablespoons of butter. Stir with a wooden spoon until you have a nice caramel. Pour into the bottom of a 13 x 9 x 2-inch baking dish and, while still warm, place the slices of soaked bread onto the caramel. Cool, cover, and refrigerate overnight.

4. Preheat the oven to 350°F.

5. Heat the remaining tablespoon of butter in a heavy-bottomed skillet over medium heat. When the butter starts to foam, add the slices of bread to the pan, caramel side down. Reduce the heat slightly and cook for 2 to 3 minutes, until crisp and golden brown. Transfer the toast to a sheet pan, caramel side down, and bake in the oven until it puffs up like a soufflé, is warm in the center, and golden brown on top, about 10 minutes.

6. Slice each piece of pain perdu in half and arrange 3 half slices on four plates, caramel side up. Serve with whatever fruit happens to be in season and warm maple syrup, and dust with confectioners' sugar, if desired.

Chef Myers' Tips

"Get the caramel to where it's truly dark; if it's light it doesn't have the depth of flavor."

"The bread is critical: use a good-quality brioche. If you can't find brioche, use challah or egg bread—either would be a good second best."

"Make sure the bread is stale and cut into thick 1-inch slices so it doesn't turn mushy in the custard overnight."

"I like to use a great single-barrel Vermont syrup."

Cinnamon Rolls

MICHAEL McCARTY [Michael's, *Santa Monica, California*]

A recipe for "Cinnamon Rolls or Schnecken" from the International Jewish Cook Book *by Florence Kreisler Greenbaum, published in 1919.*

MICHAEL McCARTY, A WONDERFUL RACONTEUR AND FRIEND to everyone, opened Michael's in 1979 when he was twenty-five. It was an instant success. Diners flocked to dine beneath the David Hockney and Jasper Johns artwork that lined the walls, to eat the new Californian cuisine, and be a part of Michael's, both the man and his restaurant, chic *je ne sais quois*.

McCarty's cinnamon rolls are perfect to bake when you invite friends over for brunch. With a little planning, you can fill your home with the mouthwatering aroma of baking cinnamon rolls. Prepare the brioche dough the day before and in the morning roll out it out, sprinkle with cinnamon, and bake in the oven. At Michael's Restaurant in Santa Monica, these sweet rolls are served as people gather for the Santa Monica Farmers' Market tour that McCarty conducts to show his customers how he uses the local produce in his seasonal menu.

CINNAMON ROLLS OR SCHNECKEN

Take half the kuchen dough. Roll one-half inch thick and spread well with melted butter. Sprinkle generously with scraped maple, brown or granulated sugar and cinnamon, then roll. Cut the roll into equal parts about one inch thick, place close together endwise in a spider, generously buttered, spread with one-fourth inch layer of brown or maple sugar. Let rise until light, and bake ten to twenty minutes in a hot oven, a golden brown. Invert the spider, remove rolls and serve caramel side up.

Brioche Dough

- ½ cup milk
- ½ ounce fresh yeast
- 3 cups all-purpose flour
- 4 large eggs, at room temperature
- ¼ cup sugar
- 1½ teaspoons coarse salt
- 1 cup (2 sticks) unsalted butter, cut into 1-inch pieces, at room temperature

To Make the Brioche Dough

1. At least 8 hours in advance or the night before, prepare the brioche dough. Place the milk in a small saucepan over medium heat and bring to 115°F on a cooking thermometer. Immediately remove from the heat and pour into a large mixing bowl.

2. Add the yeast and mix just until the yeast dissolves. Add ½ cup plus 3 tablespoons of the flour and, using a wooden spoon, beat it into the liquid. This is the "sponge."

3. When blended, pour the remaining flour on top of the sponge. Do not stir. Place the bowl in a warm, dry spot and leave, undisturbed, until you see the sponge begin to bubble up through the flour. This can take anywhere from 45 to 75 minutes, depending upon the temperature and humidity of the room.

4. Line a small baking pan with parchment paper. Set aside.

5. Place the eggs in the bowl of a stand mixer fitted with the dough hook. Mix just to blend. Scrape the flour-yeast mixture into the eggs along with the sugar and salt. Mix on low speed just until combined. Increase the speed to medium and mix until the dough begins to pull away from the sides of the bowl and form a ball. Add the butter and continue mixing until the butter is completely incorporated into the dough and the dough has, again, pulled away from the sides of the bowl and either formed a ball or begun to climb up the dough hook.

6. Scrape the dough onto the prepared baking pan, cover with a sheet of parchment paper, and place in the refrigerator for 8 hours or overnight. Do not remove it from the refrigerator until you are ready to make the rolls.

Cinnamon Rolls

1/4 cup granulated sugar

1/4 cup packed light brown sugar

2 teaspoons ground cinnamon

1/4 cup (1/2 stick) melted unsalted butter

1 large egg yolk

1/4 cup plus 2 tablespoons half-and-half

1 1/2 cups confectioners' sugar, sifted

1/2 teaspoon pure vanilla extract

Pinch of salt

MAKES 12 CINNAMON ROLLS

To Make the Cinnamon Rolls

1. Combine the granulated sugar, brown sugar, and cinnamon in a small bowl. Set aside.

2. Line a baking sheet with parchment paper. Set aside.

3. Lightly flour a clean, flat work surface. Remove the dough from the refrigerator and place it on the floured surface. Lightly sprinkle the top of the dough with additional flour. Using a rolling pin, gently roll the dough out to a 1/4-inch-thick rectangle about 18 inches long and 13 inches wide. This should be done quickly as the butter in the dough will soften and the dough will be difficult to handle.

4. Using a pastry brush, gently coat the dough with the melted butter. Sprinkle the entire surface with the sugar-cinnamon mixture. Starting from the top, roll the dough towards you, creating a log that will be about 22 inches long. Carefully transfer the log to the prepared baking sheet, cover with parchment paper, and refrigerate for 30 minutes.

5. Preheat the oven to 350°F.

6. Combine the egg yolk and 2 tablespoons of the half-and-half in a small bowl, whisking to blend well. Set the egg wash aside.

7. Lightly flour a clean, flat work surface. Remove the rolled up dough from the refrigerator and transfer it to the floured surface. Using a serrated knife, carefully cut the log crosswise into 12 equal pieces.

8. Place a clean piece of parchment paper on the baking sheet. Carefully transfer each roll to the baking sheet, leaving about 3 inches between each one. Using a pastry brush, lightly coat the top of each roll with the reserved egg wash.

9. Place the rolls in the oven and bake for about 18 minutes, or until lightly browned. Remove from the oven and set aside to cool for 10 minutes.

10. While the rolls are cooling, whisk together the confectioners' sugar, the remaining 1/4 cup of half-and-half, the vanilla, and salt to make a thin glaze. (If the glaze is too thick, add more half-and-half; if too thin, add additional sugar, a teaspoon at a time.) Drizzle the glaze over the rolls and serve immediately. The rolls are particularly good when still warm.

Huckleberry's Blueberry Bran Muffin

Zoe Nathan [Huckleberry, *Santa Monica, California*]

WHEN I FIRST CAME TO AMERICA ON A HIGH-SCHOOL EXCHANGE, I couldn't believe the mother in the family I was staying with would regularly bake a batch of muffins from scratch early in the morning. It seemed so decadent to eat cake for breakfast. I didn't stop to think about the extra time she was putting in to make them, filling the house with aromas to draw us out of bed and downstairs. Whipping up a batch of muffins is easy, especially Zoe Nathan's recipe for Blueberry Bran Muffins. "I make this muffin at Huck that sells like crazy," says Nathan, "and when I don't run it for a day, people get mad!"

Blueberry muffins are so American to me, perhaps even more so than apple pie, which can be found in Europe in many forms: Tarte tatin, apple streusel, and apple crumble. Blueberries, however, are indigenous to America. When the European settlers arrived, they incorporated the new types of available produce into their old recipes. It's

A recipe for "Graham Gems" from the Presbyterian Cook Book *compiled by the Ladies of the First Presbyterian Church, Dayton, Ohio, published in 1873.*

likely that the native blueberries, found all along the Eastern seaboard, were picked and thrown into a batch of "muffins," and so, the blueberry muffin was born.

Historically, the American muffin—to distinguish it from the English muffin—is a much closer relative to a tea cake, being sweeter, with a more cakelike batter that often includes fruit, spices, and nuts, and is baked in small pans.

A recipe for "Graham Gems" from the *Presbyterian Cook Book* (1873), is similar to Nathan's muffin recipe both in ingredients—graham flour being a whole wheat flour like bran—and in the way they are baked in little individual compartments of a special pan. Early variations of muffins and gems included bran and corn, and by the early twentieth century, flavors such as blueberry, cranberry, and apple were commonplace.

> **GRAHAM GEMS.**
> Mrs. J. F. E.
>
> Two eggs; two cups of sweet milk; one cup of Graham flour; one of wheat flour, and a little salt. Grease the pans with lard; heat them very hot; fill almost full, and bake about half an hour.

8 tablespoons (1 stick) unsalted butter, melted and cooled

1/4 cup brown sugar, plus more for topping

1/2 teaspoon salt

1 large egg

1/4 cup maple syrup

1/4 cup honey

1/4 cup canola oil

1 cup all-purpose flour

1 cup wheat germ, lightly toasted

1 teaspoon baking soda

1 cup plain full-fat yogurt

2 cups blueberries

MAKES 12 MUFFINS

1. Preheat the oven to 350°F.

2. Place cupcake liners in a 12-cup muffin pan.

3. In a large bowl, whisk by hand the butter, brown sugar, and salt. Add the egg and whisk to combine.

4. Add the maple syrup, honey, and canola oil. Whisk until emulsified.

5. Add the flour, wheat germ, baking soda, and yogurt, and whisk together just until combined.

6. Fill the muffin cups about three-quarters full. Top with lots of fresh berries. Crumble a little brown sugar on top of the fruit.

7. Bake in the oven until the cake springs back and the tops are golden brown.

Chef Nathan's Tips

"Don't mix the blueberries into the batter, just put them on top, so the muffins don't get too liquidy or soft in the center. And be generous with the fruit—as the muffin rises, the berries spread out across the top."

"The muffins are also great topped with cranberries or strawberries—depending on what's in season at the market."

"If you don't have muffin pans, put the batter in a 9-inch cake pan and bake it as a cake, then slice and serve with vanilla ice cream. It's delicious."

Gruyère Popovers

BRIAN MOYERS [BLT Steak, *Los Angeles, California*]

AT BLT STEAK, BRIAN MOYERS COMBINES HIS VAST CULINARY knowledge with the bounty of local farmers' markets to create compelling dishes that thrive on simplicity. Moyers developed a formidable skill set working with renowned chefs such as Nobu Matsuhisa, Todd English, and Richard Farnabe. His ability to adroitly move from steakhouse classics to seasonal dishes is visible in the execution of BLT's trademark dishes—of which the popovers are one—and in his weekly farmers'-market-driven blackboard specials.

LUCY'S POP-OVERS.

Two tea-cups sweet milk, two tea-cups sifted flour, heaped a little, butter size of a walnut, two eggs, and one table-spoon sugar, a little salt; bake in hot gem-pans, filled half full, for twenty minutes, and serve immediately.—*Mrs. W. A. James, Marshall,*

Mrs. W. A. James, Marshall's recipe for "Lucy's Pop-overs" from Buckeye Cookery *by Estelle Woods Wilcox, published in 1877.*

The generosity of chefs never ceases to amaze me, and Moyers is no exception. We have worked together on many projects and he always goes beyond just giving me a recipe, food, and a smile. "You should be familiar with popovers," Moyers says, when I visit him in the kitchen at BLT. "They are the same as British Yorkshire puddings." James Beard would beg to differ. "They are purely American," Beard writes in *American Cookery*. "Although the batter is almost that of a Yorkshire pudding, I do not believe that is the inspiration." Rather than making these puddings to accompany beef as the English do, they were made for breakfast. In *Buckeye Cookery* (1877), Estelle Woods Wilcox includes a recipe for "Lucy's Popovers," with the batter baked in gem pans. Almost exactly the same recipe is included in a later edition and called "Breakfast Cakes," as well as a recipe using similar batter for "Nuns Puffs (for tea)" that are cooked in a "puff pan," for which she includes an illustration.

Popovers, with their crispy, golden brown, misshapen exteriors and light, airy interiors, are served at BLT Steak instead of bread. This is closer to the English pairing of beef and Yorkshire puddings than the nineteenth-century breakfast cakes. Moyers has baked up quite a few batches. He has tweaked the recipe for the home cook—it's all in the details.

4 cups whole milk

8 large eggs

4 cups all-purpose flour

1½ heaping tablespoons salt

Nonstick vegetable spray

2¼ cups grated Gruyère cheese

High-quality unsalted butter, for serving

Coarse sea salt, for serving

MAKES 12 POPOVERS

1. Gently warm the milk over low heat and set aside. Whisk the eggs until frothy and slowly whisk in the milk (so as not to cook the eggs). Sift the flour with the salt. Slowly add this dry mixture to the egg mixture and gently combine until mostly smooth. Strain to remove any lumps and let the batter rest for at least 30 minutes at room temperature.

2. Place a popover pan in the oven. Preheat oven to 375°F. Remove the popover pan from the oven and spray with nonstick vegetable spray. Fill each popover cup three-quarters full with batter.

3. Top each popover with approximately 2½ tablespoons of the Gruyère.

4. Bake in the oven for 50 minutes, rotating the pan a half-turn halfway through, until golden brown.

5. Remove the pan from the oven and slide the popovers out. Serve immediately with a high-quality salted butter and coarse sea salt.

Chef Moyers' Tips

"We play with other flavored salts and butters: butter with a touch of molasses and finished with smoked salt is my new favorite."

"It's great to use leftovers for breakfast in a play on eggs Benedict or Florentine."

English Muffins

NANCY SILVERTON   [Osteria Mozza and Pizzeria Mozza, *Los Angeles, California*]

MAKING MUFFINS WITH NANCY
Silverton is intense, fascinating, and fun. She demonstrates how to stretch the dough: with one graceful motion she lifts, pulls, and gently lets it fall onto the counter, resulting in the perfect thickness for cutting. Out of her obsession for baking, Silverton built and sold a bread empire (La Brea Bakery) and then teamed up with Mario Batali and Joe Bastianich to create Mozza. Silverton rules the corner of Highland and Melrose—first came the Pizzeria, then the Osteria, next Mozza 2 Go, and most recently Scuola di Pizza. Upon opening in November 2006, Mozza instantly became a phenomenon. It won the popularity prize in Los Angeles in a recent Zagat poll, and no one was really very surprised.

Pizzas weren't part of the original plan, but when the space was found and it contained a pizza oven, Silverton turned her attention to making the perfect pie. The result is the distinctly chewy, slightly charred, flavorful crust of a Mozza pizza.

On any given night Silverton can be found behind the mozzarella bar, in the center of the more formal, Michelin-star dining room of the Osteria, creating her plates—bright red, oven-roasted, cherry tomatoes still on the vine, little leaves of basil, white creamy burrata oozing over the plate, a drizzle of olive oil, and a final touch of sea salt. Dressed in a pale blue apron covering a stylish outfit, her mass of tight ringlet curls pinned up high on her head as always, she flashes that omniscient smile with a twinkle in her eye. Sitting at the mozzarella bar with a glass of Flor prosecco, Silverton places a little plate on the marble: toasted baguette topped with salty lard and sweet orange uni. "Sex on toast!" she tells us and laughs.

Silverton has chosen to develop a new English muffin recipe based on one from the nineteenth-century cookbook *How We Cook in Los Angeles*. "I've never made them before and would love to try," she says. The 1894 recipe calls for one large cup of yeast. "It's clear it couldn't have been a whole cup of yeast in the old recipe," says Silverton, "that would be too much." She goes on to clarify that this cup probably refers to the sourdough starter, made of fermented flour and water, that would have been used for bread making a hundred years ago. They would replace what they took out of the starter, to keep it at a certain level. "I took a bread formula to make my sourdough starter," Silverton explains. "The next day I used a cup of the potato water and then I added other ingredients that weren't in the recipe to improve upon it and to add flavor. I used a little rye flour—I prefer the look of an English muffin that isn't chalky white; it needs a little dirtiness to it." She also added a little butter and some honey for sweetness. "I tried it without the butter and honey originally and it was just too bland." Trying to recreate the taste of a commercial English muffin, she bought a pack to taste. "They were terrible," she says, "very chemical-tasting. I remember them being so much more flavorful, and having the distinctive taste of sourdough." So she lengthened the muffin-making process to achieve this.

ENGLISH MUFFINS
Mary Roach.

One pint lukewarm potato water; 2 tablespoons mashed potato; 1 large cup yeast; flour; corn meal.

Mix like soft bread dough. When very light, roll and cut with a large cutter, sprinkle corn meal over the molding board, leave the muffins upon it until light; then bake on a pancake griddle until quite crisp.

Mary Roach's recipe for "English Muffins" from How We Cook in Los Angeles, *published in 1894.*

Silverton's long-time friend Amy Pressman happens to be at Mozza the afternoon we are testing the recipe. "You have to be very gentle with the dough," she says. "Nancy doesn't even realize how she does it because she's so experienced, but home cooks will have to play a little to get it right. But that's the beauty of it, their imperfections prove they are homemade."

The tray of English muffins comes out of the oven and we all gather round. "This one is perfect, right?" asks Silverton. But she is hypercritical about some of the others and concerned they haven't turned out as well as the batch they baked yesterday. "These will be too raw, you can feel—I can just tell." Marissa Goodman, who has worked on the recipe with Silverton, returns the tray to the oven for an additional five minutes. They huddle to discuss the nuances of the recipe: "A rye dough never feels like a white dough, there should have been more life in it, but the proportion of rye is so small, I'm not sure what was wrong with this batch."

We have to wait for the muffins to cool, which is torturous. "You'll want to eat them straight from the oven, they smell so good," says Goodman. "But you have to let them dry out a little inside before you fork them open." After ten attempts at the recipe—bigger muffins, less proof time, more butter and honey, less flour in the sponge—Silverton still isn't satisfied and the perfectionist wants to try again.

English Muffins

I made a batch of these and sent Nancy Silverton a note to say that the recipe had worked flawlessly. She replied, "Are there nooks and crannies?" Once you taste them, you will want to make them every day—or at least every Sunday morning, ready for a late, lazy brunch. Fry up an egg with some thick-cut bacon, place this on top of a little nest of baby arugula lightly tossed in lemon juice and olive oil on one half of the muffin, melt Parmigiano-Reggiano on the other half—the result: the exquisite Egg-Mozza-Muffin.

Potato Water

2 large potatoes, peeled and cut into small pieces

Sponge

1 tablespoon (1/3 ounce) active dry yeast

2 cups potato water, room temperature

1 3/4 cups bread flour

4 1/2 tablespoons dark rye flour

Dough

1 cup potato water

1 tablespoon (1/3 ounce) active dry yeast

1 sponge

4 tablespoons mashed potato

3 tablespoons honey

4 tablespoons milk powder

4 cups bread flour, plus more for dusting work surface

5 teaspoons salt

4 tablespoons (1/2 stick) unsalted butter, softened (room temperature)

Oil for the bowl

1/4 cup semolina flour

MAKES A BAKER'S DOZEN

To Make the Potato Water

1. In a medium pan, cover the potatoes with water plus 1 inch; boil until tender.

2. Drain and reserve the potato water. Mash or rice the potatoes.

To Make the Sponge

1. In a large bowl, mix the yeast and the room temperature potato water so it dissolves; then add the bread and rye flours and combine. Cover the bowl with plastic wrap. Using some additional plastic wrap, make a "rope" to tie the covering down tightly. Let it sit for 2 hours at room temperature.

2. Refrigerate overnight.

3. Remove from the refrigerator and let the mixture come back up to room temperature, about 1 1/2 hours.

To Make the Dough

1. In a large bowl of a stand mixer fitted with the hook attachment, mix the potato water and the yeast. Add the sponge, potato, honey, milk powder, and flour.

2. Mix for 2 minutes on low. Add the salt. Increase the speed to medium and mix for 6 minutes. Add the butter and mix for 2 minutes on medium.

3. Turn the dough out into a well-oiled bowl. Cover the bowl again with the plastic wrap and the plastic-wrap rope and let sit for 1 hour to rise.

4. Turn the dough out onto a floured surface and give it 4 folds, from all 4 sides. Invert it and put it back into the bowl. Cover the bowl with plastic wrap and plastic rope again and let sit for another 1 hour for a second rise.

5. Preheat the oven to 350°F.

6. Turn the dough out and stretch it by picking up opposite ends and pulling outwards gently and smoothly until the dough reaches about 3/4 inch in thickness. Then let the dough fall onto the dusted surface. One can also gently pat the dough to get the desired thickness and shape. Let it sit for 10 minutes.

7. Using a 3 1/2-inch cutter, cut out the muffins and carefully transfer them to a sheet pan dusted with semolina flour.

8. Cook the muffins on a griddle over medium heat until they puff up and are pale gold in places, about 3 minutes. Flip and cook the other side. (This is *not* to cook the muffins all the way through, but to give them a little color.)

9. Bake the muffins on a sheet pan for 15 to 20 minutes. Remove from the oven and cool completely to let the inside dry out a little. Fork open and enjoy.

Sandwiches

Lobster Roll with Yukon Gold Potato Chips

RICK MOONEN [rm seafood, *Las Vegas, Nevada*]

"I FISHED WITH MY DAD ON LONG ISLAND AS A KID. BLUEFISH was fun—you didn't get a bite, you got a strike," Moonen says. "Then there was Captain Al out of Freeport who always used to say, 'You can't hook 'em—you can't cook 'em.'" Moonen has devoted his career to advocating sustainable seafood and educating the public on the dangers of overfishing. Whether he's behind the stove in his Las Vegas restaurant or outside of the kitchen testifying in Washington, D.C. on environmental and sustainable fishing policy, Moonen is always practicing what he preaches. In 2011 the Monterey Bay Aquarium honored him as "Chef of the Year" for his work. Who better to give us his recipe for the beloved American seafood classic, the lobster roll? When I ask him if lobster is sustainable, he uses a lobsterman term and describes them as "bugs of the sea"—enough said.

The humble lobster roll: delicious and decadent, the perfect pairing of a lowbrow hot-dog bun with the gourmet's prized crustacean. The exact origin of the lobster roll is unclear and many towns along the coast of New England claim to be home to the first lobster roll. Its traditional preparation is also up for debate—some argue it should be warm, made with lobster lightly sautéed or drizzled with butter; others insist it must be cold, prepared with chilled lobster meat and mayonnaise. The soft hot-dog bun is the standard for both versions, split along the top with straight sides, often toasted, and served with a side of potato chips.

Mrs. Lincoln's Boston Cook Book (1884), has a recipe for lobster salad that is served in "nests or cups of crisp lettuce leaves." She wasn't trying to cut out carbs, she was using what was available—hot-dog buns wouldn't come into being until the early twentieth century. (And, yes, she did use mayonnaise with her lobster.) She goes on to give a recipe for "Salad Sandwiches:" "Mix a small quantity of mayonnaise dressing with finely chopped lobster. Cover a small slice of bread with lettuce and then with salad, lettuce, and bread again. Wrap them in tin foil or oiled paper and serve at picnics or when traveling." So there you have it—the precursor to the modern lobster roll.

> SARATOGA POTATOES.
>
> It requires a little plane, or potato or cabbage cutter, to cut these potatoes. Two or three fine, large potatoes (ripe new ones are preferable) are selected and pared. They are cut, by rubbing them over the plane, into slices as thin or thinner than a wafer. These are placed for a few moments in ice, or very cold water, to become chilled. Boiling lard is now tested, to see if it is of the proper temperature. The slices must color quickly; but the fat must not be so hot as to give them a dark color.

A recipe for "Saratoga Potatoes" from Practical Cooking and Dinner Giving *by Mrs. Mary Newton Foote Henderson, published in 1876.*

For his lobster roll, Moonen uses mayonnaise and crème fraîche with lots of finely chopped fresh herbs, celery, red onion, lemon juice, and zest. Moonen was very clear that the temperature has to be just right: warm bun, and cold—"but not too cold"—lobster. Moonen pairs his roll with warm, salty, homemade Yukon Gold potato chips. Mrs. Lincoln would have known potato chips as Saratoga Potatoes or Saratoga Chips, originating around the middle of the nineteenth century in Saratoga Springs, New York. A recipe from 1876 is very similar to Moonen's—right down to the bowl of ice water.

Lobster Roll with Yukon Gold Potato Chips

One bite of Rick Moonen's lobster roll, (fresh herbs, celery, onion, lemon zest, mayonnaise, and crème fraîche piled high in a toasted bun, with homemade salty Yukon potato chips on the side) will transport you to the New England coast.

For a really pretty presentation of the chip, skip soaking the slices of potato in water and sandwich an herb leaf between two slices before frying. The starch from the potato binds it and as the potato chip cooks it becomes translucent, revealing the herb inside. Any herbs can be used; the tarragon, dill, and parsley in the lobster roll would be nice, as well as chervil or sage—or a mixture.

Lobster Rolls

4 tablespoons (½ stick) unsalted butter, softened

1 tablespoon mayonnaise

1 tablespoon crème fraîche

Sea salt and freshly ground pepper

1 teaspoon chopped fresh tarragon

1 teaspoon chopped fresh dill

1 teaspoon chopped fresh flat-leaf parsley

Finely grated zest and juice of 1 lemon

One 2-pound lobster, steamed, meat diced

½ tablespoon brunoise of celery

½ tablespoon brunoise of red onion

4 top-split hot-dog buns

Yukon Gold Potato Chips

Canola oil

3 or 4 Yukon Gold potatoes

Sea salt, ground fine

SERVES 4

To Make the Lobster Rolls

1. Liberally butter the outer sides of the buns and toast on a griddle or in a sauté pan; remove and keep warm. (At rm seafood they make lobster butter—a mix of lobster roe and butter—and spread it on the outside of the bun, which gives it a nice orange color.)

2. Combine the mayonnaise and crème fraîche in a small bowl and season it with salt and pepper. Add the tarragon, dill, parsley, and lemon zest. Add the lobster, celery, onion, and lemon juice; toss gently.

3. Taste and adjust seasoning, then pile liberally into each bun and serve with the Yukon Gold Potato Chips.

To Make the Potato Chips

1. Fill a Dutch oven or other large, heavy pot halfway with canola oil and slowly bring to 350°F.

2. Fill a large bowl with cold water. Peel potatoes and thinly slice on a mandoline directly into the water. Rinse potatoes thoroughly to remove all starch, changing water if needed. Pat dry prior to frying.

3. Carefully lower potatoes into the hot oil and fry until golden brown, about 2 minutes. Using a slotted spoon, transfer the chips to a platter lined with paper towels and season with sea salt.

Hand-Cut Scottish Salmon Burgers with Curry Rémoulade and Crispy White Anchovies

MARCUS JERNMARK [Aquavit, *New York, New York*]

DESPITE A SERIOUS LACK OF SLEEP FROM HAVING A NEW BABY, Marcus Jernmark is still full of energy on the morning we meet. "I'm wearing my Happy Socks!" he tells me, revealing the Swedish-made, bright striped socks rising above his classic tan brogues.

Jernmark grew up in Gothenburg, Sweden, and in his twenty-eight years seems to have developed a passion not only for cooking, but also for promoting all things Swedish, not least the cuisine—both traditional and modern. He arrived in America to be the chef at the Swedish Consulate in New York City, young and excited to learn. In 2009, he

moved back into a restaurant kitchen when he was offered a job at Aquavit. (The twenty-five-year-old restaurant is almost as old as Jernmark, who would have been three when it opened in 1987!)

Describing Aquavit as Modern Scandinavian gives you a glimpse at the heart of this upscale New York restaurant—think dill, pickled herring, meatballs, and lingonberries, but as far removed as possible from the cafeteria at the famous yellow-and-blue home furnishings store. There are two dining areas—the Bistro, where Jernmark serves casual, crowd-pleasing comfort food; and the more formal dining room, where he can experiment with modern techniques and get more creative.

"Sweden has a five-hundred-year-old culinary tradition based on fresh ingredients served at the peak of their short seasons, combined with pickled, cured, and preserved foods that sustain us from harvest to harvest," says Jernmark. He has embraced the variety and abundance of produce in the United States that may have only been available back home in Scandinavia for a limited season.

When he cooks traditional Scandinavian food for an American palate, he tries to remain true to his roots. Blood Pudding on the menu might turn off New Yorkers, but if he names it Berkshire Pig Two Ways and serves it with bacon and lingonberries (sourced from Canada or Oregon), they will order it.

Jernmark has taken his distinctly Swedish approach to cooking and merged it with quintessential American comfort food to create a whole new take on the traditional burger. Instead of beef, Jernmark uses salmon, a popular Scandinavian protein, to fill a brioche bun. Infused with dill and a hard cheese, the pink patties are then topped with curry rémoulade and crispy anchovies. The result: an instant Swedish-American classic.

2 teaspoons olive oil, plus enough for pan-frying

1 tablespoon yellow curry powder

1 cup thick mayonnaise

1/2 cup pickled vegetable mix (available at the olive bar in most supermarkets), minced

1/2 cup plus 2 tablespoons fresh chopped chives

Salt and freshly ground white pepper

1 tin white anchovy fillets (in oil and vinegar)

1 cup all-purpose flour

2 eggs, beaten in two separate bowls

1 cup panko bread crumbs

1 pound Scottish salmon (fine, hand cut)

1 shallot, minced

1/8 cup chopped fresh dill

1/2 tablespoon Worcestershire sauce

Finely grated zest and juice of 1/2 lemon

1/2 tablespoon Skånsk mustard (or substitute Dijon)

1/3 cup Prästost cheese, coarsely grated (or substitute a good-quality American sharp cheddar)

6 brioche buns, toasted

MAKES 6 BURGERS

1. Heat the 2 teaspoons of olive oil in a medium sauté pan. Add yellow curry powder and sauté for 2 minutes, stirring constantly. Let cool.

2. Mix the cooled yellow curry powder with the mayonnaise; add the pickled vegetable mix and the 1/2 cup chopped chives. Season with salt and pepper and set aside.

3. Dip each anchovy fillet in the all-purpose flour, then in 1 beaten egg, and finally in the panko bread crumbs, making sure entire fillet is well covered.

4. Over medium heat, cover the bottom of a medium sauté pan with olive oil and pan-fry the prepared anchovies until crispy. Pat dry with paper towels and set aside.

5. In a large bowl, mix the salmon, shallot, the 2 tablespoons of chives, dill, Worcestershire sauce, lemon zest and juice, mustard, cheese, and the remaining egg. Season well.

6. Roll the salmon mixture into 2 tight logs about 2 inches in diameter and wrap in plastic wrap. Refrigerate until set, 30 to 60 minutes.

7. Once set, cut the logs into sliders about 1 inch thick.

8. Over high heat, cover the bottom of a medium sauté pan with olive oil. Pan sear the burgers until golden brown. Alternatively, grill on high heat.

9. Slather the burgers with curry rémoulade and top with crispy white anchovies. Serve on toasted brioche buns.

Truffled Crab Melt

VITALY PALEY [Paley's Place, *Portland, Oregon*]

VITALY PALEY WAS BORN NEAR KIEV, UKRAINE, AND MOVED TO New York with his parents as a boy. Switching from Julliard to the French Culinary Institute when he realized he wanted to be a chef, not a concert pianist, he went on to graduate and work in some of the best restaurants in New York—Union Square Cafe, Remi, and Chanterelle—before moving to Limoges, France, with his wife, Kimberly, to refine his skills. They returned to New York, and in 1994 the couple decided to pack up and move to Portland, in large part because the local bounty of Oregon reminded them of the life they had shared in France. They opened Paley's Place together in 1995 and have firmly established themselves at the top of the Pacific Northwest's dining scene, winning many awards since, not the least being the James Beard Award for Best Chef: Northwest, in 2005.

When I tell Paley that my father-in-law, chef Jean-Jacques Rachou, has been helping me recipe test for this book, he says he's deeply honored, if a little nervous, that someone he looked up to when he was starting out as a chef, will cook his recipe. He has nothing to be nervous about—served as a tasty supper, a stylish lunch, or cut into delicious bite-size hors d'oeuvres, Vitaly Paley's grown-up riff on the classic diner favorite, the tuna melt, is ultrasophisticated. Made with buttery brioche, sweet crabmeat, melted artisan cheese, and decadent truffles, this is a fun and easy-to-make recipe that will wow your taste buds and impress your friends. "This is not a fussy recipe," says Paley. "So making it to taste is best."

For the cheese, Paley suggests using Astraea, handcrafted by Pat Morford of Rivers Edge Chèvre in Oregon's Central Coast Range—for its excellent melting properties and because this Vietnamese cinnamon-and-chipotle-pepper-rubbed aged cheese has a slight spice that cuts through the richness of the dish. Swiss Gruyère, which is more readily available, works as well. If truffles are not in season, substitute frozen ones. Truffle butter is available from specialty food stores or online.

4 thick slices brioche, cut into circles using a 3-inch cookie cutter

4 teaspoons truffle butter, melted

1/4 cup good-quality mayonnaise

2 ounces fresh Oregon black truffles, brushed clean and coarsely chopped

1 apple, peeled, cored, and thinly sliced

Generous dash of hot pepper sauce

2 tablespoons finely minced sweet red onion

2 tablespoons finely chopped fresh flat-leaf parsley

1 tablespoon capers

Freshly squeezed juice of 1/2 lime

Kosher salt and freshly ground pepper

1/2 pound Oregon Dungeness crabmeat, squeezed dry and picked over

4 ounces Astraea or Gruyère cheese, shredded (about 1 cup)

MAKES 4 OPEN-FACED SANDWICHES

1. Preheat the broiler. Brush one side of the brioche slices with the truffle butter and set on a sheet pan, buttered side up. Broil until golden and set aside.

2. Preheat the oven to 400°F.

3. In a large bowl, mix the mayonnaise, chopped truffles, sliced apple, hot pepper sauce, onion, parsley, capers, and lime juice, and season with salt and pepper. Fold in the crabmeat to incorporate.

4. Top each slice of toast, buttered side down, with the crab salad and sprinkle with cheese. Bake in the upper third of the oven until the crab salad has warmed through and the cheese is melted, about 5 minutes. Serve immediately.

Lobster Croque Monsieur

ERIC RIPERT [Le Bernardin, *New York, New York*]

"IT'S A GOOD SANDWICH," SAYS ERIC RIPERT IN HIS TYPICAL
understated manner, referring to his decadent lobster-filled version of the classic croque
monsieur. From what everyone has told me about Ripert, this is like calling him a good
chef—huge understatement. At the risk of sounding cliché, it might be more accurate to
say that he's a good person. Those who know Ripert can't say enough nice things about
him. Within minutes of shaking his hand I understand what they mean. I, too, feel as if
I'm drunk on Ripert Kool-Aid. With best-selling books, TV shows, three Michelin stars
for his restaurant, and a best friend in Anthony Bourdain, no less—in person, he lives up
to everything I've heard about him and so much more.

Ripert never stops smiling, a big white toothy grin. He's humble about all he has
achieved and gracious when paid a compliment about his book, a specific recipe, or his
restaurant. His celebrity status has changed nothing. "When you are inside the restaurant," he says, "there is no such thing as a celebrity chef, and I am mostly here. Luckily
TV doesn't take that much time." I suspect that it's not the kitchen that is keeping him
grounded, it's just who he is.

When I meet with Ripert at Le Bernardin, he is excited to
look back through time to see his recipe in a historical context. He
has a collection of old cookbooks at home—mostly French—that
he likes to read for inspiration. He tells me he will look through
them for early croque monsieur recipes. Perhaps the simplicity of
the sandwich means it never made it into the likes of *Escoffier* (he
pulls out his copy from the shelf—it's not there). Or perhaps it's
too lowly? It's hard to find references to its first cousin, the American grilled cheese sandwich, with or without meat, in any of the
early American cookbooks. Perhaps the closest recipes are those
for Welsh rarebit—a mixture of cheese, butter, and often ale that's
melted together in a pan, spread on toast, and sometimes broiled.

Ripert's recipe is an adaptation of a croque monsieur that
was on the menu at Le Bernardin with smoked salmon and caviar
instead of the classic ham. "I like croque monsieur a lot," he says. "It always reminds me
of my grandmother and cooking with her. She used to have a press with a heart shape and
we would press it into the bread and it would make a design on the sandwich."

"The recipe itself is very easy," says Eric. "Cooking the lobster is the most challenging part. You have to kill the lobster and make sure that it doesn't suffer, at least as little
as possible. I think it's difficult because it's an animal that's alive in front of you. It's not
like you buy a steak of lobster, so this can be emotional for a lot of people. If you are an
omnivore, it's a good experience because it gives you much more respect for the ingredient
as you see the entire living animal."

Lobster Croque Monsieur

Eric Ripert's take on the classic grilled cheese sandwich and its close relative from across the Atlantic, the croque monsieur, is beyond gourmet, *c'est magnifique!*

1 lobster (1½ pounds)

5 ounces Gruyère cheese

8 slices pain de mie (or good-quality white bread)

1 tablespoon lemon confit, rinsed well and finely minced (optional)

1 tablespoon chopped fresh chives

8 tablespoons (1 stick) unsalted butter, softened

SERVES 4

1. To cook the lobster, bring a pot of salted water to a boil (the water should be well-seasoned but not salty). Kill the lobster by inserting a knife in the head, just behind the eyes, and cutting down between the eyes. Add the lobster to the water and simmer for 7 minutes. Remove the lobster from the water and allow it to cool. Once cool, remove the claws and tail from the lobster, crack the shells, and carefully remove the meat, keeping it intact. Trim the end of the tail and pull out the vein. Cut the tail and claws into ¼-inch-thick slices, discarding the fatty claw meat inside the pincers. Cover and keep refrigerated until ready to assemble the croque monsieurs.

2. Using a vegetable peeler, slice the Gruyère cheese very thinly.

3. Lay the bread out on a table. On 6 slices, place the Gruyère cheese in an even layer, and on top of this place the sliced lobster, using a mix of tail and claw on each piece of bread. Sprinkle the lobster slices with lemon confit and chives. Close the sandwiches. Using a serrated knife, cut off the crusts. (You may make this recipe up to this point a few hours in advance, wrap it in plastic wrap, and refrigerate.)

4. Before serving, spread the softened butter evenly on the outsides of the sandwiches. Preheat a nonstick sauté pan over medium-high heat. Add the sandwiches to the pan, Gruyère side down, and sauté for 2 minutes. Turn them over and sauté for 1 minute, or until nicely browned on the lobster side.

5. To serve, slice the croque monsieur on the diagonal, then on the diagonal again, making four triangles. Arrange the triangles on a plate. Repeat for the other three sandwiches. Serve immediately.

Lemon Confit

Lemon confit is made using an old technique for preserving lemons that originated in Morocco and is a favorite condiment of Ripert's—make a jar of it once and you can use it year-round.

6 lemons

Kosher salt

1. Cut the lemons in quarters, but not all the way, and pack in kosher salt in a sterilized canning jar (a 1-quart canning jar will hold all 6 lemons).

2. Refrigerate for at least 1 month, but preferably 3 months to a year. Remove a lemon whenever you need it, discard everything but the rind, rinse well, and mince finely for the sandwich.

Chef Ripert's Tip

"Let the bread become golden brown and crunchy and then repeat with the other side to make sure the bread doesn't get soggy. You want the crunch on the outside with the moist middle. "

Outdoor Grilled Cheese Sandwich with Nectarine Chutney

CURTIS STONE [*Los Angeles, California*]

JOHN MONTAGU, FOURTH EARL OF SANDWICH, GAVE HIS TITLE
to a filling between two pieces of bread during a twenty-four-hour gambling spree in
1762, when he didn't want to leave the gaming table to eat and ordered something he
could eat with his hands. Despite its British origins, Americans,
always drawn to anything convenient, adopted the sandwich
and created countless versions—many becoming quintessen-
tially American—the hamburger, hot dog, breakfast sandwich,
BLT, and PB & J, to name just a few. And then there's the gooey,
crunchy, golden grilled cheese—made of individually wrapped
slices of orange processed cheese that are placed between two
slices of white bread and heated on the stovetop in a frying pan.
Mexicans have quesadillas, the French have croque monsieur,
Italians make panini, the British have cheese on toast, and the
Welsh have rarebit (somehow managing to include beer with
their cheese). Across the globe, people turn to melted cheese and
bread for a satisfying, easy-to-make comfort food.

Grilled cheese cooked outside on the grill seems so obvious, and I thank my friend, Australian chef Curtis Stone, for
introducing me to it. Stone invites me over to show me how it's
done. When I arrive, he's in the kitchen laughing at viral videos
on his iPad and we share our favorites. He takes me on a tour of
his new home in Los Angeles, which is undergoing some con-
struction before he moves in, and then we head to the backyard
to make an outdoor grilled cheese sandwich together.

Preparing the sandwich takes Stone no time; he makes
it all look supereasy, partly because everything has been beautifully prepared, but mostly because Stone is in his element—
cooking outside. The hardest part is slicing the ciabatta to get
two long, thin, even pieces of bread. "I feel that a sandwich
shouldn't be about the bread but what goes in it," says Stone, "so
cut the bread thin." He then rubs the bread liberally with garlic
before piling on the cheese, chutney, and arugula and sliding it
into his outdoor pizza oven.

If you don't have access to an outdoor oven, gas grill, or
charcoal grill and you are indoors, use a panini press or bake in an indoor oven or under
the broiler. "You can even use a griddle pan on the stove and put a brick on top!" says
Stone.

The sandwich comes out of the oven sizzling and oozing melted cheese. Stone
picks up a slice and bites into it, long strings of cheese stretching from his mouth to the
sandwich.

Grilled Cheese Sandwich

1 ciabatta loaf (about 12 inches long by 4 1/2 inches wide)

Extra-virgin olive oil, for brushing

Salt and freshly ground pepper

1 large clove garlic, cut in half

4 tablespoons Dijon mustard

1 cup Nectarine Chutney

8 ounces Buckaroo cheese (Cowgirl Creamery), rind trimmed, sliced 1/8 inch

4 ounces Red Hawk cheese (Cowgirl Creamery), rind trimmed, sliced 1/8 inch

2 cups baby arugula

Nectarine Chutney

2 teaspoons canola oil

1 teaspoon yellow mustard seeds

1 small white onion, finely diced

2/3 cup sugar

1/3 cup white wine vinegar

1 teaspoon finely chopped peeled fresh ginger

1/4 teaspoon hot red pepper flakes

4 firm but ripe nectarines (about 1 1/2 pounds total), pitted, cut into about 1-inch pieces

1/2 teaspoon salt

Makes 3 cups

SERVES 4

To Make the Grilled Cheese Sandwich

1. Heat the outdoor oven or grill to medium-high heat.

2. Using a large serrated knife, trim 1/8 inch off the top and bottom of the ciabatta. Then cut the ciabatta horizontally in half, so you have two long slices of bread about 1/2 inch thick.

3. Brush the top and bottom of the ciabatta with olive oil, season lightly with salt and pepper, and rub with the garlic clove. Place the ciabatta slices, oiled side down, on the grill and cook until just barely golden brown, rotating but not turning over to toast evenly, about 3 minutes.

4. Remove the ciabatta from the grill and reduce the heat to low. Spread one toasted side of the ciabatta with mustard and spoon the chutney over the other.

5. Over the mustard, place the Buckaroo and Red Hawk cheeses. Scatter the arugula on top of the cheese and cover with the top half of the ciabatta, chutney side down, and press firmly to hold the sandwich together. Lightly brush the top of the sandwich with oil.

6. Place the sandwich, oiled side down, in the oven or on the grill over the burner on low heat and close the hood.

7. Cook until the cheese melts and the bread is golden brown, rotating the sandwich as needed to brown evenly, about 8 minutes per side.

8. Transfer the sandwich to a cutting board. Using a serrated knife, cut the sandwich into 8 pieces and serve immediately with Nectarine Chutney.

To Make the Chutney

1. Heat the oil in a heavy bottomed saucepan over medium heat. Add the mustard seeds and sauté until they begin to pop, about 30 seconds.

2. Add the onion and sauté until tender and translucent, about 4 minutes.

3. Stir in the sugar, vinegar, ginger, and pepper flakes. Simmer until the sugar dissolves.

4. Add the nectarines and cook about 10 minutes, stirring occasionally, until the nectarines are tender but still firm enough to hold their shape; the syrup should thicken slightly. Stir in the salt.

Chef Stone's Tips

"Rubbing the bread with garlic is important. What you don't want are pieces of garlic on the bread, because they will burn—you just want the flavor."

"The chutney should stay good in the refrigerator for up to a week."

Vetri's Reuben Sandwich

MARC VETRI [Vetri, *Philadelphia, Pennsylvania*]

"FOR THOSE OF YOU WHO DON'T KNOW MARC, HE PROBABLY cooks the best pasta in this country." Now if this were his father talking (which would be very unlikely, because Sal Vetri likes his Italian food a little more American than Italian, and his son's food is a little too Italian for his old-school spaghetti-and-meatballs taste), you might take such a compliment with a pinch of salt, but when it's Joe Bastianich singing his praises, it's like being given four stars from the *New York Times*. I ask Tom Colicchio if he has any recommendations for chefs. "You *have* to get Marc Vetri."

Marc Vetri opened Vetri, his intimate forty-seat restaurant in the heart of Center City Philadelphia, in 1998. It's been a runaway success ever since, one of the hardest reservations to get, partly because of its diminutive size and mostly because it's so damn good. His outstanding Italian cuisine, with innovative flavor combinations and artful presentations, has captured diners' imaginations and propelled Vetri to the forefront of culinary trends. I ask Vetri if he'd ever expand. "If anything, I'd like to make it even smaller." With two more restaurants and a gastropub on the way, he has expanded across Philadelphia, but Vetri, the restaurant, remains the same—and just as popular as ever.

Vetri didn't want to be a chef: "I wanted to be a rock star, so I studied music in Los Angeles and paid my way by cooking." Realizing that the guitar wasn't going to be his ticket to fame and fortune, he bought a one-way ticket to Lombardy, Italy, to apprentice in a Bergamo restaurant. From Philadelphia to Los Angeles to Lombardy to New York and finally back home to Philadelphia, Vetri gathered knowledge and skills along the way that he now brings to his cooking and all his restaurants. His flavors are simple yet pronounced. "Cooking is about finding high-quality regional ingredients," he says, "then using the simplest techniques to convey their purity." Think Italian food with whimsy. As for gaining rock-star status, Ferran Adrià recently pronounced chefs to be the new rock stars of the world, and when Vetri needs his guitar fix he gets together to jam with none other than Bastianich and Colicchio.

When I contact Vetri for a recipe, he comes back with this: "How about an old-school Reuben sandwich—just an initial thought," and he includes a little history about the Reuben and where it originated. The classic Reuben, created by Arnold Reuben in the early twentieth century, consists of pastrami or corned beef, sauerkraut, and Swiss cheese, grilled between slices of rye bread. Vetri keeps the cooking to a minimum and the preparations straightforward, but gives it an Italian twist, serving his favorite deli meat, mortadella, instead of pastrami on a homemade bialy—a Yiddish roll a bit like a bagel, which is baked rather than boiled.

Vetri's Reuben Sandwich

This is one easy sandwich to make—even baking the bialys is a piece of cake. The mortadella with the melted cheese is perfectly matched by the acid in the salsa rossa, the crunch of the slaw, and the spicy pickles. Pile the fillings high and then squish the sandwiches in the pan to make what we now refer to as rock-star Reubens.

Bialys

4 3/4 cups bread flour

1 1/2 teaspoons salt

2 1/4 teaspoons (1 envelope) active dry yeast

1/2 onion, minced

1 tablespoon olive oil

Poppy seeds, for sprinkling

Sea salt, for sprinkling

Makes a baker's dozen

Salsa Rossa

2 red bell peppers, roasted, skins removed

3 tablespoons bread crumbs

1/4 cup olive oil

1/3 cup mayonnaise, plus extra

Sherry vinegar

Salt and freshly ground pepper

Makes about 1 1/3 cups

Spicy Pickles

1/4 cup white wine vinegar

2 whole jalapeños

1 tablespoon kosher salt

1 teaspoon sugar

1 clove garlic

1 teaspoon whole black peppercorns

1 teaspoon whole coriander seeds

1 cucumber, peeled and thinly sliced

Makes about 1 1/2 cups

Slaw

1/2 head savoy cabbage, thinly sliced

1 tablespoon white-wine vinegar

1 teaspoon sugar

3 tablespoons olive oil

To Make the Bialys

1. Heat 1 3/4 cup water to 130°F. In a stand mixer fitted with the hook attachment, mix the flour, salt, yeast, and hot water. Knead for 10 minutes on low speed, adding additional water/flour, if needed, to form a soft, smooth dough.

2. Cover and proof for 1 hour in a warm place.

3. Cook the onion for 30 minutes over low heat in olive oil and set aside.

4. Weigh out 3-ounce balls (13 total) of dough and let them rest for 30 minutes.

5. Preheat the oven to 450°F.

6. Shape the balls of bialy dough into rounds with center indentions. Fill with the onion and then sprinkle with the poppy seeds and sea salt. Place the rounds on an oiled sheet pan and bake for 12 minutes, or until golden brown.

To Make the Salsa Rossa

1. Place the roasted peppers and bread crumbs in a blender and blend until smooth. Slowly drizzle in the olive oil to emulsify.

2. Mix the salsa rossa with the mayonnaise, adding more mayonnaise if needed.

3. Season with sherry vinegar, salt, and pepper.

To Make the Spicy Pickles

1. Combine all the ingredients except the cucumber slices and bring to a boil.

2. Pour the boiling liquid over the cucumber slices and let sit for 1 hour. Set aside in the refrigerator.

To Make the Slaw

Mix together all the ingredients and marinate for 1 hour.

To Assemble and Serve

1. Slice each bialy in half crosswise and place the salsa rossa, slaw, pecorino cheese, and mortadella inside.

2. Melt the butter in a cast-iron skillet over medium heat. Place the bialys in the pan and press with another pan or a brick. Flip after about 3 minutes and cook another 5 minutes, or until the cheese is melted and the crust is golden brown.

3. Slice and serve with the spicy pickles on the side.

3 tablespoons chopped fresh
   flat-leaf parsley

Salt and freshly ground pepper

Makes about 2 cups

Assembly for one bialy

1 tablespoon Salsa Rossa

1 ounce Slaw

1 ounce young soft pecorino
   cheese, thinly sliced

3 ounces mortadella
   (preferably Italian), very
   thinly sliced, almost shaved

1 tablespoon unsalted butter

Spicy Pickles on the side

Chef Vetri's Tips

"I leave the jalapeños whole and serve them with the sandwich, but not
everyone will eat them."

"If you don't use all the bialy rolls, you can use them for other sandwiches."

Bacon Burger with Chipotle Mayo

MICHAEL SCHLOW [Radius and Tico, *Boston, Massachusetts*]

FRESH OFF THE RED-EYE FROM SAN FRANCISCO, I MEET WITH
restaurateur and chef Michael Schlow at his newest restaurant—Tico, serving American cuisine with strong Spanish, Mexican, and South American influences. Born in Brooklyn and of Jewish heritage, Schlow moved to Boston in 1995 and has been on the cutting edge of the city's culinary scene ever since. With five restaurants, each featuring a different type of cuisine, I ask him if there's anything left for him to do? "Perhaps a burger joint or a gourmet diner." This James Beard Award-winning chef has just been in Miami grilling up burgers at the South Beach Wine and Food Festival's annual Rachael Ray Burger Bash. This year his Schlow burger featured cheddar, crispy onions, and horseradish-black pepper sauce.

The hamburger—a national dish of sorts—is certainly one of America's biggest cultural exports, with burger joints popping up all over the globe. German immigrants are responsible for first bringing Hamburg steak—a minced beefsteak patty that originated in Hamburg—across the Atlantic. Boston native Mrs. Mary Lincoln was cooking up burgers in 1884, which she called "Broiled Meat Cakes" and "Hamburgh Steak." The origin of the hamburger bun is less certain—many have claimed posthumously that their family members were the first to add the bun. Then along came the "Cheese Hamburger" in the '20s in Pasadena and the "Cheeseburger" in Colorado. In the '50s, Dick and Mac McDonald ran a

> *Hamburgh Steak.* — Pound *a slice* of *round steak* enough to break the fibre. Fry *two* or *three onions*, minced fine, in *butter* until slightly browned. Spread the onions over the meat, fold the ends of the meat together, and pound again, to keep the onions in the middle. Broil **two or three minutes.** Spread with *butter, salt,* and *pepper.*

tight business focused on burgers, fries, and shakes in San Bernardino, California, which caught the attention of Ray Kroc who had the vision to see restaurants across the country all serving the limited menu. The rest—as the cliché goes—is history.

A recipe for "Hamburgh Steak" from Mrs. Lincoln's Boston Cook Book by Mrs. Mary J. Lincoln, published in 1884.

Schlow took to the grill at Tico. Flames leapt into the air as he made us a burger to share. Each juicy patty of meat was topped with crispy bacon and some chipotle mayonnaise. With a large portion of fries on the side, I was in burger heaven.

Bacon Burger with Chipotle Mayo

Michael Schlow serves a mean burger at his restaurant Tico. He mixes olive oil in with the meat which makes it extra juicy. He also uses a 20 percent fat content in the ground beef to make the burgers hold together and give them a meatier flavor. Topped with bacon and a smoky chipotle mayo this is deliciousness in a bun.

Chipotle Mayo

1 cup mayonnaise

1 tablespoons chipotle peppers

2 tablespoons freshly squeezed lime juice

2 tablespoons chopped fresh cilantro

2 tablespoons honey

Salt and freshly ground pepper

Makes about 2½ cups

Burgers

1 pound plus 2 ounces 80% lean ground beef

2 tablespoons extra-virgin olive oil

Salt and freshly ground pepper

2 thick slices of good-quality Vermont or English cheddar cheese

2 hamburger buns, split in half

3 slices cooked apple wood–smoked bacon, crisp not burnt, cut in half

MAKES 2 BURGERS

To Make the Chipotle Mayo

1. In a small bowl, combine all the ingredients, cover, and refrigerate overnight to develop the flavors.

2. The next day, strain the mayo and season with salt and pepper.

To Make the Burgers

1. In a medium bowl, combine the ground beef with the olive oil, salt, and plenty of pepper.

2. Divide the meat in half and make 2 patties. Refrigerate the patties if you aren't grilling immediately.

3. Heat the grill to high. Remove the patties from the refrigerator and let stand at room temperature for 7 minutes. Brush the grill with olive oil. Grill the burgers for 1½ minutes (for rare). Give the burgers a quarter-rotation through 90 degrees to give them crosshatched grill marks, and cook for another 1½ minutes. If you like your burgers a little more well-done, increase the cooking time from 3 minutes per side to 4 minutes.

4. Flip the burgers over and grill for 1½ minutes. Rotate the burgers through 90 degrees to "grill mark" them, and cook for another 1½ minutes.

5. Transfer the burgers to the grill's top shelf or to a cooler section of the grill and cover each one with a slice of cheese. Turn the grill off and shut the lid for 4 minutes.

6. After 4 minutes, the cheese will be melted and the burger cooked rare to medium rare. Toast the buns, cut side down, on the grill, if desired. Spread plenty of chipotle mayo on the buns. Place a patty on each. Top with crispy bacon slices.

7. Serve with French fries and ketchup on the side.

Chef Schlow's Tips

"Ask the butcher for 80% lean ground meat—this is the most important part of the recipe!"

"Buy the best buns you can get; I prefer brioche buns."

"Don't make the patties more than an hour in advance of grilling."

The Humm Dogg

DANIEL HUMM [Eleven Madison Park, *New York, New York*]

DANIEL HUMM GREW UP IN SWITZERLAND, MOVING TO AMERICA to work as the executive chef at Campton Place, San Francisco. There he was discovered by Danny Meyer, who brought him to New York to head up Eleven Madison Park. "The menu is set up to offer the best possible experience for the diner," Humm explains. "Each dinner is designed from the choice of just the main ingredients, so we have control." The dining room is magnificent—vast floral displays of orange gerbera suspended in individual water containers stretch up to the extremely high ceilings. Humm is extremely proud of two Michelin stars, four stars from the *New York Times*, being named Best Chef of New York City (2010) by the James Beard Foundation, and making it onto the S. Pellegrino World's 50 Best Restaurants in 2010. Humm is in love with New York—the culture, the history, the food—although he still returns to Europe often for culinary adventures and to indulge in his other passion, bicycle riding.

I was pleasantly surprised when Humm asked to do a hot dog. "Shocking for me to give you a hot dog," he says, laughing at the thought of it. On getting to know him and his passion for Americana, in particular New York, it makes sense. He created this "haute dog" with truffle and celery relish for PDT, a little bar on the Lower East Side that you enter through a phone booth—the front of the bar is a hot-dog shop. Next up—a New York street vendor hot-dog stand? With the supersuccessful Shake Shack from Meyer just across the street in Madison Park, you know that just about anything is possible.

The many stories about who invented the first hot dog and where it originated stretch back through history. Frankfurters, or "franks," were born in Frankfurt, Germany, five years before Columbus set sail to discover the New World. "Weiners" comes from the German name for Vienna, where a butcher who trained in Frankfurt made sausages called weiner-frankfurters. To add to the puzzle, the frankfurter was also sometimes called a "dachshund sausage" or a "bundewurst" (dog sausage) after the dog breed, due to its similar shape. Franks and weiners were brought to America by German immigrants in the nineteenth century, and America's love of a sausage in a bun took off. In the 1860s, frankfurters were being sold in milk rolls with sauerkraut from hand-pulled wagons in New York. An urban myth that dog meat was used in the sausage in the late 1800s led to the hot-dog carts being called "dog wagons" by college students on East Coast campuses.

We will never know for certain why eating hot dogs turned into a national pastime and became a cherished tradition at baseball games, amusement parks, fairs, and on the streets of big cities. Americans today consume more hot dogs than ever—90 percent are eaten with mustard—the very yellow variety, as well as pickle relish, and sauerkraut. Humm's dog is wrapped in bacon and topped with celery relish, truffle mayonnaise, and melted Gruyère (a nod to his homeland).

Pickled Mustard Seeds

¹/₄ cup mustard seeds

¹/₂ cup white balsamic vinegar

1 teaspoon salt

¹/₂ teaspoon sugar

Makes about ¹/₂ cup

Celery Relish

¹/₂ cup brunoise of celery

1 cup brunoise of celery root

1 tablespoon Pickled Mustard Seeds

¹/₂ cup brunoise of sour pickle

2 tablespoons sherry vinegar

2 tablespoons white balsamic vinegar

Salt

Makes 1 pint

Truffle Mayonnaise

1⁷/₈ cups (15 ounces) canola oil

2 large egg yolks

1 chopped truffle

Salt

Dash of lemon juice

Dash of truffle oil

Makes 1 pint

Assembly

6 potato hot-dog buns

6 hot dogs

6 slices bacon

6 tablespoons Truffle Mayonnaise

6 ounces Gruyère cheese, grated

6 ounces Celery Relish

1 recipe Yukon Gold Potato Chips (page 48)

MAKES 6 HOT DOGS

To Make the Pickled Mustard Seeds

1. Bring a medium saucepan of water to a boil. Add the mustard seeds, and cook for 30 seconds. Strain the seeds through a fine mesh strainer and rinse well under cold water. Transfer to a medium bowl.

2. Bring the vinegar, salt, and sugar to a boil in a small saucepan over medium heat. Pour the liquid over the mustard seeds and allow to cool at room temperature. Cover and leave at room temperature overnight.

To Make the Celery Relish

1. Blanch and shock the celery and celery root.

2. Toast the pickled mustard seeds in a pan.

3. Mix the cooked and cooled celery, celery root, and mustard seeds with the pickle. Season with the sherry and balsamic vinegars, adding salt as needed.

To Make the Truffle Mayonnaise

Emulsify the oil very slowly into the egg yolks until creamy and white. Add the chopped truffle and season with salt, lemon juice, and truffle oil.

To Assemble and Serve

1. Toast the hot-dog buns.

2. Pierce the hot dogs with a fork several times and wrap each one with a single slice of bacon. Heat a sauté pan over medium-high heat. Place the bacon-wrapped hot dogs in the pan and cook, turning often, until the bacon is crisp and has rendered most of its fat.

3. Spread 1 tablespoon of truffle mayonnaise on each bun. Place a bacon-wrapped hot dog in each. Top with 1 ounce of the Gruyère cheese.

4. Place the hot dogs in an ovenproof dish under the broiler to melt the cheese.

5. Remove and top each with 1 ounce of celery relish. For some added crunch on the plate, serve with Yukon Gold Potato Chips.

Pulled-Pork Sandwich with Parsley Sauce, Pink Pickled Onions, and Creamy Cucumbers

MICHAEL SCHWARTZ [Michael's Genuine Food & Drink, *Miami, Florida*]

"I LOVE TO BARBECUE," SAYS MICHAEL SCHWARTZ. "BUT I'M IN no way a pit master." For his pulled-pork sandwich, Schwartz gives the classic preparation a subtle makeover by lightening up the pork, replacing the barbecue sauce with a parsley sauce, and adding some zing with pickled onions and creamy cucumbers. There's nothing subtle about the colors: the hot pinks and verdant greens are more commonly found on a Lily Pulitzer sundress than in a sandwich. Schwartz, as is his fashion, leads us away from the expected mango of Miami Beach and into a whole new chapter of Floridian comfort food.

Michael's Genuine Food & Drink is Schwartz's eponymous restaurant, with its low-key vibe, in the Design District of Miami. The winner of the 2010 James Beard Award Best Chef: South, Schwartz is at the forefront of the farm-to-table movement. For his second Michael's, in the Cayman Islands, his "locovore" philosophy has led to partnerships with the islands' fishermen and farmers, just as it has in South Florida.

Schwartz moved to Miami Beach in the early 1990s. Before this he had worked in restaurants from the East to West coasts, starting out in Philadelphia as a busboy at age sixteen. Schwartz is very involved with his community, and like other chefs who are part of Michelle Obama's Chefs Move to School initiative, he adopted a local elementary school where he plants vegetables, cooks healthy food, and shares his knowledge of healthy habits with the students. The vibrant colors and exciting flavors of Schwartz's sandwich are sure to please any kid—not that adults won't be equally tempted.

I can't stop thinking about layering pork, pickles, and cucumbers again soon—it has become my vice, a Miami vice.

Pulled-Pork Sandwich with Parsley Sauce, Pink Pickled Onions, and Creamy Cucumbers

This pulled-pork sandwich packs a punch, both visually and in flavor. "It's sure to be a crowd-pleaser," promises Michael Schwartz (one of his favorite sayings). Although there are several stages to making this dish, they are all very straightforward, and the finished pulled pork topped with hot pink pickles is my family's new favorite lunch.

Parsley Sauce

1 cup fresh flat-leaf parsley leaves, washed, dried, and firmly packed

3 tablespoons capers, drained and rinsed

2 anchovies in oil, drained

3 cloves garlic, coarsely chopped

1/2 teaspoon freshly ground black pepper

1/2 cup extra-virgin olive oil

Makes about 3/4 cup

Pink Pickled Onions

2 cups unseasoned rice vinegar

1/2 cup sugar

2 bay leaves

1 teaspoon mustard seesd

2 small red onions (about 1 pound), sliced into 1/4-inch-thick rounds and separated into individual rings

Makes about 2 cups

Creamy Cucumbers

1 English cucumber

1 tablespoon kosher salt

1/4 cup Greek-style yogurt

2 tablespoons heavy cream

1 teaspoon chopped garlic

1 teaspoon chopped fresh mint

Freshly squeezed juice of 1 lemon

Freshly ground pepper

Makes about 2 cups

To Make the Parsley Sauce

Put all ingredients in a blender. Purée until the mixture is completely smooth and bright green. The sauce should be wet and slightly soupy in consistency.

To Make the Pink Pickled Onions

1. Combine the vinegar, sugar, bay leaves, and mustard seeds in a medium saucepan with 1 cup of water. Slowly bring to a simmer over medium-low heat, stirring occasionally to dissolve the sugar.

2. Put the onion in a heatproof container and pour in the hot liquid. Toss to coat evenly; the onion rings should be completely submerged in the liquid. Cover and cool to room temperature. Chill before serving.

To Make the Creamy Cucumbers

1. Cut the cucumber in half lengthwise. Scoop out the seeds with a teaspoon. Slice the cucumber very thinly with a mandoline or a sharp knife. Put the cucumber slices in a medium stainless-steel or glass bowl; add the salt and mix thoroughly. Set aside for 10 to 15 minutes. Transfer the cucumber to a colander and rinse thoroughly. Press down the cucumber with your hands to remove excess liquid, and then blot with paper towels to dry.

2. Put the cucumber slices back in the bowl and add the yogurt, cream, garlic, mint, and lemon juice. Toss to combine; season with pepper. Refrigerate until ready to use.

To Make the Pulled Pork

1. Preheat the oven to 300°F.

2. In a mortar and pestle or spice grinder, combine the fennel, coriander, red pepper flakes, chili powder, and cinnamon. Grind until you have a spice powder. Put the spice powder in a small bowl and mix in the salt and pepper.

3. Place the pork, fat side up, in a roasting pan. Using a sharp knife, score the surface of the meat with small slits. Rub the spice mixture all over the pork, inside and out, being sure to get in the incisions. You can cover the pork and let it marinate for a few hours or overnight, or cook it immediately. If you decide to marinate the pork in the fridge, be sure to take it out 1 hour before you put it in the oven so it can come to room temperature before cooking.

4. Pour in enough water to just film the bottom of the roasting pan; this will add moisture to the pork while it roasts. Cover the pan tightly with aluminum foil. Slow-roast the pork for 2 hours. Increase the oven temperature to 425°F and continue to roast for another hour, until the meat is falling apart. Transfer the pork to a serving platter, tent with foil, and allow to rest for 10 minutes. Using 2 forks, shred the pork.

Pulled Pork

¹/₄ cup fennel seeds

1 tablespoon coriander seeds

1 tablespoon hot red pepper lakes

1 tablespoon chili powder

1 tablespoon ground cinnamon

¹/₄ cup kosher salt

1 tablespoon freshly ground black pepper

1 boneless pork shoulder (about 5 pounds) trimmed of excess fat

To Serve

8 brioche buns

Soft unsalted butter, for toasting buns

¹/₄ cup Parsley Sauce

1 cup Creamy Cucumbers

¹/₂ cup Pink Pickled Onions

MAKES 8 SANDWICHES, WITH LOTS OF LEFTOVERS

To Assemble and Serve

1. Cut the brioche buns, spread with butter and toast.

2. Pile some pulled pork onto the buns. Drizzle with parsley sauce, top with creamy cucumbers, some pink pickled onions, and the top of the bun.

Chef Schwartz's Tips

"The pickled onions keep for months stored in covered container in the refrigerator."

"The subrecipes here are super versatile and should become staples in your kitchen."

Soups
&
Stews

Tomato Soup and Salad

ALICE WATERS [Chez Panisse, *Berkeley, California*]

LISTENING TO ALICE WATERS TALK ABOUT THE PLEASURE OF
biting into a ripe summer tomato off the vine is like listening to poetry for the palate—my mouth is watering. Such a stickler for only cooking seasonally, when she watched *Julie and Julia* apparently her one comment was that Julia Child would not have found basil in the Paris market—it would have been out of season.

Shelling beans together, we shared a moment thinking about Rose Gray from the River Café who had recently died. Peas in a pod, Gray and Waters both adopted a foreign cuisine (Italian and French respectively) and transformed the notion of cooking in their homelands to be simpler, authentic, and delicious.

Waters has chosen to share two dishes—one salad and one soup—both deeply soothing in very different ways.

Tomato soup is a quintessential American comfort food, usually eaten with a grilled cheese sandwich. I like the notion that Waters takes the bread of the sandwich and uses this to thicken her soup in the Italian tradition of *Pappa al Pomodoro*. Cheese is used to garnish the soup, along with basil leaves and olive oil. The best tomatoes for Waters' soup are ripest when the weather is warmest, so she suggests serving the soup hot or cold.

Given Waters' high-profile political work, it seems fitting to look back at a trio of old recipes for tomato soup from the *White House Cook Book* (1887) by Mrs. F. L. Gillette. Like Waters' recipe, these three variations from the nineteenth century are an ode to simplicity, combining few ingredients with straightforward preparation.

She also showcases the tomatoes in their raw state. "When tomatoes are plentiful, this salad is on the menu at Chez Panisse every day, varying slightly with the many possible garnishes," says Waters. "There is usually a mix of tomatoes of different colors, sizes, and flavors. Garlic croutons are always present—slices of *levain* bread or torn-up, bite-size pieces, oiled, toasted, and rubbed with garlic while still warm from the oven. They are best mixed in with the tomatoes so that they absorb the juices." Waters' recipe for the perfect tomato salad is more a set of ideas than strict weights and measures, not unlike early American recipes.

TOMATO SOUP. No. 1.

Place in a kettle four pounds of beef. Pour over it one gallon of cold water. Let the meat and water boil slowly for three hours, or until the liquid is reduced to about one-half. Remove the meat and put into the broth a quart of tomatoes, and one chopped onion; salt and pepper to taste. A teaspoonful of flour should be dissolved and stirred in, then allowed to boil half an hour longer. Strain and serve hot. Canned tomatoes, in place of fresh ones, may be used.

TOMATO SOUP. No. 2.

Place over the fire a quart of peeled tomatoes, stew them soft with a pinch of soda. Strain it so that no seeds remain, set it over the fire again, and add a quart of hot boiled milk; season with salt and pepper, a piece of butter the size of an egg, add three tablespoonfuls of rolled cracker, and serve hot. Canned tomatoes may be used in place of fresh ones.

TOMATO SOUP. No. 3.

Peel two quarts of tomatoes, boil them in a sauce-pan with an onion, and other soup vegetables; strain and add a level tablespoonful of flour dissolved in a third of a cup of melted butter; add pepper and salt. Serve very hot over little squares of bread fried brown and crisp in butter.
An excellent addition to a cold meat lunch.

Three recipes for "Tomato Soup" from the White House Cook Book *by Fanny Lemira Gillette, published in 1887.*

Tomato Soup and Salad

Alice Waters' thick tomato soup is a version of the Italian classic *Pappa al Pomodoro* and her simple suggestions for a tomato salad are a play on a *Caprese*; a perfect pairing for a September supper when tomatoes are still abundant but the chill of fall is fast approaching.

Tomato and Bread Soup

2 small onions

4 to 6 cloves garlic

1/2 to 3/4 cup fine-quality, extra-virgin olive oil

Salt

2 pounds very ripe tomatoes, cored and roughly chopped

1 small bunch basil (about 1/4 pound), leaves picked, stems reserved

2 to 2 1/2 cups bread crumbs

Parmigiano-Reggiano cheese

SERVES 6

To Make the Tomato and Bread Soup

1. Peel and dice the onions and peel and chop the garlic. In a sauté pan, sauté the onions in about 1/2 cup of the olive oil until soft. Add the garlic and some salt and cook a few minutes more.

2. When the onions and garlic are done, remove and set aside one-third of the mixture. Add the tomatoes to the remaining onion mixture along with the basil stems and cook for about 15 minutes to make a nice tomato sauce. Pass through a food mill and return to the pan.

3. Add the reserved onions and garlic to the tomato sauce. Over very low heat, stir in about 1 1/2 cups of the bread crumbs. After 10 minutes, turn off the heat and let the soup sit for 10 minutes. As the bread crumbs absorb the liquid, the soup will slowly thicken. The dryness and density of the bread crumbs, the soupiness of the tomatoes, and your own personal preference will dictate how much bread to add. The denser the crumbs, the longer the soup takes to thicken and the less you will need. If you have very dense bread, make finer crumbs and cook the soup more slowly. If the soup thickens too much, thin it out with a little water.

4. Chop a handful of the basil leaves and stir them into the soup, with a little more olive oil if you like, and taste and adjust the seasoning.

5. Serve hot or cold, garnished with a thread of olive oil, the grated cheese, and a whole basil leaf, if you wish.

To Make the Tomato Salad

Choose the best tomatoes you have that are fully ripe but not too soft. Slice large tomatoes in wedges or slices, or cherry tomatoes in half. Moisten with balsamic vinegar (how much will depend on the sweetness and acidity of the tomatoes), season with salt and pepper, and drizzle generously with fine olive oil. Mix gently to keep the tomatoes intact and garnish with any of the following, singly or in combination: basil leaves, torn, cut into a chiffonade, or left whole; garlic croutons; slices of fresh mozzarella or the tiny bocconcini mozzarellas; sliced red onion; brandade- and tapenade-topped croutons.

Chef Waters' Tips

"Make sure you choose very ripe tomatoes, or the soup may be too acidic."

"The best bread crumbs to use for this are from light, white Italian-style bread that is fairly dry and finely crumbled."

Strawberry Gazpacho

DAVID KINCH [Manresa, *Los Gatos, California*]

JAMES BEARD AWARD-WINNER DAVID KINCH IS ALL ABOUT *TERROIR* and his sense of place on the Californian Coast. His partnership with Cynthia Sandberg and Love Apple Farm in the Santa Cruz Mountains ensures a year-round supply of bio-dynamic produce for his two-Michelin-star restaurant, Manresa. From the farm to his table via his kitchen, where he works his magic, Kinch gives every plate his highly personal haute cuisine touch.

Cold soup may not be the first dish that jumps to mind as a comfort food, but think of a hot summer's day in coastal California and how soothing a cup of chilled gazpacho soup would be. This is not your everyday gazpacho either—instead of tomatoes Kinch uses ripe strawberries. The resulting flavor profile is indeed familiar and yet new, more complex, and subtle. A cold soup made from strawberries that isn't a dessert is definitely an unexpected twist, but whoever decided that tomatoes were the only fruit to be given savory status?

"The idea of the gazpacho came about after a discussion and tasting of a bowl of strawberry purée and a bowl of tomato purée next to each other," says Kinch. "I realized that it was very hard to distinguish the two from each other. In fact, if you didn't know what you were tasting, you might mistake the flavor of strawberry as a super-ripe tomato purée."

How We Cook in Los Angeles (1894) includes a section that's all about growing strawberries in your garden year-round in Southern California—"200 hundred plants will be sufficient for an ordinary family." Given the large quantity of strawberries called for in Kinch's recipe it might be time to get digging. For those without a green thumb, it's definitely worth a trip to your local farmers' market to buy the ingredients. "Ripeness is key when it comes to selecting the strawberries," says Kinch. The riper the strawberries, the better the soup. This soup combines the flavors of summer—a food memory to draw upon for comfort as the winter months roll around.

5 pounds ripe strawberries, hulled

1/2 pound white onion, thinly sliced (about 1 onion)

1/2 pound red bell peppers, cored, seeded, and thinly sliced (about 2 medium peppers)

5/8 pound cucumbers, peeled, seeded, and thinly sliced

1 clove garlic, peeled, thinly sliced

1 cup fresh tarragon leaves

1/2 cup extra-virgin olive oil

6 tablespoons balsamic vinegar

Fine sea salt

Croutons, for garnish (optional)

Cubed cucumber for garnish (optional)

SERVES 10

1. To make the consommé, place half the strawberries in a large bowl and wrap tightly with plastic wrap. Place the bowl over a double boiler and simmer until the strawberries have given up their liquid, about 2 hours. The strawberries will look like they have given everything up—pale and soggy in a vibrant red liquid, the consommé.

2. Strain the consommé, letting it drain without pressing and refrigerate.

3. Crush the other half of the strawberries by hand over a bowl. Add the onions, bell peppers, cucumbers, garlic, tarragon, extra-virgin olive oil, and balsamic vinegar. Cover and marinate overnight in the refrigerator.

4. Purée strawberry-vegetable mixture in a blender, then strain. Adjust the thickness by thinning the purée with the strawberry consommé.

5. Season with fine sea salt and serve chilled topped with croutons or little cubes of cucumber (they do a number of variations at Manresa).

Chef Kinch's Tips

"You can use any type of cucumber, but given a choice, I would use small garden cucumbers."

"Take the seeds out of the cucumbers and remove the white pith of the red peppers; these are not pure flavors."

"Make sure the bowls or glasses you choose to serve the soup in are really well chilled."

"The covered soup will keep well in the refrigerator for several days."

Spiced Corn Broth with Scallops, Noodles, and Herbs

JODY ADAMS [Rialto, *Boston, Massachusetts*]

JODY ADAMS' PHILOSOPHY ON FOOD IS SIMPLE and straightforward: it should be both delicious and affordable. "I am thrilled with our country's growing desire to learn where our food comes from, to support small farms, and to buy sustainably. The knowledge that's presented by people like Michael Pollan and movies like *Food, Inc.* is great. While recognizing that, to say that we should all be eating from our local farmer and planting stuff is just unrealistic. So how can we really look at feeding our nation in a way that people get the best they can get and not pay a fortune for it?"

Adams practices what she preaches—she likes to cook using meat or fish protein as an accent because it's a healthy and economically practical approach. "I can go for days without animal protein but I also think we need it—and it's delicious!" The Italian approach to food, Adams contends, is really the one that makes the most sense in terms of the body and the environment.

"I don't do complicated," says Adams. "Rialto is an Italian restaurant." She does, however, incorporate many culinary influences from her travels abroad into her dishes, including a recent trip to Cambodia—"I was struck by how similar Cambodian food was to Italian food, in that it was about taking the best of what's available—mostly plants and lots of herbs—and using less meat." She was particularly taken by their approach to soups: "Everything goes into a bowl—vegetables, rice noodles, with a hot broth poured over it—and that is how it's cooked."

Adams applies this Asian technique to a classic corn chowder recipe from New England, and the result is a lighter, more sophisticated soup that is equally satisfying. Old American recipes for corn soups and chowders are thick and heavy, laden with cream or milk, flour, and butter. Fannie Farmer's "Corn Soup" in the section "Soups Without Stock," in the *Boston Cooking-School Cook Book*, is a good example of this.

Adams's spiced corn broth with scallops, noodles, and fresh herbs is a refreshing and delicious take on the rich, stodgy corn soups of one hundred years ago. "This is an August recipe," says Adams, "an end-of-the-summer finale, when local corn is at its peak."

Corn Soup.

1 can corn.	2 tablespoons butter.
1 pint boiling water.	2 tablespoons flour.
1 pint milk.	1 teaspoon salt.
1 slice onion.	Few grains pepper.

Chop the corn, add water, and simmer twenty minutes; rub through a sieve. Scald milk with onion, remove onion, and add milk to corn. Bind with butter and flour cooked together. Add salt and pepper.

A recipe for "Corn Soup" from the Boston Cooking-School Cook Book *by Fannie Merritt Farmer, published in 1896.*

Spiced Corn Broth

1/2 pound rice vermicelli noodles

1 1/2 cups fresh corn kernels, stripped from cobs, cobs reserved (3 to 4 ears)

2 tablespoons extra-virgin olive oil

1 large white onion, cut into 1/4-inch-thick slices (about 2 cups)

4 stalks lemongrass, sliced crosswise into 1/2-inch pieces

4 cloves garlic, smashed and peeled

2 tablespoons thinly sliced fresh ginger

Kosher salt and freshly ground pepper

1/2 pound sea scallops, trimmed of tough muscle and sliced 1/4 inch thick; reserve the muscle

4 cups fish stock or 2 cups high-quality, low-sodium boxed chicken stock

2 cups bottled clam juice

2 ounces pancetta, cut into 1/4-inch dice

1 tablespoon thinly sliced garlic (3 to 4 cloves)

1 tablespoon finely julienned fresh ginger

1 tablespoon minced anchovy (about 4 fillets)

1 tablespoon light brown sugar

1/4 to 1/2 teaspoon hot red pepper flakes

Freshly squeezed juice of 1 lime

3 scallions, ends trimmed, green and white parts sliced diagonally as thinly as possible

1 cup ripe tomato, cut into 1/4-inch dice (about 6 ounces)

1 cup thinly sliced peeled cucumber

Accompaniments

1 lime, quartered

Asian fish sauce and hot sauce

1 small bunch each of mint, cilantro, and basil

SERVES 4

---

1. Soak the noodles in warm water according to the package directions (3 to 10 minutes, depending on thickness). After they've softened, drain and use a pair of kitchen scissors to snip them into 2-inch lengths. Set aside.

2. Cut the corn cobs into 1-inch lengths.

3. Heat 1 tablespoon of the olive oil in a large saucepan over medium-high heat. Add the onions, lemongrass, smashed garlic, and sliced ginger, and season with salt and pepper. Sauté until the vegetables begin to brown around the edges, about 4 minutes.

4. Add the corn cobs, scallop muscles, stock, clam juice, and 3 cups of water. Bring to a boil, then lower the heat and simmer for 35 minutes. Strain into a bowl; you should have about 6 cups of corn broth.

5. Return the saucepan to the stove over medium heat. Add the remaining tablespoon of olive oil, the pancetta, sliced garlic, and julienned ginger, and cook until the pancetta starts to render its fat and the vegetables are tender, about 3 minutes. Stir in the anchovy, sugar, and pepper flakes.

6. Return the broth to the saucepan, increase the heat to high, and bring it to a boil. Lower the heat and simmer for 10 minutes.

7. While the broth is simmering, toss the scallops with the lime juice.

8. When the broth has simmered for 10 minutes, add the soaked noodles to heat through.

9. In the bottom of four warm soup bowls, layer the corn kernels, scallions, tomato, cucumber, and scallops.

10. Scoop the noodles out of the broth with a pasta spider and distribute them evenly among the four bowls. Pour the broth over the noodles and serve. Offer guests lime wedges, fish sauce, hot sauce, and fresh herbs so everyone can finish their soup to taste.

Chicken Soup

TOM COLICCHIO [Colicchio & Sons, *New York, New York*]

"THIS IS WHAT I DO ON DAYS LIKE TODAY," SAYS TOM COLICCHIO, "I make chicken soup." It's blizzard conditions outside and it's taken five minutes for me to defrost as we sit together at Colicchio & Sons, the stylish restaurant he opened when his second son was a newborn. He tells me he is expecting a third son and jokes that he won't have to change the name from "& Sons" to "& Sons & Daughter"—"I would have done

that, too!" Colicchio's chicken soup is his go-to recipe at home; he cooks it up about twice a month for his family. He has never put it on the menu at Colicchio & Sons, which Sam Sifton described as having "an aesthetic that is entirely American." Sifton went on to say that "it appropriates all that has come to it, without apology" in his three-star *New York Times* review.

When Colicchio is in town and not on set as the chief judge on *Top Chef*, he's at his restaurants, although the James Beard Outstanding Chef of 2010 is the first to admit he cooks a lot less these days. Colicchio hates the term "celebrity chef," and finds it funny that movie stars, who he considers real celebrities, ask to meet him. We talk about apps for the iPad—he's not that impressed with the cooking ones to date. He enjoys reading the blog "Ideas in Food"—"There's a lot of information and the photography is great." However, the lack of ethics on a lot of the Internet food sites angers him. "They make stuff up, they claim they are journalists but it's tabloid and they don't check facts or even care. Horrible."

People have turned to chicken soup as a cold remedy for centuries around the world. Dubbed "Jewish Penicillin," chicken soup was even given as a prescription in England, and the Chinese also believe it helps to restore health. Recently science is catching up to tradition, and studies show that the soup does indeed have anti-inflammatory properties and thins mucus, plus the steam helps to decongest, the vegetables contain lots of healthy nutrients, and the light broth is easy to digest.

In medieval times in Europe, the soup was eaten separately from the chicken, which is how Colicchio suggests serving his dish. Across the world, starch has been added to the soup; rice noodles, pasta, potatoes, or dumplings can all be served with it.

Colicchio's chicken soup is restorative and bursting with flavor. "The hardest part of the recipe is the cutting of the chicken. I like to start the chicken in the water and cook for forty minutes before I add the vegetables, and then I add the pasta shells at the end." Once you've tried this simple and straightforward recipe, I'm certain you'll never go back to canned or boxed soup again.

1 chicken, quartered, with bones intact (do not remove the breast meat from the breastbone and include necks and giblets)

2 carrots, peeled and halved

2 celery stalks, washed and halved

2 leeks, washed well and halved

2 parsnips, peeled and halved

1 onion, peeled and halved

1 sprig fresh thyme

Kosher salt and freshly ground pepper

1 1/2 cups small shell pasta (optional)

Freshly grated Parmigiano-Reggiano cheese (optional)

Extra-virgin olive oil

Coarse sea salt

SERVES 4

1. Place 1 gallon of water and the chicken in a stockpot and bring to a simmer over medium heat. Simmer gently, skimming regularly, until the broth is fragrant, about 30 minutes.

2. Add the vegetables and thyme and continue to simmer for another 20 minutes. Season with salt and pepper.

3. Bring a large pot of salted water to a boil over high heat. Add the pasta and cook until al dente, about 8 minutes. Drain and divide the cooked pasta among four bowls.

4. Remove the chicken with a slotted spoon and place on a serving dish. Ladle the broth and vegetables over the pasta in the bowls and serve with the grated Parmigiano-Reggiano, more freshly ground pepper, and a drizzle of extra-virgin olive oil, if desired. Sprinkle the chicken with coarse sea salt and serve alongside the soup.

Walnut Matzo-Ball Soup

CRAIG STOLL [Delfina, *San Francisco, California*]

I HAD HOPED FOR A RECIPE FROM CRAIG STOLL FOR PIZZA— full-flavored authentic Italian food is what this James Beard award-winning chef is best known for at his restaurant Delfina. For ten minutes he tells me in great detail and with such passion that a pizza recipe involves so much that the accompanying text would be a book in and of itself. Instead we turn to his heritage.

Stoll grew up in New York, the son of forward-thinking Jewish parents who were passionate about food. They would dine at the best restaurants at home and abroad; at one point they even took Szechuan cooking lessons. This education instilled in their son a desire to grow up to be a chef. After a formal education at the Culinary Institute of America, Stoll packed his bags for Italy to do what his parents had shown him by example: glean all he could through total immersion. As Craig Stoll was thinking about a new dish to introduce on the menu at Delfina for Passover, he tapped into his heritage and came up with this comforting soup with his family's nutty twist.

Although traditionally a Passover dish, matzo-ball soup is served at every holiday in Stoll's family. "For years I tried to figure out where the walnut in my mother's matzo balls came from," he says. "Not even my grandmother knew why or when it began. Since the recipe for the matzo balls themselves is essentially the one from the side of the matzo-meal box, I referred to it last year when I went to make the soup at Delfina for Passover. The recipe instructs the cook to form balls with the batter 'the size of a walnut.' I recalled that my grandmother employed a German cook whose English was limited. I suspect that she misunderstood the walnut reference to literally mean 'Place a walnut in the center of each ball.' Whatever the story, we continue to do so and have always loved the results."

A recipe for matzo balls is found in *"Aunt Babette's" Cook Book: Foreign and Domestic Receipts For the Household: A valuable collection of receipts and hints for the housewife, many of which are not to be found elsewhere* (1889). Although not the first Jewish cookbook (Esther Levy's *Jewish Cookery Book* was published in 1871), it is interesting that *"Aunt Babette's"* is much more assimilated, and contains many nonkosher recipes using pork and shellfish. Interestingly, the recipe for matzo balls is in the chapter titled "Easter Dishes," which also includes instructions on how to make a seder plate and set the table for Passover. She says the matzo *kloesse,* "are very nice for soup." Given Stoll's family tradition of walnuts, it's lucky the German cook wasn't using Aunt Babette's recipe, which says to "form into little balls the size of marbles."

> **MATZO KLOESSE.**
> Soak some matzos about half an hour, and press out all the water. Heat some goose oil in a spider; cut up part of an onion very fine, heat it with the goose oil and dry the matzos in it. Put the matzos in a bowl; break in five or six eggs, a large handful of matzo flour, some salt and grated nutmeg and a very little ground ginger. Mix this thoroughly into the dough. Grease your hands, and form into little balls the size of marbles. You can make enough at once to last a few days. Keep in an ice-chest. Another way is to use all matzo flour, moistening the flour with scalding soup stock and proceed as above. These are very nice for soups.

A recipe for "Matzo Kloesse" From "Aunt Babette's" Cook Book by "Aunt Babette," published in 1889.

Walnut Matzo-Ball Soup

Stoll points out that "quantities are perhaps more than you'll need, but my mother never feels that there is enough unless we have copious amounts of leftovers." And just like the Stoll family, you don't have to save this comforting soup for Passover—make it part of your family get-togethers and start a new tradition.

2 gallons flavorful chicken stock

1 large chicken (about 4-pounds)

2 pounds additional chicken necks and backs

10 whole black peppercorns

2 or 3 bay leaves

1 head garlic, split in half

3 sprigs thyme

3 sprigs parsley

Kosher salt

5 medium carrots

2 bunches of celery, just the pale inner hearts and leaves

1 medium onion

1 cup toasted, halved walnuts

1 1/2 cups matzo meal

6 large eggs, lightly beaten

2 tablespoons chopped fresh curly parsley

1 tablespoon chopped fresh dill

SERVES 12

1. In a 12-quart or larger stockpot, combine the first eight ingredients. Add a small amount of kosher salt. Bring to a boil and immediately turn down to a simmer. Skim the top once with a ladle and discard the scum. Simmer for about 2 1/2 hours, or until the chicken is falling apart.

2. While the soup is simmering, scrape the carrots, cut in half lengthwise and slice into 1/4-inch-thick half-moons. Set aside. Pull the leaves off of the celery hearts and set aside. Slice the stalks of celery on the diagonal, 1/4 inch thick. Combine with the carrot and set aside. Peel the onion and cut in half from root to tip. Slice in half again and slice the quarters 1/8 inch thick. Combine with the carrots and celery.

3. Using a ladle, skim as much fat as possible off the top of the soup; reserve and refrigerate. Using a combination of a skimmer and tongs, gently remove the chicken from the pot. Place on a platter to cool. Strain the soup through a fine-mesh sieve, pour it back into the pot, and allow it to cool before refrigerating overnight.

4. Pull the skin off of the chicken. Pull the meat off of the bones. By hand, shred the meat into bite-size pieces along the grain of the meat (a piece should fit on a soupspoon). Discard the sinew, veins, and cartilage. Pack the chicken meat tightly in a bowl and cover tightly with plastic wrap. Refrigerate overnight.

5. The next day, remove the soup and the reserved chicken fat from the refrigerator. With a soupspoon, scrape the fat off of the top of the soup and combine it with the previously reserved fat. This is the *schmaltz*. Allow the fat to warm but not liquefy in the vicinity of the stove. Remove 8 cups of stock from the pot and bring to a simmer in a second, wide pot. Skim the foam and fat from the top. Check and adjust the salt if necessary.

6. Pour the matzo meal into a large mixing bowl. Add a pinch or two of kosher salt and whisk together well. Add the eggs, 6 tablespoons of the schmaltz, and 6 tablespoons of the cooled chicken broth. Mix until the batter *just* comes together. The batter should be stiff enough to just form a ball but it will be somewhat difficult to work with. A loose batter is part of the secret to light, fluffy matzo balls. Refrigerate the mixture for 20 minutes.

7. Fill a small bowl with cool tap water. Dip your hands in to wet them. Grasp a walnut in one hand and then scoop up enough batter to form a 1-inch ball around the walnut; gently drop it into the simmering soup. Repeat, until you have four or five matzo balls in the pot at one a time. Simmer gently for about 20 minutes, until the balls have fluffed up and are floating. When cut in half, the matzo ball should be moist all the way to the center—but there should not be an undercooked core around the walnut. You may have to sacrifice one in order to test the doneness. When done, transfer the cooked matzo balls to a large platter. Keep them covered between batches.

8. While the matzo balls are cooking, add the cut vegetables to the main pot of soup and cook until soft. When done, add the chicken and the matzo balls. Simmer until both the chicken and the matzo balls are heated through. Add the chopped parsley and chopped dill, simmer 5 more minutes, and serve.

Steamed Pork Meatball Soup

Harold Dieterle [Kin Shop, *New York, New York*]

WITH AN ICE STORM FORECAST FOR later that night, Harold Dieterle's new restaurant Kin Shop in Manhattan's Greenwich Village was the perfect antidote to a brutally cold winter's evening. Warm, comforting, and with intense umami, one mouthful of his spicy pork meatball soup and concerns about adverse weather conditions instantly melt away. I'm warmed from within. Kin Shop is a Thai restaurant, but perhaps more Thai-American, in that tried-and-true way this country has of adopting ingredients and dishes from around the world and adapting them for the American palate—serving up equal measures of comfort and heat. Dieterle has spent time in Thailand and it shows in the authentic depth of flavor in his dishes. He's not afraid to serve his customers something with a little more spice than the usual Americanized version of pad Thai.

Dieterle credits his mother for first inspiring him to be a chef, as they cooked traditional Sicilian Sunday suppers together. Home economics classes at school, a series of *stages* in Spain, and studies at the Culinary Institute of America in Hyde Park, New York paved Dieterle's path to becoming a chef. After graduating from culinary school, he went to work in restaurant kitchens in and around New York City until reality television came calling.

Dieterle competed in and won the first season of Bravo's *Top Chef* back in 2006. The following year, helped by his winnings, he opened his first restaurant, Perilla, in the West Village. The seasonal menu at Perilla is American based with Dieterle's Italian roots shining through. The chef loves to play with the flavors of Asia and calls Perilla "a New American restaurant with Asian influences." I can't help but think this could describe Dieterle—a new American chef with Asian influences.

Dieterle is riding the wave of the American palate's growing demand for more intense and exotic flavors. "You could add egg noodles to the meatball soup," he says. "But it's pretty satisfying just the way it is." Perhaps one hundred years from now spicy Thai meatball soup, with or without noodles, will feel as American as spaghetti and meatballs.

1 onion, very finely chopped

5 cloves garlic, very finely chopped, plus 2 tablespoons minced fried garlic for garnish

1 pound ground pork butt

1 tablespoon coarsely chopped fresh basil

2 tablespoons chili sauce, such as Sriracha or Sambal

1/4 cup panko bread crumbs

2 large eggs, lightly beaten

Salt and freshly ground pepper

2 tablespoons minced fresh ginger

2 quarts pork stock

1/4 cup black sweet soy sauce, such as Kwong Hung Seng

1/4 cup fish sauce

1 teaspoon blended oil, 90% canola and 10% olive

8 pieces baby bok choy, split

SERVES 4

1. In a sauté pan, cook the garlic and onion in a bit of oil. Chill briefly, and then add to the ground pork.

2. Mix together the basil, chili sauce, bread crumbs, and beaten eggs and combine with the pork. Form the mixture into 1-ounce meatballs and steam until cooked through, about 20 minutes.

3. In a large saucepan, cook the minced ginger in oil.

4. Add the pork stock and season with the fish sauce and soy sauce.

5. Add the pork meatballs and braise for 30 minutes.

6. Taste and adjust the seasoning, add the bok choy to the soup, and cook for about 3 minutes.

7. Divide the soup equally among four bowls and garnish each with some fried garlic.

Gratinéed French Onion Soup

ALAIN DUCASSE [Benoit, *New York, New York*]

AS I TURN THE CORNER ONTO FIFTY-FIFTH STREET FROM SIXTH
Avenue to visit Benoit, I am filled with emotion. It has been five years since I last made my way here, back when it was *la grande dame* La Côte Basque and I was visiting my father-in-law in his restaurant. This is where I got married back in 1998, where we celebrated birthdays and reveled with our friends at black-tie dinner parties upstairs in the private rooms—never before had La Côte Basque seen hula hooping on the tables—and given that it's now Alain Ducasse's domain, I doubt it ever will again.

I push round in the revolving door, the very same one from La Côte Basque and before that Henri Soulé's Le Pavillon (Rachou took the door, along with the murals, when he moved the restaurant down the street to this location). A who's who of the rich and famous have passed through this door—presidents and royalty, movie stars, writers, and captains of industry. The space is so familiar and yet completely different. Unlike my previous visits, no one knows me and I can't head straight back to the kitchen to have the chef fix me a little lunch. Ducasse has transformed the space into his version of a Parisian bistro, Benoit. "A French bistro is the steak house *à la française*," he says, "but for New Yorkers we have adapted the proposal to put forth lighter, fresher, market-driven options. Also, on this side of the Atlantic Ocean organs are not necessarily featured on bistro menus around town."

Born on a farm in southwest France, Ducasse began working in restaurant kitchens when he was sixteen and rose up through the ranks to the very top of the culinary world. Not satisfied with his worldwide empire, he sought out a presence in New York to further his insatiable ambitions, beginning with the *très* elegant Alain Ducasse at the Essex House in 2000. "While each region has drawn from its *terroir*—the climate, soil, and sun—to yield singular products," says Ducasse, "the flair and individuality of the multiple cultural influences in the United States have set the stage for modern cuisine."

32. SOUPE A L'ONION.

ONION SOUP. (*Lean—Clear.*)

PROPORTIONS.—For five persons:

Onions............................12 (somewhat according to the size).
Butter......................2 tablespoonful.
Flour............................1 tablespoonful
Bread.............................½ lb.
Rasped cheese...................½ lb.
Water............................2 to 3 quarts.
Time.—1 hour.

PREPARATION.—1st. Have about 12 fine slices of bread and ½ lb. of rasped cheese, Parmesan preferred, place some slices on the bottom of a dish that can be put in an oven, pour over a bed of cheese, then a bed of bread, etc., finishing by a bed of bread but preserving enough cheese for a last bed. 2d. Chop about 12 onions, let them cook slowly in a sauce pan with about 2 tablespoonful of butter until a light brown, add while stirring 1 tablespoonful of flour, stir the whole for a while, then add 2 quarts of water. 3d. Allow to cook for 5 minutes. 4th. Pour this soup through a strainer on the bed prepared as above. 5th. Pour over the dish a last bed of cheese, and let it bake until a light brown.

CAUTION.—In serving this soup take care to give each guest some of the crust, dry and palatable.

NOTE.—You may have a good family soup by doing only as indicated in the 2d. and 3d. and serving it with some toast and rasped cheese.

A recipe for "Soupe A L'Onion" from La Cuisine Française. French Cooking for Every Home. Adapted to American Requirements *by Fraçois Tanty, published in 1893.*

Memories of simple food and the flavors of his grandmother's cooking feed into his ideas of what he likes to cook for himself at home if he wants something comforting. "Pasta, with olives, tomato paste, and pesto. The three are a classic combination of Mediterranean tastes: olive, tomato, and basil. No cheese." He also tells me he's rather partial to American sandwiches. "There is nothing like a freshly made bacon, lettuce, and tomato club sandwich. Straightforward, satisfying, refreshing."

I am curious if Ducasse's menu at Benoit differs from that which he'd serve in Paris. "Gratinéed French onion soup corresponds perfectly to the American palate," he says. "Perhaps one might consider this dish to be synonymous with the classic grilled cheese; both being gorgeously cheesy."

Long before Julia Child, French cooking found its way across the Atlantic and was extremely fashionable. Thomas Jefferson returned from Paris with handwritten recipes for the food he had eaten and fallen in love with. Americans wanted to emulate French cooking both in restaurants and at home, and many regular dishes were elevated simply by being given French-sounding names. A little book published in 1893, *La Cuisine Française. French Cooking for Every Home. Adapted to American Requirements* by François Tanty is an interesting example particularly because, unlike Escoffier's *Le Guide Culinaire*, it is aimed at the American home cook, with the cooking being "a little less refined [than traditional French cooking], but quite as palatable." In Tanty's recipe for "Soupe A L'Onion," half a pound of "rasped cheese" (rasped is an old-fashioned way of saying grated), is layered with bread, and then the soup is poured over it, and it's baked in the oven—the cheese melts and makes a perfect bubbling top, not unlike what we find today at Alain Ducasse's New York bistro.

1½ **pounds medium onions, halved lengthwise, then thinly sliced lengthwise**

4 **tablespoons (½ stick) unsalted butter**

¼ **cup dry white wine**

2 **quarts beef broth**

Cheesecloth sachet filled with 4 whole cloves, 3 bay leaves, 1 tablespoon crushed black pepper, 1 sprig fresh thyme, and ½ head of garlic, tied with kitchen twine

6 **slices of baguette, cut on the diagonal ¼ inch thick**

¼ **cup port wine**

2 **tablespoons Swiss cheese, grated**

½ **pound Gruyère, Comté, or Emmental cheese, grated**

Salt

SERVES 6

1. In a 4- to 5-quart heavy-bottomed pot over high heat, cook the onions in the butter with a little salt, uncovered, stirring frequently, until the onions are deep golden brown, about 5 minutes.

2. Lower the heat and cook the onions until very soft.

3. Stir in the white wine and cook, stirring for 2 minutes. Stir in the broth and the cheesecloth sachet and simmer, uncovered, stirring occasionally for 30 minutes.

4. While the soup simmers, position a rack in the middle of the oven and preheat the oven to 350°F.

5. Arrange the slices of baguette in a single layer on a large baking sheet and toast them in the oven until completely dry, turning them over once, about 15 minutes.

6. Remove the bread from the oven and heat the broiler. Place six 8- to 10-ounce, ovenproof soup crocks or ramekins onto a shallow baking sheet.

7. Discard the sachet from the soup, and just before serving, stir in the port wine.

8. Divide the soup evenly among the soup crocks, then float a toast in each. Sprinkle enough Gruyère and Swiss cheese mélange to cover the top of each crock, allowing the cheese to hang over the rim.

9. Broil the filled soup crocks 4 to 5 inches from the heat source until the cheese is melted and bubbly, 1 to 2 minutes.

Modern Mock Turtle Soup

MICHAEL VOLTAGGIO [ink., *Los Angeles, California*]

NO STRANGER TO THE LIMELIGHT, MICHAEL VOLTAGGIO WON the Emmy-winning season six of *Top Chef*, beating out none other than his older brother, Bryan. In a recent post on their website, the younger Voltaggio shared photographs showing what the two like to eat as a midnight snack when they are hanging out together—a chicken and potato chip sandwich followed by Ritz crackers with Nutella for dessert. Somehow, the Voltaggio brothers make even the most lowbrow of foods look appealing.

I wanted to give Voltaggio a challenging recipe to contribute and selected the most whimsical of all the old dishes, mock turtle soup. Recipes for this consommé with beef are numerous in early American cookbooks and yet it is no longer even heard of today. At the end of the nineteenth century, mock dishes were very popular—I've even come across a mock apple pie recipe made with crushed crackers and lemon juice. *The Great Western Cook Book* (1857) by Angelina Maria Collins is written for the "Ladies of the West" and contains a recipe for "Mock Turtle Soup" that calls for a boiled calf's head, eggs, the juice of two lemons, and "a half pint of wine when ready to serve."

MOCK TURTLE SOUP.

Take the upper from the lower part of a calf's head, and put both in a gallon of water and boil till tender.

Strain the liquor, let it stand till next day, and take off the fat. Hang it over the fire three-quarters of an hour before serving it, and season it with salt, cloves, pepper, mace, and sweet herbs, tied in a bag. Add half a pint of rich gravy. Darken it with browned flour or fried sugar. Then put in the yolks of eight eggs boiled hard, the juice of two lemons, and force-meat balls. When ready to serve, add half a pint of wine.

A recipe for "Mock Turtle Soup" from the Great Western Cook Book *by Angelina Maria Collins, published in 1857.*

In the final throes of opening his new restaurant ink. when we meet, Voltaggio is excited to show me the space. The name comes from his signature tattoo but more importantly it comes from the notion that ink on the page is the basis for all creativity. "If you get an idea, you write it down in ink. I also like the idea of the Rorschach test when you hold up blots and interpret them." At the restaurant there are blots of ink on the floor. "I think even the dishes themselves could be seen like a Rorschach test—you'll eat something and it will be different to you than it is to me."

"His dishes are thoughtful," says chef Tom Colicchio about Voltaggio's food, "they make sense. He's trying to make good food, and he uses techniques to that end. His food is new and it's different, but it's not that far away from tradition." Voltaggio considers his modern style of cooking to be specific to Los Angeles: "In this city you can eat almost anything from around the world without having to travel, and I wanted to tap into that melting pot."

Not one to do things by half-measures, Voltaggio has put a lot of thought into this recipe. "When I started to research mock turtle soup, I found that most were broth based rather than cream based." His resulting beefy consommé is full of flavor, which he achieves by using a pressure cooker. "It gives a cleaner faster flavor, it's not muddy tasting," he says. "The pressure cooker is the most important part of the recipe—and at around one hundred dollars, it is a small investment for an amazing tool. I use it for everything."

A warm steaming wave of beef aroma laced with a hit of lemon wafts up from the bowl. Even the most squeamish of eaters (that would be me) will forget the pigs foot or beef cheek, and tuck in.

Modern Mock Turtle Soup

Michael Voltaggio brings this classic American soup back to life. The addition of the kombu and bonito flakes gives the broth an essence of seawater, "something turtley," Voltaggio says. The pressure cooker's intense steam heat cooks the broth faster, tenderizes the meat, and produces a tastier, healthier soup.

Stock for Consommé

1 onion

3 pounds Wagyu beef cheek meat, whole

1/4 cup vegetable oil

Sea salt

1 cup red wine

5 1/4 pints chicken stock

2 carrots, peeled and cut into large dice

1 celery root, peeled and cut into into large dice

1 turnip, peeled and cut large dice

1 sheet dried kombu (about 2 ounces)

1 bay leaf

3 whole cloves

1 pig's foot

3 egg whites

1/3 ounce bonito flakes

Quail Egg Garnish

10 quail eggs

Madeira-Lemon Drops

1 1/2 cups grapeseed oil

2 sheets gelatin

1 teaspoon agar agar

1 tablespoon sugar

6 1/2 tablespoons freshly squeezed lemon juice

1 cup Madeira

Extra-virgin olive oil, for drizzling

Micro chives, for garnish

SERVES 5

To Make the Stock for Consommé

1. Cut the onion in half. Place the halves, flesh side down, in a dry skillet. Cook over high heat until the onion halves are very black on the flesh side. Turn the heat off and leave the onion halves in the pan until needed.

2. Remove all the silverskin from the beef cheek. Add the vegetable oil to a pressure cooker pot and place over high heat. Season the cheek meat with salt and sear the cheek meat in the hot oil on all sides. Add the red wine and deglaze the inside of the pot removing all the the brown bits stuck to the bottom of the pot. Add the chicken stock and bring to a low simmer.

3. Add the carrots, celery root, turnip, kombu, bay leaf, and cloves to the pressure cooker. Add the blackened onion halves and the pig's foot. Seal the lid on the pressure cooker and cook on high pressure for 1 hour.

4. Release the pressure. Carefully remove the beef cheek without breaking it. Set it on a parchment paper–lined baking sheet and chill in the refrigerator until it sets up hard enough to slice.

5. Strain the stock through a sieve into another pot and discard the vegetables and the pig's foot (or eat it as a snack!). Allow the stock to cool almost to room temperature.

6. In a mixing bowl, whisk the egg whites until frothy, and fold in the bonito flakes. Mix the bonito-egg white mixture into the stock and return the pot to the stovetop. Over medium-low heat, cook just until the egg whites coagulate and form a raft on the surface. Reduce the heat to low and leave, undisturbed, until the raft is solid and the liquid underneath is clear. Poke a hole in the raft very carefully, trying not to break bits of it into the broth. Using a ladle, strain the consommé through a colander lined with a coffee filter into another pot.

To Make the Quail Egg Garnish

1. In a small saucepan, cover the quail eggs with cold water and place over medium heat. When the water comes to a boil, start timing and boil for 6 minutes.

2. Prepare an iced water bath. Using a slotted spoon, remove the eggs from the boiling water and transfer to the chilled ice bath. When cooled, carefully break each shell, release the cooked egg, and refrigerate.

To Make the Madeira-Lemon Drops

1. Place the grapeseed oil in a pint-size container; something with height for when you drop in the lemon drops. Put the grapeseed oil in the freezer at least 1 hour before starting.

2. Place the gelatin sheets into a container of ice water until softened. Mix together the agar agar, lemon juice, sugar, and Madeira, put into a small saucepan, and bring to a boil. Pour the mixture into the jar of a blender and blend on low

speed. Remove the gelatin from the ice water and squeeze out the excess water. Drop the softened gelatin sheets into the Madeira mixture. Pour the contents into a plastic squeeze bottle.

3. Remove the grapeseed oil from the freezer. Place the oil, in its container, directly into another bowl of ice in order to keep it as cold as possible. Secure the squeeze bottle in your hand. Release drops of the liquid from the squeeze bottle into the cold oil while moving your hand back and forth across the surface of the oil. The liquid should bead up in the oil as it drops and become tiny, caviar-like orbs at the bottom of the oil. Refrigerate until ready to serve.

To Assemble and Serve

1. Remove the cheek meat from the refrigerator. Cut 15 thin slices from the cheek. Arrange 3 of the thin slices of meat in the center of each of five bowls. Bring the consommé to a boil.

2. Using a slotted spoon, carefully place 2 poached quail eggs in each of the five bowls on top of the meat.

3. Using the slotted spoon, remove some of the Madeira drops from the grapeseed oil and transfer to a paper towel–lined tray to drain off excess oil. Place about a teaspoon of the drops on and around the cheek meat.

4. Drizzle a little bit of extra-virgin olive oil over the meat. Season with sea salt. Garnish with micro chives. Pour the boiling consommé over the garnish tableside.

Oyster Belly Chowder with Homemade Oyster Crackers

ROB EVANS [Hugo's, *Portland, Maine*]

DISCUSSING CHOWDERS, LOBSTERS, SOUPS, AND STEWS WITH
Rob Evans from Hugo's in Portland, Maine, is an education in and of itself. There were so many nuances that I really hadn't grasped until he started pointing them out. There's traditional New England chowder with cream, and Manhattan chowder with tomatoes; there is clear broth chowder from Rhode Island, usually made with fish, as well as the pale pink Long Island clam chowder that is a subtle fusion of both the creamy and tomato varieties. Chowder and lobster was all I ate when visiting a foggy Maine back in the late '90s. We took the ferry across from Portland to the charming Peaks Island to visit a friend and his grandparents for lunch. My plate was filled with the whole orange creature, tools at the ready next to it, and nothing else, just melted butter for dipping. I would have to work hard to crack into the crustacean to get to the perfectly cooked morsels of white succulent flesh. Back in Portland, my husband and I needed something to take the edge off the pure protein lunch. Local clam chowder, thick with vegetables, cream, and chewy briny bivalves, and topped with deliciously crunchy crackers, hit the mark.

"How about a chowder with oysters rather than the usual clams?" asks Evans. "And we can even make the oyster crackers for the top." New England native Evans, winner of the 2009 James Beard Best Chef: Northeast, with his wife Nancy, resurrected Hugo's in Portland, and put it up there with some of the best restaurants in America.

His beautiful, delicate plates of food and exciting twists on old favorites showcase seasonal local produce. "We are lucky that Maine is full of great products," says Evans. He likes to show respect to the farmers by listing them on the menu. "These things don't just come out of a vacuum, there are these people working really hard to produce great ingredients for us." Evans didn't go to culinary school, but he obviously picked up a thing or two from his time spent working at the French Laundry and the Inn at Little Washington, before Hugo's.

OYSTER CHOWDER.
Lewis G. Evans.

Fry out three rashers of pickled pork in the pot you make the chowder; add to it three potatoes and two onions, both sliced; cover with water; boil until they are nearly cooked; soak two or three dozen crackers in cold water a few minutes, then put into the pot a half can of best oysters, one quart of milk and the soaked crackers. Boil all together for a few minutes; season with salt, pepper, and butter. Fish Chowder can be made in the same way by using fresh fish instead of oysters.

Another Evans, who lived one hundred years before Chef Evans, wrote this recipe for "Oyster Chowder" in the *Presbyterian Cook Book* (1873), published in Dayton, Ohio.

Evans' recipe for a delicious New England chowder is really straightforward to make. And who knew it was so easy and so fun to make up a batch of oyster crackers? I have experimented with different cutters and like the little stars—especially good for a Fourth-of-July party. I also made up some using letter cutters for my children.

Lewis G. Evans' recipe for "Oyster Chowder" from the Presbyterian Cook Book, *compiled by the Ladies of the First Presbyterian Church, Dayton, Ohio, published in 1873.*

Oyster Belly Chowder with Homemade Oyster Crackers

This thick and creamy soup tastes of the seaside. Apart from the easy preparation, I love this oyster cracker recipe—baking them was one of the highlights of cooking for the book. The little crackers puff up in the oven to whatever shape you choose. Be creative and turn your chowder into an alphabet soup.

Oyster Crackers

1 envelope active dry yeast (about 1/4 ounce)

1/4 cup whole milk, warmed in a bowl in the microwave to 120°F, plus more as needed

1/2 cup all-purpose flour, plus more as needed for dusting

1/4 teaspoon salt

Oyster Belly Chowder

24 oysters

1 tablespoon bacon fat or pork fat

1/4 cup small diced celery

1/4 cup minced shallot

1/4 cup small diced carrot

1 tablespoon all-purpose flour

1 cup heavy cream

1 bay leaf

1 sprig thyme

1/2 cup small diced potato

1/2 teaspoon Worcestershire sauce

1/8 teaspoon Tabasco sauce

1 tablespoon chopped fresh flat-leaf parsley

1 tablespoon chopped celery leaf

1/4 teaspoon finely grated lemon zest

Salt

SERVES 4

To Make the Oyster Crackers

1. Sprinkle the yeast into the warm milk in the bowl and mix together. Let bloom for about 5 minutes.

2. Combine the flour and salt in the bowl of a stand mixer fitted with the paddle attachment. Add the warm milk-yeast mixture and combine. Adjust the consistency to make a smooth dough by adding a little extra flour or milk as needed.

3. Switch to the dough hook and knead in the stand mixer for 2 minutes.

4. Form the dough into a ball, place in a bowl, cover, and let rise for 1 hour. The dough should double in volume.

5. Preheat the oven to 425°F.

6. Roll out the dough, using a rolling pin or with a pasta machine, dialed to the first setting. Rest 1 minute between rolls. Roll 4 to 5 times to get it very thin.

7. Punch out the crackers with a small fluted cutter and transfer to a baking sheet lined with parchment paper, leaving a small amount of space between each cracker. Let rest 10 minutes, uncovered.

8. Bake the crackers for 6 minutes in the preheated oven, rotating the baking sheet halfway through the baking time.

9. Cool the crackers on a wire rack.

To Make the Chowder

1. Shuck the oysters and reserve 1 cup of liquid.

2. Trim the oyster bellies and set aside. Add the trimmings to the oyster liquid and bring to a simmer for 1 minute. Strain the oyster liquid through a fine-mesh sieve and set aside. Discard the trimmings.

3. In a 2-quart pan over medium heat, add the bacon fat, celery, shallots, and carrots and sweat them for 2 minutes. Add the flour, stir, and cook for 2 minutes more.

4. Add the cream, bay leaf, thyme, potato, Worcestershire sauce, Tabasco, and reserved oyster liquid. Simmer for 10 minutes. Reduce the heat to low.

5. Add the parsley, celery leaf, lemon zest and season with salt.

To Serve

1. Place 6 oyster bellies in each of four soup bowls and place in the oven for 1 to 2 minutes to gently warm the oysters.

2. Divide the chowder evenly among the bowls and top with homemade oyster crackers.

Mushroom Soup with Mushroom Hash

JOSIAH CITRIN [Mélisse, *Santa Monica, California*]

WE ARE OUT TO SEA AND THE WATERS ARE A LITTLE CHOPPY.
Seven days in to his annual juice fast, Josiah Citrin is not in the finest of moods. The chef's hunger, plus the rocking boat, sharpens his tongue. He's well respected by the other chefs who are fishing on the boat, many of whom are his friends and even some who have worked in his kitchen. This trip came about because after Donato Poto of Providence came fishing with me for a story for *edible Los Angeles*, he told Citrin and some other chefs about the outing during their weekly coffee at the Santa Monica Farmers' Market. They all wanted to go fishing, too. so I obliged.

The chefs have all brought food to share on the boat. Citrin makes a small open-faced sandwich, using an olive dip, some prosciutto, and a little cheese from the Cheese Store of Beverly Hills. He then adds the pièce de résistance—shaved truffles from the Truffle Brothers—and hands it to me. Now this is something I would break a fast for.

Rated number one in Los Angeles by *Zagat* since 2000 and the recipient of two Michelin stars, Josiah Citrin's restaurant Mélisse is a chic, fine-dining experience; something that is increasingly hard to find these days, especially in L.A. His food is exquisite—each plate a work of art with lots of colorful components. The white table-clothed dining room is ultrasophisticated and has a unique feature: on special occasions the ceiling retracts, and you can dine under the stars *en plein air*. Heavenly.

At Mélisse, Citrin serves a mushroom soup with a quenelle of truffle mousse and roasted chestnuts. Here he has pared down his recipe to give a simpler but no less flavorful and warming incarnation, serving it over a molded circle of mushroom hash and garnishing it with a pretty green sprig of chervil.

How We Cook in Los Angeles (1894) has a recipe for mushroom soup which instructs you to boil the mushrooms for two hours! I'm not sure what will be left to "press through a fine colander" but so glad we now have Citrin a century later with his refined soup.

Citrin and I shop for mushrooms together at the Santa Monica Farmers' Market. The locally foraged black mushrooms look good, he thinks, as do the chanterelles. "The good thing about this recipe," he says, "is that you use the best mushrooms you can find and you can even add some dried mushrooms to the mix for added depth of flavor." I'm thinking a sprinkling of the truffles from the boat would be a nice extravagant addition, too.

MUSHROOM SOUP
Mrs. Hugh W. Vail.

One tablespoon flour; 1 tablespoon butter; 1 quart milk; 1 pint mushrooms.

Melt flour and butter until very smooth, (do not brown), add the milk slightly heated to the flour and butter. Stir constantly in a double sauce pan until it becomes thick like cream.

To prepare the mushrooms. Peel and boil for two hours; when cold, press through a fine colander, and stir into the previously prepared soup until well heated through. Serve.

Mrs. Hugh W. Vail's recipe for "Mushroom Soup" from How We Cook in Los Angeles, *published in 1894.*

Mushroom Soup with Mushroom Hash

Josiah Citrin's velvety soup has such depth of flavor—it's earthy and almost meaty in its complexity. The little round of hash adds another dimension of texture. This is definitely one for my vegetarian mother next time she visits—an homage to our days of mushroom foraging together when I was a girl.

Mushroom Soup

2 tablespoons (¼ stick) unsalted butter

1 small sweet onion, peeled and sliced

2 cloves garlic, halved

1 leek, white part only, sliced

3 pounds cremini mushrooms, washed and sliced

4 pieces dried porcini

¼ cup peeled and diced celery root (about ¼-inch dice)

1 green apple, peeled and diced

1 cup mushroom broth

2 cups chicken stock

1 bouquet garni

¼ cup heavy cream

Sea salt and freshly ground pepper

Mushroom Hash

Grapeseed oil

2 fingerling potatoes, peeled, diced, and held in water

6 cremini mushrooms, washed and cut into small dice

1 shallot, cut into brunoise

1 tablespoon unsalted butter

Sea salt and freshly ground pepper

Fresh flat-leaf parsley, chopped

To Serve

2 tablespoons (¼ stick) unsalted butter

6 chervil sprigs

SERVES 6

To Make the Mushroom Soup

1. Melt the butter in a heavy-bottomed pot set over medium-low heat. Add the onions, garlic, and leek and sweat them, stirring often, for 5 minutes, or until translucent. Add the diced celery root and apple and sweat them, stirring often, for 3 minutes, Add the mushrooms and mix well. Increase the heat to medium and cook for 5 minutes, stirring often.

2. Add the mushroom broth, chicken stock, and bouquet garni and bring to a boil. Season lightly with salt and freshly ground pepper. Reduce to a simmer and cook for 20 minutes. Add the cream and dried porcini and bring to a boil. Reduce to a simmer and let cook for 15 minutes.

3. Transfer the soup in batches to a blender and purée on high speed until very smooth. Strain through a chinois or a fine-mesh sieve and season to taste with salt and pepper. Keep warm until ready to serve, or cool and reheat just before serving.

To Make the Musshroom Hash

1. Add grapeseed oil to a depth of ¼ inch in a heavy nonstick sauté pan. Heat the oil over high heat. Add the potatoes and sauté until golden.

2. Add the mushrooms and sauté for 5 minutes more, stirring every 30 seconds. Season with salt and pepper. Add the butter, shallots, and chopped parsley and sauté for 45 seconds, stirring well.

To Assemble and Serve

1. Bring the soup to a boil and add the butter.

2. Blend with an immersion blender until light and airy.

3. Place a 2-inch ring mold in the center of six warmed soup plates. Pack the molds with the mushroom hash; remove the ring mold. Garnish with a chervil sprig.

4. Give the soup a final blend and ladle it into the soup plates.

Chef Citrin's Tips

"Select the best-looking mushrooms at the market; if you can get wild mushrooms these will impart the most flavor."

"The soup can be prepared a day in advance and refrigerated."

"Be sure the potatoes are dried well before adding them to the sauté pan."

Gumbo Z'Herbes

LEAH CHASE [Dooky Chase's Restaurant, *New Orleans, Louisiana*]

"IT'S THE OLD POT THAT MAKES THE GOOD SOUP," GOES THE
old Creole proverb. As I listen to octogenarian Leah Chase reminisce about growing up in
Louisiana and her days spent in strawberry fields picking "culls"—the overripe fruit, too
sugary and squishy to ship North—to make strawberry wine, I am truly drawn into the
Queen of Creole Cuisine's world. Born in 1923 in New Orleans, it's so enlightening to be
talking history with someone who lived it, rather than reading about it in a book.

In 1946, Chase married the son of Dooky Chase's owners, just three months after they met. She started working at the restaurant in the 1950s after their children were all of school age, and she's been there ever since. The restaurant is a rich and vibrant scene; people come for the food, the art, and the music. Many jazz greats have played here and eaten Chase's food. She is a living legend, and I mean that quite literally, feeding presidents (she scolded President Obama for putting hot sauce in her gumbo!) and other such luminaries as Martin Luther King, Jr. (Dooky Chase was a gathering place for the civil rights movement in the 1960s). She has inspired Disney films (*The Princess and the Frog*) and been honored so many times that the list takes up two pages of her biography. She has four children, sixteen grandchildren, and four great-grandchildren, and let's not forget she still runs the restaurant.

Gumbo z'Herbes is a dish usually reserved for Lent and, in particular, for Maundy or Holy Thursday; the Thursday before Easter—the day when Christians commemorate the Last Supper. The basis for a gumbo is either okra or filé and a really thick brown roux. Chase makes her gumbo with filé, many varieties of slow-cooked greens, and lots of meat.

So much superstition and voodoo comes together in Chase's dish. "You can never use an even number of greens—it's considered very unlucky," she says very firmly. "And you can never use thirteen, very, very unlucky. So I use nine greens in my gumbo, based on a recipe handed down to me from my grandparents. Like anything, we have outgrown some of the things and it has been adapted." The recipe, for instance, calls for peppergrass, a wild herb Chase used to forage. It still grows in the South but won't be found in your local supermarket so Chase suggests substituting with watercress. "It has a peppery taste to it but more green and herb-like."

Recipes for gumbo in old American cookbooks are numerous, dating back to Mary Randolph's *Virginia House-wife* (1824). In Lafcadio Hearn's *La Cuisine Creole* (1885), there are nine recipes for gumbo, including one with the title "Remarks on Gombo of Okra or Filee" that describes the soup as "an economical way of using up the remains of any cold roasted chicken, turkey, game, or other meats."

The person Chase most admires for his wisdom, among the thousands she has met, is Howard Thurman: "If you sit quiet, and think," he said, "you will see what you can do and how you can do it." It strikes me that Chase rarely sits quiet for very long—there are always pots to scrub, sauces to stir, and guests to feed.

REMARKS ON GOMBO OF OKRA OR FILEE

This is a most excellent form of soup, and is an economical way of using up the remains of any cold roasted chicken, turkey, game, or other meats. Cut up and season the chicken, meat, or other material to make the soup; fry to a light brown in a pot, and add boiling water in proportion to your meat. Two pounds of meat or chicken (bones and all), with a half pound of ham, or less of breakfast-bacon, will flavor a gallon of soup, which, when boiled down, will make gombo for six people. When the boiling water is added to the meat, let it simmer for at least two hours. Take the large bones from the pot, and add okra or a preparation of dried and pounded sassafras leaves, called filee. This makes the difference in gombo. For gombo for six people use one quart of sliced okra; if filee be used, put in a coffee-cupful. Either gives the smoothness so desirable in this soup. Oysters, crabs, and shrimp may be added when in season, as all improve the gombo. Never strain gombo. Add green corn, tomatoes, etc., etc., if desired. Serve gombo with plain-boiled rice.

"Remarks on Gombo of Okra or Filee" from La Cuisine Creole by Lafcadio Hearn, published in 1885.

Gumbo Z'Herbes

Jadin loin, gombo gaté—"When the garden is far, the gumbo is spoiled." An old Creole saying. Given the large number of green ingredients in this dish, it is definitely one to make after a trip to the local farmers' market. Leah Chase's gumbo is so steeped in history and folklore it's a shame to have it only one day of the year—and don't forget to always use an odd number of greens!

1 bunch mustard greens

1 bunch collard greens

1 bunch turnip greens

1 bunch watercress

1 bunch beet tops

1 bunch carrot tops

1 bunch spinach

½ head lettuce

½ head green cabbage

2 medium onions, chopped (about 3 cups)

4 cloves garlic, crushed and chopped

1 pound smoked sausage

1 pound smoked ham

1 pound brisket, cubed

1 pound stew meat

1 pound hot sausage (chaurice)

5 tablespoons all-purpose flour

1 teaspoon fresh thyme leaves

1 teaspoon cayenne pepper

Salt and freshly ground pepper

1 teaspoon filé powder

SERVES 8 TO 10

1. Clean the greens under cold running water, making sure to pick out any bad leaves and rinse away any grit. Chop the greens coarsely and place in a 12-quart stockpot along with the onions and garlic, and cover with cold water (about 1½ gallons). Bring the mixture to a boil, reduce to a simmer, cover, and cook for 30 minutes.

2. Strain the greens and reserve the cooking liquid.

3. Cut all the meats, except the chaurice, into bite-size pieces (about 1-inch pieces) and place in the 12-quart stockpot with 2 cups of the reserved liquid. Steam over high heat for 15 minutes.

4. Meanwhile, cut the chaurice into bite-size pieces and cook in a skillet over high heat to render the fat, about 10 minutes. Remove the chaurice, keeping the grease in the skillet, and set aside.

5. Blend the greens in a food processor until puréed.

6. Place the skillet of chaurice grease over high heat and add the flour. Cook the roux until the flour is cooked, about 5 minutes; it does not have to be brown. Pour the roux over the meat mixture and stir to combine.

7. Add the puréed greens to the meat in a stockpot and add 2 quarts of the remaining reserved liquid. Simmer over low heat for 20 minutes. Add the chaurice, thyme, and cayenne, stir well, and season with salt and pepper; the smoked meats contain a lot of salt so go easy. Simmer for 40 minutes. Stir in the filé powder and remove the gumbo from the heat. Serve over steamed rice.

Rabbit Stew with Chanterelles and Biscuits

SUSAN SPICER [Bayona, *New Orleans, Louisiana*]

AS HER INSPIRATION, SUSAN SPICER chose to modernize a rabbit pie recipe from Lucidio Hearn's *La Cuisine Creole* (1885). The subheading for the book reads: *A Collection of Culinary Recipes From Leading Chefs and Noted Creole Housewives, Who Have Made New Orleans Famous for Its Cuisine.* Fast-forward one hundred years and Spicer is just that—a leading chef who has helped make New Orleans renowned for its cuisine with her restaurant Bayona. Spicer opened Bayona in 1990, housed in an eighteenth-century cottage in the French Quarter.

The first chef I meet with in New Orleans, she is not only very welcoming, but also extremely helpful with all her local knowledge and connections. She has given younger chefs, for example Donald Link, the helping hand they needed to become established. Together, she and Link started Herbsaint eleven years ago. Spicer has since relinquished her share to Link, and in addition to Bayona, she is now concentrating on her new venture, Mondo, in Lakeview, the neighborhood she has called home for twenty years. She was the inspiration for the chef in the HBO series *Treme* and acts as a consultant for the show.

In the small kitchen at Bayona, Spicer prepares kumquats with a young female cook, joking together in a manner far removed from the formal kitchens in France where Spicer trained in the '80s and where young cooks would have cowered in the presence of "Chef."

An 1885 rabbit pie recipe calls for "two or three young squirrels or rabbits" cooked up with mushrooms, parsley, and shallots. Once the dish is light brown, "throw in a glass of white wine." Spicer's pie has chanterelle mushrooms, added at the end—and no squirrels for today's American home cook, but a simple biscuit topping on a rich stew of rabbit and chanterelles. Rabbit is a great meat to use for a stew—it's low in fat and cholesterol, high in protein, has a mild flavor, and is highly sustainable. The Romans consumed a lot of rabbit and decreed that young maidens should be fed rabbit to make them more beautiful and more willing.

Stew

5 tablespoons olive oil

6 hind legs of rabbit, or 1 whole rabbit cut into 6 to 8 pieces

Salt and freshly ground pepper

3 cups chicken stock

2 bouquet garni of thyme, sage, parsley stems, and a bay leaf tied together

2 onions, 1 quartered and 1 diced

2 whole cloves

2 celery stalks, diced

1 medium carrot, peeled, split lengthwise, and cut into 1/2-inch pieces

2 medium turnips, peeled and diced

1 clove garlic, minced

1 teaspoon chopped fresh thyme

1/2 teaspoon chopped fresh sage

4 tablespoons all-purpose flour

1 cup milk or cream

2 tablespoons (1/4 stick) unsalted butter

1/2 pound fresh chanterelle mushrooms, washed and scraped (gills can be dirty)

Biscuits

2 cups sifted all-purpose flour

2 teaspoons baking powder

1/2 teaspoon salt

4 tablespoons (1/4 stick) unsalted butter or shortening

3/4 cup whole milk or buttermilk

SERVES 6

To Make the Stew

1. Heat 2 tablespoons of the olive oil in a large skillet or Dutch oven over medium-high heat until hot but not smoking. Season the rabbit well with salt and pepper and place the legs in the hot pan, turning to brown on all sides. For the best results, don't overcrowd the pan and try not to fuss with the pieces until they have a chance to brown.

2. Pour off the excess oil and add the chicken stock, 1 bouquet garni, and 1 onion, quartered and pierced with the cloves. Add enough water to just cover the rabbit; bring to a boil. Reduce the heat and simmer, covered, either on top of the stove or in a 350°F oven, turning once or twice, until the rabbit meat is tender and coming away from the bone, about 40 minutes.

3. Remove the pot from the heat, cool, and drain, reserving the liquid (you should have 4 cups; add additional chicken stock if necessary). When cool enough to handle, pick the meat off the bones and set aside. Discard the bones. Skim any excess fat off the reserved broth.

4. Heat 3 tablespoons of the oil in an 8- to 12-quart stockpot or other heavy-bottomed ovenproof pot or Dutch oven over medium heat. Add the diced onion, celery, carrot, and turnips, and cook for about 7 minutes.

5. Add the garlic, thyme, and sage, then sprinkle in the flour and stir 2 to 3 minutes. Whisk in the milk or cream, then 1 cup of the reserved stock and bring to a boil. Whisk in the remaining stock and add the remaining bouquet garni.

6. Return to a boil, then reduce heat, add the rabbit meat and a little salt, and simmer gently, stirring from time to time, about 12 minutes, until the vegetables are tender when pierced with a paring knife and the stew has a slightly thick, creamy consistency.

7. In a sauté pan, heat the butter; when hot, sauté the chanterelles over medium-high heat until the liquid they release has evaporated and they start to turn brown and get a little bit crispy. Season with salt and add to the stew.

8. Remove the stew from the heat; taste and adjust the seasoning. Serve with warm biscuits. (If you prefer a biscuit topping, instead of rolling out the biscuit dough, drop spoonfuls of dough onto the cooked stew and bake for 15 minutes at 400°F.)

To Make the Biscuits

1. Preheat oven to 450°F.

2. Sift the flour once; measure; add the baking powder and salt; sift again. Cut in the shortening. Add the milk all at once; stir carefully until the flour is dampened, then stir a bit more vigorously until the mixture forms a soft dough.

3. Turn out on a lightly floured board and knead 30 seconds.

4. Roll out the dough to 1/2-inch thick. Cut with a floured biscuit cutter. Bake on an ungreased cookie sheet for 12 to 15 minutes.

Beef Stew with Herbs and Spices

CHRISTIAN CAIAZZO [Osteria Stellina, *Point Reyes Station, California*]

AN HOUR NORTH OF SAN FRANCISCO, AFTER A DRIVE ACROSS
the Golden Gate Bridge and through stunning countryside, I arrive at the tiny coastal
town of Point Reyes Station, the home of Christian Caiazzo's restaurant Osteria Stellina.
With fresh seafood straight out of the bay, locally raised organic meats, and artisan cheeses
from the Cowgirl Creamery, all the components for following the Slow Food manifesto
are here in Marin County. On top of this Caiazzo has started cultivating the field next to
his house, growing produce for the restaurant.

Caiazzo, still dressed in his kitchen apron, takes me on a tour of the small farm.
"Soon we'll have fresh eggs," he says, as we pass a half-built chicken coop. "I made it big
enough to house lots of hens. I'm going to clad it in reclaimed wood when I get the time."
As well as chickens, he plans to raise goats and keep bees. He's not sure about pigs, as
much as he's into cooking snout-to-tail; he has two young children who are sensitive to
pet piggies ending up as pork sausages.

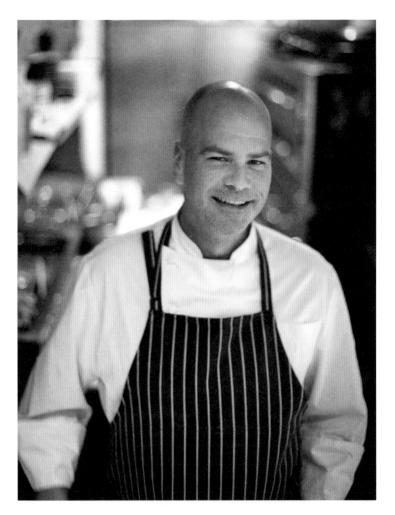

The sun is low in the sky, about to
disappear behind the magnificent rolling
hills. In the distance you get a glimpse of
the inlet where the oysters that are served
in his restaurant are harvested. This is
where Caiazzo has chosen to call home,
and you can understand why. He rattles
off a list of newly planted vegetables,
pointing to rows of thin green onion leaves
just beginning to sprout and some colorful
stalks of chard. He proudly shows me his
fava beans and snaps off a shoot for me to
try. "They taste like peas," he says. "We
use these in salads."

Few things are more comforting
than a bowl of Caiazzo's rustic beef stew.
The flavors of the meat are slowly cooked
out to form a rich gravy with hints of cinnamon and cloves. For a spicier stew, just
add an extra pinch of hot red pepper flakes.
At Stellina, the stew is served alongside a
creamy polenta—mashed potatoes would
work nicely, too.

3 pounds beef shoulder cut into 1- to 1½-inch cubes

3 tablespoons olive oil

7 cups good-quality beef stock (preferably homemade)

1 tablespoon chopped garlic (about 3 cloves)

Pinch of hot red pepper flakes

2 whole cloves

1 large cinnamon stick

2 carrots, chopped into ¾-inch pieces

1 Spanish onion, chopped into ¾-inch pieces

4 celery stalks, chopped into ½-inch pieces

2 tablespoons chopped fresh flat-leaf parsley, stems removed

1 tablespoon chopped fresh thyme leaves

1 tablespoon chopped winter or summer savory leaves

1 fresh bay leaf (or 2 dried bay leaves)

1 cup red wine

Salt and freshly ground pepper

SERVES 6

1. Thirty minutes to 1 hour prior to cooking, generously season the cubed beef with salt and pepper. Place in a colander to drain the liquids. Pat the meat dry with paper towel just before cooking.

2. Preheat the oven to 450°F. Place a large, heavy-bottomed roasting pan in the oven for 5 minutes to preheat. Add the olive oil to the hot pan, return the pan to the oven, and when the oil begins to smoke, remove the pan from the oven, and add the meat. Spread the meat out and return the pan to oven to evenly brown the meat. Every 5 minutes, stir the meat but be careful not to over stir. When the meat has a bit of color around the edges, remove the pan from the oven.

3. Pour the beef stock into a large pot and place over low heat. Adjust the temperature as necessary to keep it just below a boil.

4. Using a slotted spoon, remove the meat from the roasting pan and set aside. Place the pan on the stovetop over medium heat, quickly add the garlic, and stir with a wooden spoon. Stir in the pepper flakes, cloves, and cinnamon stick. Cook for 2 minutes, then add the carrots, onions, and celery. Sauté the vegetables for about 3 minutes. Add 1 tablespoon of the chopped parsley and season with salt and pepper to taste. Stir in ½ tablespoon of the chopped thyme and ½ tablespoon of the chopped savory and continue to sauté. When the vegetables have softened and the onions are translucent, about 5 minutes, add the bay leaf and the remaining parsley, thyme, and savory. Deglaze the pan with the red wine, reduce the heat, and simmer until the liquid has reduced by half.

5. Return the meat to the roasting pan and pour the hot stock over the meat. Stir and return the pan to the oven.

6. Once the stew begins to bubble, 5 to 10 minutes, reduce the oven temperature to 375°F; the stew should be just below a simmer. Cook for about 1½ hours; the cooking time depends on the tenderness of the beef. Stir the stew after 45 minutes and check that the liquid is reducing and the meat is tenderizing.

7. The stew is ready when the beef is fork-tender, and the liquid has reduced by about half and has thickened. Remove the stew from the oven and remove and discard the cinnamon stick and bay leaf. Taste and adjust the seasoning and let the stew rest for 5 minutes before serving.

Old World Goulash

WOLFGANG PUCK [Spago, *Beverly Hills, California*]

KNOWN FOR PUSHING BOUNDARIES WITH THE FOOD HE creates in his many restaurants, Wolfgang Puck will often look backwards when he cooks at home. For comfort food in particular, he turns to the traditional Austrian food of his childhood. "Goulash, a beef stew that goes back to the Austro-Hungarian Empire, is my idea of old-world comfort food—from my past life," he says. Vienna was the capital of the Austro-Hungarian Empire, so it's not surprising that the food lives on beyond the borders that have shifted with time and politics. Seasoned heavily with both sweet and hot paprika, this rich, satisfying dish is beautifully balanced in flavor.

"We start this dish with the same amount of onion as beef," says Puck. "To this you add the two kinds of paprika, marjoram, caraway seeds, garlic, and a little tomato paste, and then you cook it really slowly. I also add a little touch of balsamic vinegar to it, which isn't traditional Austrian, but I like it."

Puck grew up learning how to cook by watching his mother, a chef in the Austrian town where he was born. With her encouragement, he began his formal training at the age of fourteen. Puck then moved to France to work in some of the finest kitchens in the world, including Maxim's in Paris, the Hôtel de Paris in Monaco, and one of my most favorite restaurants—L'Oustau de Baumanière in Les Baux de Provence. (This three-Michelin-star restaurant is a must for anyone who is lucky enough to be in the region.) Puck did all this before he was twenty-four, when he decided to leave the fancy French restaurants and the goulash of his childhood behind and seek his fortune in America.

Goulash recipes can be found in the cookbooks from the late 1800s—often called Hungarian goulash. The basic principles of stewing up lots of beef and onions with paprika remain unchanged. Puck suggests serving the dish with potatoes, rice, or spätzle on the side. *The Neighborhood Cook Book* from 1914 contains three recipes for goulash, and in *Foods of the Foreign-Born* (1922), Bertha M. Wood includes goulash made with beef, veal, pork, pork kidneys, and potatoes, but makes no mention of the all-important paprika.

With this dish, Puck shares something about his origins with his children and passes on his love of food. His sixteen-year-old son already wants to follow in his father's footsteps. "You have to care and have passion for food to be a chef—you can't teach this." His two younger children, ages four and five, love to help out in the kitchen, and the family will all join in when he prepares a meal at home. "Last night we all cooked together—even the little ones helped. And today my son is taking lobster with curry ginger sauce to school in his lunchbox." No peanut-butter-and-jelly sandwiches for the Puck kids. "I don't care for the taste," he says.

If I had the choice, I think I'd eat goulash and spätzle leftovers for lunch as well.

2 tablespoons vegetable oil

1 pound onions, peeled and finely chopped

1 tablespoon sugar

3 tablespoons sweet paprika

2 teaspoons hot paprika

3 tablespoons tomato paste

1 tablespoon minced garlic

1 tablespoon chopped fresh marjoram

1/2 teaspoon chopped fresh thyme

2 teaspoons (or more) kosher salt

1/2 teaspoon freshly ground pepper

3 pounds boneless beef shank, well trimmed and cut into 1-inch cubes

3 cups organic chicken broth

2 tablespoons balsamic vinegar

1 tablespoon caraway seeds, toasted in a dry skillet over medium-low heat until fragrant, 1 to 2 minutes, and coarsely ground

SERVES 6 TO 8

1. Heat a heavy stockpot or Dutch oven over high heat. Add the oil. When the oil is hot, add the onions and sugar; sauté, stirring occasionally, until the onions look glossy, about 3 minutes. Reduce the heat to medium and continue to cook, stirring frequently, until the onions are golden, 5 to 10 minutes longer.

2. Add the sweet and hot paprika, tomato paste, garlic, marjoram, thyme, salt, and pepper. Sauté, stirring continuously, for 1 minute. Stir in the beef cubes, chicken stock, balsamic vinegar, and caraway seeds, along with 1 cup of water. Bring the liquid to a boil and then reduce the heat to low to maintain a gentle simmer. Partially cover the pot and simmer, stirring occasionally, for 1 1/2 hours, or until the meat is very tender. Turn off the heat and skim off the liquid fat glistening on the surface. Taste and adjust seasoning with salt and pepper. Serve hot with spätzle, dumplings, potatoes, rice, or kaiser rolls.

Salads
&
Sides

Deconstructed Caesar Salad

GRAHAM ELLIOT [Graham Elliot, *Chicago, Illinois*]

THE LARGER THAN LIFE, HEAVILY TATTOOED, YOUNG GRAHAM Elliot bounces around his restaurant kitchen with the energy and playfulness of a giant puppy, his eyes twinkling behind his signature designer white glasses. The walls are lined with neatly arranged rows of spice jars, glass measuring beakers more commonly found in a laboratory, copper pots and pans of every sort, an oversized fork and spoon, and bright color-block paintings by a local artist. I feel like I have stepped from the chic grown-up dining room through the looking glass into an *Alice in Wonderland* playground complete with a tiny set of pots suitable for Barbie.

Elliot is having fun "juxtaposing four-star cuisine with humor and accessibility" to give the world "bistronomy." His ever-changing menu reflects this: it's an expression of who he is and his belief that cooking is an art form. Elliot takes American classic food

and popular culture as his foundation, and then gets creative: instead of a bread basket he serves truffle and Parmesan popcorn; he garnishes Wisconsin cheddar risotto with Cheez-It crackers; his deconstructed Caesar salad comes with savory brioche "Twinkies;" and his indoor campfire s'mores (made with graham crackers, of course) hark back to childhood memories of roasting marshmallows in the great outdoors.

A baker in Illinois invented Twinkies in 1930. He filled a soft cake with vanilla cream and wrapped it for convenience, creating an iconic American snack food. Elliot makes his own savory version using brioche to pair with that other classic American staple—the Caesar salad. Caesar Cardini is generally credited as creating the first one when he ran out of ingredients on a busy Fourth-of-July weekend in 1924 in Tijuana, Mexico. Cardini brought the salad across the border to California, and it has since grown in popularity to be a staple in restaurants everywhere. With or without anchovies (Cardini opposed the use in his recipe), the salad is frequently turned into a more substantial dish by serving it topped with grilled chicken, steak, or shrimp.

Deconstructed Caesar Salad

Here you have, in all its crunchy, creamy, cheesy deliciousness, an entirely modern Graham Elliot "bistronomic" version of a Caesar salad with brioche "Twinkies" and anchovies. Just as roses are painted red in *Alice in Wonderland*, the lettuce is painted with the vivid green dressing before being rolled in Parmesan fluff. If you can't find Little Gem lettuce, a brand of heirloom romaine lettuce developed in the nineteenth century, baby romaine works just as well. In recipes such as this one, where ingredients are left raw, it's imperative to get the best quality you can find—for the Parmesan cheese I recommend using an aged Parmigiano-Reggiano.

Salad and Parmesan Fluff

2 heads Little Gem lettuce

4 ounces Parmesan cheese, for fluff

Dressing (recipe below)

12 Brioche "Twinkies"

8 fillets Spanish anchovies

Freshly ground pepper

Dressing

1 egg yolk

1 tablespoon shallot, finely chopped

2 cloves garlic, finely chopped

2 tablespoons sour cream

1 teaspoon Dijon mustard

1/2 bunch flat-leaf parsley (about 1 cup)

3 tablespoons freshly squeezed lemon juice

2 ounces Parmesan, grated

1 cup canola oil

1 teaspoon anchovy oil

Brioche "Twinkies"

2 ounces cream cheese

3 ounces mascarpone cheese

2 tablespoons half-and-half

2 ounces Parmesan, grated

1/2 tablespoon shallot, finely minced

1 tablespoon garlic, finely minced

Salt

1/2 loaf of brioche, uncut (about 8 inches)

8 tablespoons (1 stick) unsalted butter, melted

SERVES 4

To Make the Salad and Parmesan Fluff

1. Cut each head of lettuce in quarters, lengthwise. Soak the eight pieces in cold water to remove any dirt. Pat dry. Set aside for plating.

2. Using a Microplane, carefully grate the Parmesan over a bowl to make the Parmesan fluff. Set aside for plating.

To Make the Dressing

1. Place the egg yolk, shallot, garlic, sour cream, mustard, parsley, and lemon juice in a high-speed blender and purée until smooth.

2. Add the Parmesan and purée for 1 minute. Combine the canola and anchovy oils and add them to the blender in a slow steady stream while puréeing. Pause every 10 seconds to make sure the oil is fully incorporated. If the dressing gets too thick, add a tablespoon of water. Transfer the dressing to a bowl, cover, and refrigerate.

To Make the Brioche "Twinkies"

1. Preheat the oven to 350°F.

2. In a food processor, combine the cream cheese, mascarpone, half-and-half, Parmesan, shallot, and garlic; blend until fully incorporated. Season with salt. Using a silicone or plastic spatula, fill a pastry bag with the filling. Set aside.

3. Using a serrated knife, remove the crusts from the brioche. Cut 12 rectangular cubes, 1 x 1 x 1 1/2 inches. Melt the butter in a small saucepan and brush on all sides of the brioche bricks.

4. In a nonstick sauté pan, gently brown the brioche bricks over medium heat. Remove them from the pan and transfer to paper towels to absorb any excess butter.

5. Using a rounded wooden spoon end, hollow out the brioche cubes. Try and do this with only 1 hole, to retain the shape. To make the "Twinkies" pipe in the filling, making sure they are stuffed full. Place in the oven, hole side facing up, for 3 minutes to warm the centers.

To Plate

1. Using a pastry brush, coat each piece of lettuce generously with dressing and roll in Parmesan fluff. Arrange 2 pieces of lettuce per plate.

2. Place 3 "Twinkies" on each plate next to the lettuce.

3. Garnish each piece of lettuce with Spanish anchovies and freshly ground pepper.

New World Chinois Chicken Salad

WOLFGANG PUCK [Spago, *Beverly Hills, California*]

"YOU HAVE TO GO TO NEW YORK TO MAKE MORE MONEY," Wolfgang Puck's friend told him back in the early 1970s. "The plan was to work in America for ten years and then return to Europe to open a restaurant. I had seen America in the movies—the big cars and everything, and I thought they must all be rich over there and I wanted to see for myself. I think I got lucky and moved at the right time and to the right place."

"I was very difficult when I was young, not easygoing like I am today maybe!" Puck laughs. Charles Masson, of La Grenouille in New York, helped him find a job in Indianapolis. As a racing fan and having lived in Monte Carlo, Puck thought Indianapolis sounded appealing, so he took the Greyhound. Stepping off the bus, he looked around and had a *Wizard of Oz* moment: "This is certainly not Monte Carlo!"

With manifest destiny Puck moved west in 1975 to become a pioneer in California cuisine, beginning at Ma Maison and then opening his first restaurant, Spago, in 1982. "I served three-star cusine in a less-formal atmosphere—there wasn't any other restaurant in L.A. doing this back then. We had really good local ingredients, probably better than any fancy restaurant, yet we grilled them or roasted them in a wood-burning oven and served them simply." He also frequented the fish market downtown, where the Japanese sushi chefs shopped. "When I opened Spago, I put a tuna sashimi on the menu and we were the first Caucasian restaurant to serve raw tuna. Today everybody has it."

Long before fusion became fashionable, Puck tapped in to Asian influences after Spago opened in Tokyo. He wanted to do something new and came up with the idea of a Chinese-style restaurant. "I'd never studied in China, I wanted to make Western food mixed with Chinese ingredients and cooking techniques, a combination of East and West, which became Chinois on Main." Another first. "Not just a few dishes, but the whole restaurant."

Puck considers the idea of comfort food to be very conventional—"It's either chicken soup, fried chicken, or meatballs. But I really think with the Chinese Chicken Salad, it's a modern comfort food and very American. People eat differently today in this country than they did fifty years ago." His Chinese Chicken Salad is great for the summer, especially somewhere like Southern California, which he calls home. "It has some spice and great raw ingredients, which you can always find at the farmers' market," says Puck. "It's comforting for the senses. It has all the different ingredients, a little tang, a little spice, and some crunch—it has everything."

Vinaigrette

⅓ cup soy sauce

½ cup rice wine vinegar

⅓ cup Chinese mustard

1 egg yolk

2 tablespoons honey

1 tablespoon sesame paste

2 tablespoon chopped pickled ginger

1 tablespoon chili oil

Salt and freshly ground pepper

¾ cup peanut oil

Salad

1 medium mango, julienned

5 cups napa cabbage, julienned

2 medium carrots, peeled, julienned

1 head radicchio, julienned

4 cups mixed greens or watercress

3 pounds cooked skinless chicken breast, cooled and cut into small pieces

2 cups crisp fried wonton chips

2 tablespoons toasted sesame seeds

SERVES 6

1. To make the vinaigrette: In a blender, mix soy sauce, rice wine vinegar, Chinese mustard, egg yolk, honey, sesame paste, ginger, and chili oil, adding some salt and pepper for seasoning. Blend thoroughly. Slowly add peanut oil. Taste and adjust the seasoning.

2. To make the salad: In a large salad bowl, mix together all the salad ingredients except for the sesame seeds. Add half the vinaigrette and taste. If desired, add more vinaigrette a little at a time, making sure that salad is not overdressed.

3. Divide the salad equally among the six plates and sprinkle each with sesame seeds.

Chef Puck's Tips

"Crisp up the ingredients in ice water and dry them well."

"The chicken is best cooked just before you serve the salad, and then cut and never refrigerated. It absorbs the flavors and makes it more tender. Mix all the greens together and then cook the chicken and when you are ready, mix it all up."

Cobb Salad

MICHAEL McCARTY [Michael's, *Santa Monica, California*]

"THE COBB SALAD IS, WITHOUT A DOUBT, THE MOST FREQUENTLY requested lunch dish at both Michael's New York and Michael's Santa Monica," says Michael McCarty. "Our guests can't seem to get their fill—every time we take it off the menu, they demand it back!" In 1989, he opened a Michael's in New York. Long before I knew I would one day end up living in California, I'd eat lunch there and feel like I was headed west for the afternoon, tucking into the Cobb salad while eavesdropping on the exciting conversations and deals conducted around me by the literati of New York.

Bob Cobb created the Cobb salad in 1937 at the Brown Derby in Hollywood when he raided the refrigerator late one night for a midnight snack. "I'll tell you the story of how I got the recipe from Sally Cobb herself back in the '70s," says McCarty. He then follows up with this e-mail: "*And don't forget, it was sally cobb herself who introduced me to the 'cobb' in 1979, a great story, chow, mlm.*" I'm still waiting.

McCarty suggests arranging the salad like a traditional French *salade composée* with the dressing drizzled over at the table and tossed. At the restaurant they mix it in the kitchen before taking it to the table—either way this is one very filling salad.

COBB SALAD

SERVES 4–6

½ head of lettuce
½ bunch watercress
1 small bunch chicory
½ head romaine
2 medium-sized tomatoes, peeled
2 breasts of boiled roasting chicken
6 strips crisp bacon

1 avocado
3 hard-cooked eggs
2 tbs. chopped chives
½ cup fine grated imported Roquefort cheese
1 cup Brown Derby Old-fashioned French Dressing

Cut finely lettuce, watercress, chicory, and romaine and arrange in salad bowl. Cut tomatoes in half, remove seeds, dice finely, and arrange in a strip across the salad. Dice breasts of chicken and arrange over top of chopped greens. Chop bacon finely and sprinkle over the salad. Cut avocado in small pieces and arrange around the edge of the salad. Decorate the salad by sprinkling over the top the chopped eggs, chopped chives, and grated cheese. Just before serving mix the salad thoroughly with French Dressing.

1½ cups olive oil

½ cup balsamic vinegar

¼ cup chopped fresh chives

Sea salt and freshly ground pepper

1 pound chicken tenders, all fat and sinew removed

3 tablespoons peanut oil

¾ pound mesclun

10 ounces cherry tomatoes, halved lengthwise

2 avocados, peeled, pitted, and diced

4 hard-boiled eggs, peeled and chopped

½ pound bacon lardons, cooked and chopped

½ pound crumbled Maytag blue cheese

SERVES 4

1. Combine the oil, vinegar, and chives in an attractive container with a tight-fitting lid. Season to taste with salt and pepper. Cover and vigorously shake to blend. Set aside.

2. Season the chicken with salt and pepper. Heat the peanut oil in a frying pan over medium-high heat. When very hot, add the chicken and sauté, turning occasionally, for about 6 minutes, or until cooked through and nicely browned. Transfer to a platter and set aside.

3. Place an equal portion of mesclun in each of four large shallow bowls. Cut the chicken tenders crosswise into thin slices and arrange an equal portion of chicken down the center of the greens. Place a line of the halved cherry tomatoes on one side of the chicken and a line of the diced avocado on the other side. Place a line of chopped egg next to the tomatoes and a line of lardons next to the avocado. Sprinkle the crumbled blue cheese over all.

4. Serve with the dressing on the side, or drizzle a moderate amount over the top as you serve, asking diners to toss their salads immediately.

Poached Alaskan King Crab with Cucumber, Wild Golden Char Roe, Floral Cream, and Tangerine Lace

CURTIS DUFFY [Avenues, *Chicago, Illinois*]

CURTIS DUFFY IS A VERY SERIOUS YOUNG CHEF DOING EXTRA-
ordinary things in Chicago. His cooking style is incredibly intellectual and forward thinking—he takes an ingredient, refines it, pairs it with another, and then adds an unexpected
twist using modern techniques, but never forgets the integrity of the ingredient. He uses
science intelligently to create dishes that are memorable for their beauty and the balance
of the flavor combinations. "My philosophy at Avenues is about celebrating the purity of

products. I like finding the best ingredients possible and showcasing them in a way that is unique and fun for the diner."

Duffy grew up in Cleveland, Ohio, and was encouraged to follow a career as chef from an early age. Following college, he worked for a while in Dublin, Ohio, before moving northwest to learn from best in the kitchens of Chicago, first at Charlie Trotter's, then as a pastry chef at Trio where he met Grant Achatz, who gave Duffy the position of Chef de Cuisine when he opened Alinea.

Duffy calls his ability to imagine ingredients coming together and knowing what they will taste like a chef's "mind palate." Nowhere is this gift showcased better than in his dish of poached Alaskan King crab. This is the dish that had everyone talking weeks after the James Beard Awards Gala in 2010, when he served a paired down version to 1,200 hungry guests post-awards. It's a modern interpretation of a classic seafood salad. After shrimp, crab is the most common crustacean on America's plates; blue or soft-shell crabs, Dungeness crab, and Alaskan King crab are just three of the 4,400 edible species found in America, all cooked up in the many regionally specific dishes. Duffy doesn't use mayonnaise, often called for in the recipes for crab salad of the late 1800s, but instead gets the richness from the flavors and textures of the floral cream, cucumber consommé, and a citrus puree with the crabmeat and crunchy cucumber.

A recipe from 1788, originally published in England by Richard Briggs and republished in America in 1792 as the *English Art of Cookery, According to the Present Practice*, is an excellent example of crabmeat salads of the early colonial period. It contains a short recipe on how to dress a crab, using oil and vinegar, a little mustard, pepper, and salt.

Skip forward 130 years to a recipe for "Crab Meat and Tomato Jelly Salad" from Alice Bradley's book for *Luncheon and Supper Guests* (1922), and the crab salad has come a long way from oil and vinegar. Bradley's recipe includes half-inch cubes of tomato jelly made using tomato juice, vinegar, lemon juice, gelatin, and sugar. The flavor profile to this dish is not dissimilar to Duffy's salad with the acid and sugar, and the old recipe is also playing with texture using the jelly cubes and the mayonnaise in the same way Duffy is with his accompanying textural components.

Instructions for dressing a crab from the English Art of Cookery, According to the Present Practice *by Richard Briggs, published in 1788.*

To dress a Crab.

BOIL the crab well in salt and water, and when cold break it up, mix the meat in the inside of the shell well together, break the large claws, take out the meat, and cut it fine, lay it over the shell-meat as handsome as you can in the shell, put it in the dish, split the chine in two, and put at each end; crack the small claws and put them round; mix some oil and vinegar, a little mustard, pepper, and salt.

CRAB MEAT AND TOMATO JELLY SALAD

In a salad bowl lined with
Lettuce leaves, arrange separate piles of
½ pound crab meat
3 hard-cooked eggs, chopped (use silver knife so white will not discolor)
2 roots celery or
½ pound endive cut in small pieces, and
Tomato jelly cut in cubes. Between piles place
Green pepper free from seeds and cut in strips. Make a nest of heart leaves of lettuce in center and fill with
Mayonnaise dressing.

The salad ingredients may be mixed lightly together, when salad is being served, or only those ingredients that are desired may be served to each person.

A recipe for "Crab Meat and Tomato Jelly Salad" from For Luncheon and Supper Guests *by Alice Bradley, published in 1922.*

Poached Alaskan King Crab with Cucumber, Wild Golden Char Roe, Floral Cream, and Tangerine Lace

This recipe takes time and effort to prepare, there are a lot of small components that go in to it, but everything can be done well in advance. The salad is built at the last minute to produce something that is not only stunning to look at but fun to eat. Just as an ice fisherman has to break through the ice to get to the fish below, here you break through a translucent sugar layer, which itself is holding pretty morsels of food, to get to the seafood in the bottom of the glass.

Citrus Stock

2 lemons, halved

2 limes, halved

2 lime oranges, halved

2 grapefruit, halved

2 kaffir lime leaves

1/2 bottle white wine

2 quarts water

Sugar Tuiles

1/2 cup fondant

1/2 cup glucose

1/2 cup isomalt

Crab Salad

2 Alaskan King crab legs

2 seedless cucumbers

1 tablespoon simple syrup

Salt

1 cups half-and-half

2 1/4 cups sugar plus more as needed

1 tablespoon house-made floral water

1 1/2 teaspoons agar agar

3 calamansi fruit

1 tablespoon olive oil

1 cup rice wine vinegar

1 cup water

Golden char roe

Tangerine lace

1/2 red jalapeño, cut into fine strips

Fleur de sel

Shichimi togarashi (optional)

4 sugar tuiles

SERVES 4

To Make the Citrus Stock

1. Simmer all the citrus fruits together for 20 minutes.

To Make the Sugar Tuiles

1. In a small pan, heat the fondant, glucose, and isomalt to a hard crack stage (300°F). Pour it out onto a nonstick silicone mat and let cool.

2. Place the hardened sugar into a blender and blend into a powder. Place the powdered sugar into a small chinois and tap out even-layered rounds of sugar onto the mat in the appropriate diameter for the glass serving dishes that are being used.

3. Preheat the oven to 250°F and melt the sugar circles. Cool and remove from the mat. Store in an airtight container.

To Make the Salad

1. Lightly poach the crab legs in the citrus stock and slice into 1/2-inch pieces.

2. Purée 1 cucumber with the simple syrup and salt to taste in a blender for 1 minute. Rest the purée for 15 minutes in the refrigerator. Strain through a coffee filter to remove the pulp and refrigerate the remaining cucumber juice until cold.

3. Combine the half-and-half, 2 tablespoons of the sugar, salt to taste, house-made floral water, and agar agar in a small pan. Bring to a boil and simmer for 3 minutes. Strain into a bowl and place into another bowl filled with ice. Once the mixture is chilled and firm, place it into a blender and process to a smooth cream. Taste and adjust the seasoning. Set aside.

4. Blend the calamansi fruit until smooth. Sweeten with a bit of sugar until the puree is well balanced. Drizzle in the olive oil and season with salt.

5. In a small pan, combine the rice wine vinegar, 2 cups of the remaining sugar, and the water and bring to a boil. Cook to dissolve the sugar, refrigerate, and reserve.

6. Cut the remaining cucumber into small plugs (mini cylinders), cover with the well-chilled vinegar mixture, and let marinate for 1 hour.

7. Place the crab into a serving glass, layer some of the char roe on top, add the cucumber consommé and 2 of the pickled cucumber plugs. Pipe the floral cream and calamansi puree into the bowl and add a few pieces of tangerine lace. Place the "lid," or sugar tuile, over the top of the glass and add the remaining roe, a few pools of both purees, and tangerine lace. Add the jalapeño, fleur de sel, and togarashi. Serve immediately, and eat by breaking the sugar tuile into the glass.

Chef Duffy's Tips

"Togarashi is not vital to the dish, but it does give the dish a nice touch of spice. Tangerine lace is a citrus-flavored herb."

"The salad can be made without the sugar tuiles—which are extremely challenging to make!"

Brussels Sprouts and Chorizo

BILL KIM [Belly Shack, *Chicago, Illinois*]

THE BELLY SHACK IS A CASUAL LITTLE PLACE LOCAT-ed under the El tracks in the Logan Square neighborhood of Chicago. It's an Asian-Latin fusion restaurant, combining owner Bill Kim's Korean heritage with that of his Puerto Rican wife—plus a large sprinkling of American and international street food influences thrown in: kimchee, chimichurri, tostones, hot-and-sour soup with hominy, aromatic roasted squash, flat breads, kogi, a hot dog topped with pickled green papaya, and an Asian pork meatball sandwich. For dessert there's soft-serve vanilla ice cream with mint brownie bits, salty bacon, and crumbled cookies, or Vietnamese cinnamon caramel. This is what happens when you take a childhood memory and give it a gourmet twist—pure heaven, and no one seems to notice that it's snowing outside.

Bill Kim, dressed in jeans, a long-sleeved Belly Shack T-shirt, and a dark gray beanie, is friendly and welcoming, instantly ordering up several dishes for me to try. I have finished a long day as a food judge at a casting—tasting 200-plus dishes—and the last thing I really want to do is eat more. But then a bowl of Brussels sprouts is put in front of me, and one sniff of the aroma has me reaching for chopsticks and taking a bite. It's delicious—spicy, acidic, and crunchy all at once. I can't stop eating, and within minutes I'm licking the bowl.

Belly Shack is a well-deserved recipient of a Michelin Bib Gourmand award. The dining room and open kitchen is hip and vibrant—graffiti street art covers the chipboard panels and black walls with slogans such as *Eat It* and *Enjoy More, Use Less*. This is street-culture cuisine that's been elevated by a high-end chef in the way that Warhol helped Basquiat rise to the top of the New York art scene.

---

2 tablespoons vegetable oil

3 tablespoons unsalted butter

1½ pounds Brussels sprouts, peeled and quartered

⅓ pound Mexican chorizo

Freshly squeezed juice of 1 lime

¼ cup brown sugar

¼ cup fish sauce

½ tablespoon sambal oelek

¼ cup fresh cilantro leaves

¼ cup chopped crushed tortilla chips

SERVES 6

1. In a wok or large skillet, heat 1 tablespoon of the oil and 1 tablespoon of the butter. Sauté the sprouts in batches over medium-high heat until tender and caramelized. Cool and set aside.

2. In a small pan, sauté the chorizo until cooked through. Strain off the excess oil and cool.

3. In a small bowl, pour the lime juice over the brown sugar and mix to dissolve. Add the fish sauce and sambal. Add 2 to 3 tablespoons of water as needed to balance.

4. Prior to serving, heat the remaining tablespoon of oil in a large sauté pan. Add the chorizo and sauté for 1 minute. Add the Brussels sprouts and heat until warm. Add half of the lime-sugar mixture, adding more as needed to taste. To finish, stir in the remaining 2 tablespoons of butter until melted.

5. Divide among 6 bowls and garnish with cilantro leaves and tortilla chips.

Double-Baked Potatoes

DOUGLAS KEANE [Cyrus, *Healdsburg (Sonoma), California*]

A JAMES BEARD BEST CHEF OF THE PACIFIC, THE RECIPIENT OF
two Michelin stars, and the owner of one of *Gourmet*'s top fifty restaurants of America,
Douglas Keane is someone who has made it his business to raise the bar and give diners
a compelling reason to bypass the gastronomic destinations of Napa and head north to
Sonoma. Cyrus, with its beautiful soft golden dining room and opulent floral displays,
harks back to a level of sophistication rarely found in restaurants these days. A caviar and

champagne cart may sound decadent—
and it is, but it's good to know there's still
a home for such exquisite fine dining in
America.

There's nothing stuffy about Keane
or his restaurant as he gives me a tour of
the front and back of the house. We enter
the kitchen through automatic glass sliding doors and he explains that though he
doesn't believe in open kitchens, he still
wants his customers to get a glimpse of
what is going on. He also welcomes visi-
tors in his kitchen, should they request it.
"I don't think chefs belong in the dining
room," he says. Out the back and along an
alley he shows me his bakery—the staff is
busy preparing bread and other pastries.

The atmosphere is warm and friendly as they joke that he should have warned them there might be a visitor taking photographs.

What I really like about Keane is his lack of pretension. He is doing such a good job that it's almost as if he doesn't have to prove himself, and this is reflected when we discuss his recipe. He gravitates to the baked potato and turns around a double-stuffed creation from everyday ingredients—no champagne or caviar needed, although a glass of bubbly might pair well with it.

Recipes for baking and then re-stuffing potatoes are common in the regional cookbooks of the 1800s, and the technique remains unchanged. Miss Ida A. Maynard's recipe in *How We Cook in Los Angeles* (1894), calls for removing the flesh of the baked potato, mashing it with butter, hot milk, salt and pepper to taste, then re-stuffing the skins with this mixture and browning it in the oven.

Keane's version of a stuffed baked potato elevates it from simple side dish to entrée. The addition of aged cheddar cheese, sour cream, scallions, garlic, bacon, and pickled peppers makes it a delicious and satisfying meal in itself. As with all things of such simplicity it's key to get the best-quality ingredients; the better quality the aged cheddar, the better the resulting potato.

4 large Russet potatoes, washed and dried

2 tablespoons olive oil

1 teaspoon salt, plus a pinch

2 tablespoons unsalted butter, softened

1 cup bacon, diced

1 bunch scallions, white and green parts separated, thinly sliced

1 clove garlic, smashed and chopped with a pinch of salt

1 cup sour cream

2 tablespoons Dijon mustard

2 cups aged cheddar, shredded

1 cup pickled pepperoncini peppers, sliced

Salt and freshly ground pepper

MAKES 4 POTATOES

1. Preheat the oven to 350°F.

2. On a sheet pan, rub the olive oil and 1 teaspoon of salt all over the skins of the potatoes. Place in the oven for 1 1/2 hours, until soft in the middle.

3. Remove from the oven and allow to cool just enough to handle. Cut the potatoes in half lengthwise and scoop out the flesh, leaving behind a 1/4-inch-thick layer of potato lining the skins. Mash the scooped-out warm potato with soft butter.

4. Increase the temperature of the oven to 500°F and place the potato skins back inside for 5 minutes to crisp up.

5. Meanwhile, in a small sauté pan, render the bacon on low heat until soft. Add scallion whites and garlic and cook until soft. Add the sour cream, mustard, and cheese and whisk to make a sauce. Add the scooped-out potato and mix well. Season with salt and pepper.

6. Stuff the potato skins with the potato mixture and place back in the oven for 3 minutes to heat through.

7. Serve topped with scallion greens and sliced peppers.

Sweet Potato Gratin

STEPHANIE IZARD [Girl and The Goat, *Chicago, Illinois*]

"IZARD IS A TYPE OF GOAT FROM THE PYRENEES MOUNTAINS," says Stephanie Izard, explaining the connection between her name and that of her restaurant. "And of course I had to put goat on the menu." Affectionately referred to as "The Goat," Izard's restaurant is the hottest reservation to score in Chicago. It seems diners can't get enough of her smoked goat pizza, pig's ear slaw, and escargot ravioli. This petite young chef has moved beyond being famous as the winner of *Top Chef*, season four, to being one of *Food & Wine*'s Best New Chefs 2011. Expectations were high for the opening of her first restaurant, and Izard didn't disappoint, with her eclectic menu of flavors from around the world, and her nose-to-tail omnivore-inspired dishes from closer to home. The lively space, bursting with hip guests, fun artwork, and loud music, has an open kitchen that stretches from one side of the room to the other. Diners get the opportunity to watch Izard and her team prepare the small plates of food everyone is so crazy for.

Izard's sweet potato gratin with blue cheese and crispy onions is a good example of her dishes—never fussy, always flavorful, and particularly original in the combinations of ingredients. The sharpness of the blue cheese pairs beautifully with the sweetness of the potato, and adds a depth of flavor that is bold and immensely satisfying. This earthy red vegetable with the bright orange flesh graces dinner tables across America over the holidays. I've never understood the whole tradition of marshmallow topping—but baked with sugar and spice and all things nice, Americans love their sweet potatoes.

Mrs. Lincoln's Boston Cook Book (1884) states: "Sweet Potatoes may be baked or boiled. They are better baked." There are many recipes for sliced sweet potatoes in early American cookbooks—often called "escalloped"—and sweet potatoes and regular potatoes are regarded as interchangeable, as pointed out by Fannie Farmer. In *Favorite Dishes,* a collection of recipes put together by women across America to celebrate the great World's Columbian Exposition held in Chicago in 1893, there are two recipes for escalloped potatoes. The fair was held to commemorate the 400th anniversary of Columbus setting sail to discover the New World, where potatoes, corn, and tomatoes were discovered and brought back to Europe, forever changing the culinary landscape of the globe.

I like to cook Izard's creamy gratin in a casserole. As soon as it comes out of the oven, bubbling hot, I carefully divide it up in little individual serving bowls or ramekins, making sure the slices of sweet potato stay in place. To include the perfect element of texture and flavor for this immensely rich dish, I then add little mountains of onions.

Scalloped Potatoes.

From Mrs. BERIAH WILKINS, of District of Columbia, Fifth Vice-President, Board of Lady Managers.

Slice six raw potatoes as thin as wafers. This can be done with a sharp knife, although there is a little instrument for the purpose, to be had at the house furnishing stores, which flutes prettily as well as slices evenly. Lay in ice water a few minutes; then put a layer in the bottom of a pudding dish, and over this sprinkle salt and pepper and small bits of butter; then another layer of potatoes and so on until the dish is full. Pour over this a pint of milk, stick bits of butter thickly over it, cover the dish, set it in the oven, bake half an hour. Remove the cover if not sufficiently brown.

Mrs. Beriah Wilkins

Mrs. Beriah Wilkins' recipe for "Scalloped Potatoes" from Favorite Dishes *by Carrie V. Shuman, published in 1893.*

1 large spanish onion, thinly sliced on a mandoline

1 cup masa

Vegetable oil, for deep frying

1 cup heavy cream

1/2 cup (3 ounces) chopped smoky blue cheese

1/4 teaspoon hot red pepper flakes

1/4 teaspoon brown sugar

1/2 teaspoon salt, plus more for seasoning

1 1/4 pounds sweet potatoes, peeled and thinly sliced on a mandoline

SERVES 6 TO 8

1. Toss the onions with the masa flour until well coated. Shake off excess flour. Pour the oil into a deep, heavy-bottomed pot to a depth of 2 inches. Heat the oil to 350°F over medium-high heat. Carefully add the onions to the pot, and deep-fry until golden brown. Transfer with a slotted spoon to paper towels to drain.

2. In a heavy-bottomed saucepan, bring the cream to almost a simmer. Slowly add the blue cheese while whisking until just incorporated. Whisk in the pepper flakes, brown sugar, and salt. Remove from heat and set aside.

3. Preheat the oven to 300°F.

4. Toss the sweet potato slices with a pinch of salt. Lay a third of the sweet potatoes in the bottom of a casserole dish and top with a third of the cheese sauce. Sprinkle with a quarter of the onions. Repeat to form three layers.

5. Bake the casserole in the oven for about 45 minutes, covered, and an additional 15 minutes, uncovered. Cook until the cream has reduced and thickened, and the gratin is set.

6. Remove from oven and finish with the remaining crispy fried onions.

Chef Izard's Tips

"I highly recommend finding a smoky blue cheese for this dish rather than a regular blue cheese, for the extra depth of flavor it imparts. I like to use Rogue River Smokey Blue from Sonoma, California."

"Save time by planning ahead—you can make the sauce the day before to cut down on prep time."

Farro with Spring Onion and Asparagus

JOHN SUNDSTROM [Lark, *Seattle, Washington*]

JOHN SUNDSTROM MAKES A POINT OF NOT ONLY COOKING seasonally at Lark, but also cultivating relationships with his local farmers, artisans, and foragers, many of whom he calls friends. Sundstrom uses emmer farro from Bluebird Grain Farms in Winthrop, northeast of Seattle. "It's the best I've ever tried," says Sundstrom. At Lark, they also have a kitchen garden right out the back door where they grow herbs, rows of raspberries, blueberries, cardoons, tomatoes, peppers, and several types of greens.

Sundstrom's simple and satisfying dish of farro and asparagus, is a great way to enjoy vegetables because, like rice in a risotto, the farro provides substance and lends itself to whatever happens to be in season. If the mushrooms or squash look particularly good at

the farmers' market, they can make a great substitute for the spring onions and asparagus. Farro also happens to be high in protein and low in gluten, but best of all, this nutritious, nutty grain tastes great.

Spring onions are often confused with the more common green onion or scallions. The spring onion has a rounded and defined bulb and is larger than the more slender and delicate green onion or scallion. The flavor of the spring onion has more bite and is hotter on the palate. "Even though this is a really great vegetarian dish," says Sundstrom, "the farro also pairs very nicely with meat. Red wine braised shortribs or herb roasted pork loin would be excellent served over the farro as well." .

1 tablespoon unsalted butter

1 teaspoon minced garlic

1 cup spring onions, split and grilled until tender

1 cup asparagus, peeled, blanched in milk until tender, and sliced into 2-inch lengths

1 pound Bluebird Grain Farms farro

1 cup mascarpone cheese

1 ounce fresh chives, minced

Sea salt and freshly ground pepper

SERVES 6

1. In a medium saucepan, melt the butter over medium heat, add the garlic and spring onions, and sauté until the garlic is just golden. Add the asparagus, toss to mix, season. Set aside and keep warm.

2. In a large saucepan or small stockpot, combine the farro with enough cold water to cover and 1 tablespoon salt; simmer until tender, about 30 minutes.

3. Drain the farro into a large bowl.

4. Fold in the mascarpone and chives, and season with salt and pepper.

5. To serve, divide the farro among six individual casserole dishes or bowls, smooth the surface lightly, and spoon the onion-and-asparagus mix on top.

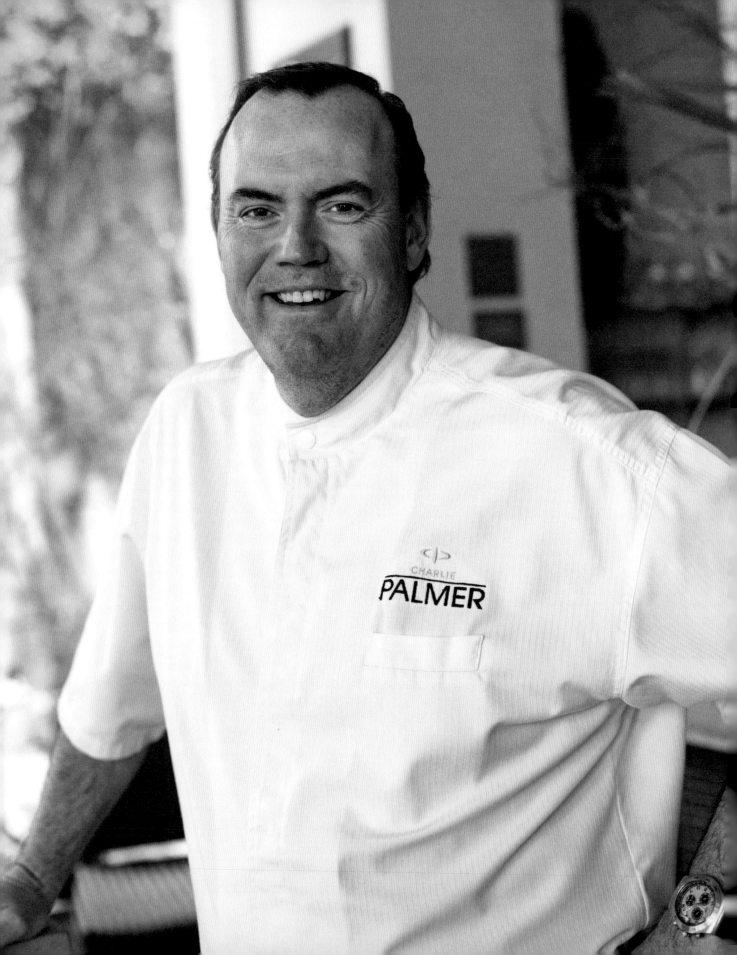

Baked Beans and Spoon-Bread Cobbler

CHARLIE PALMER [Aureole, *New York, New York*]

CHARLIE PALMER—YOU'D SPOT HIM ANYWHERE BECAUSE OF his height—walks across the lobby of the Hotel Healdsburg in Sonoma's wine country to greet me. He's a warm man with a big smile and a down-to-earth, no-frills demeanor. "Bonjour!" he says, and we head over to his restaurant Dry Creek Kitchen. "Does Didier remember me taking him to soccer games?" he asks. Palmer's first job was in the kitchen at Le Lavandou, my father-in-law's first restaurant, and he would take my husband, Didier, out to watch the local team on Sundays. Funnily enough, Didier had wondered the same thing, and remembers Palmer well and fondly. Palmer was part of the original team that worked at La Côte Basque back in the '80s, with Rick Moonen, Waldy Malouf, David Bouley, Kerry Simon, Sam Hazen, Keith Luce, and Todd English—most of whom were just starting out.

Palmer's big personality can be seen in his progressive American cuisine. Using French techniques, he builds big, bold, rambunctious flavors, often with an unexpected twist. He opened his signature restaurant, Aureole, back in 1988, and now runs an empire of restaurants, wine shops, and even a hotel. When he's not traveling around the country to visit his various enterprises, he can be found at his home in the Sonoma countryside, where he's been known to shoot wild turkeys from his porch.

If sleeping under the stars is your thing, then this recipe from Palmer, a fellow lover of the great outdoors, is for you. As American as the cowboys who cooked them up in a cast-iron pot over a campfire, baked beans are easy to make, nutritious, and so popular in Boston that the city was nicknamed "Bean Town." Baked beans are more commonly made on the stovetop than in the oven as the name would imply.

Baked Beans.

Pick over the beans the night before, and put them in warm water to soak, where they will be kept warm all night. Next morning pour off the water, and pour on boiling water, and let them stand and simmer till the beans are soft, and putting in with them a nice piece of pork, the skin gashed. Put them into the deep dish in which they are to bake, having water just enough to cover them. Bury the pork in the middle, so that the top will be even with the surface. All the garden beans are better for baking than the common field bean. They must bake in a moderately hot oven from two to three hours.

A recipe for "Baked Beans" from Miss Beecher's Domestic Receipt Book *by Catharine Esther Beecher, published in 1850.*

Used around the world in various forms through history, beans were one of the earliest crops that man cultivated. Originating in Mexico, beans were first grown in North America by Native Americans. Early American cookbooks contain many recipes for baked beans. Catharine Esther Beecher, a pioneer in culinary education and home economics, gives a lovely, simple recipe in the third edition of her book *Miss Beecher's Domestic Receipt Book*, published in 1850.

Palmer's hearty baked beans are made with a few more spices and sugar and topped with a spoon bread cobbler. This is certainly a major improvement on the canned baked beans doled out by dinner ladies at my English boarding school, and one that my little cowboys love.

Baked Beans and Spoon-Bread Cobbler

Topped with bright yellow spoon-bread, Charlie Palmer's sweet and spicy baked beans are epic in flavor and lovely to look at. Best eaten while watching a John Ford western and dreaming of riding off into the sunset in Monument Valley.

Beans

1 pound navy beans, also known as haricot beans or white beans

4 cloves garlic, halved

2 bay leaves

1/2 pound slab bacon, diced (rind reserved)

2 cups diced onion

1/2 cup molasses

1/2 cup maple syrup

1/2 cup packed dark brown sugar

1/2 cup ketchup

2 tablespoons Worcestershire sauce

1 tablespoon dry mustard

1 teaspoon salt

Pinch of ground cloves

1/4 teaspoon ground cinnamon

1/2 teaspoon coarsely ground pepper

Spoon Bread

4 large eggs, separated

1 1/2 teaspoons salt, plus a pinch for the egg whites

3 cups whole milk

1 cup yellow cornmeal

1 1/2 tablespoons granulated sugar

Pinch of cayenne pepper

3 tablespoons unsalted butter

2 teaspoons baking powder

SERVES 6 TO 8

To Make the Beans

1. Rinse the navy beans, cover with plenty of water, and soak overnight.

2. The next day, drain the beans and transfer to a large ovenproof pot. Cover with fresh water and add the garlic cloves and bay leaves. Bring to a simmer and continue to cook for 50 to 60 minutes, or until they are tender—times may vary depending on the exact type of dried bean used. Take a few of the beans out with a large spoon and blow on them with a few quick puffs; if that is enough force to separate the outer skin they are finished. Remove from the heat and set aside to cool in the liquid while assembling the remaining ingredients.

3. Render the bacon until golden and crisp and then add the onions. Sweat the onions until tender, 7 to 10 minutes.

4. Add the remaining ingredients to the pot with the bacon and onions and bring to a simmer, stirring well.

5. Strain the beans, reserving the cooking liquid and discarding the bay leaves. Add the beans to the bacon-onion mixture with 3 cups of the reserved cooking liquid, and mix to incorporate. Cover and bake at 300°F for 2 1/2 to 3 hours.

To Make the Spoon Bread

1. Preheat the oven to 350°F.

2. Whip the egg whites to soft peaks with a pinch of salt and set aside.

3. Scald the milk in a medium saucepan.

4. Combine the cornmeal, salt, sugar, and cayenne; whisk into the milk over low heat. Add the butter and continue to mix (switch to a silicone or plastic spatula) constantly for 8 to 10 minutes over low heat.

5. Remove the cornmeal from the heat and incorporate the egg yolks and baking powder.

6. Fold the whipped egg whites into the cornmeal mixture.

7. Place the warm baked beans in a 2-quart ovenproof casserole, a 10-inch cast-iron pan, or individual ramekins in an even layer.

8. Top with the spoon bread and transfer to the oven to bake for 50 to 60 minutes, rotating halfway through, until a toothpick inserted into the spoon bread comes away clean. If using ramekins, the spoon bread will take less time to cook—about 30 minutes.

Chef Palmer's Tip

"Bake on a cookie sheet lined with aluminum foil, as the baked beans may bubble up over the sides the same as a traditional cobbler would."

Small
Plates
&
Snacks

Boneless Chicken Wings with Green-Olive Purée and Jicama Guacamole Wraps

JOSÉ ANDRÉS [The Bazaar, *Los Angeles, California*]

SMALL PLATES OF TAPAS GRACE BOTH THE MODERN AND TRADI-tional menus at The Bazaar. José Andrés enjoys playing with his food—especially American comfort food. At a recent talk he gave with Ferran Adrià and Juan Mari Arzak in Los Angeles, he mentioned his love of chasing the food trucks in Los Angeles and frequenting Umami Burger. "The melting pot of America is the most powerful university a young cook can attend," he said. "With very little money you can learn the world one plate at a time right here." Just like his food, this Spaniard with the big personality, this king of the quip, likes to show off and deliver the unexpected. When the panel was asked what home cooks could learn from the best chefs in the world, Arzak replied, with his usual one-word wisdom: "Humility." "I don't endorse this myself," Andrés retorted, in one of many moments of self-parody.

The Bazaar is a wonderful playground for all the senses, where anything and everything can happen. There are cotton-candy machines to wrap morsels of foie gras on a stick, caviar cones rather than ice-cream cones, and "Dragon's Breath" popcorn—liquid nitrogen–soaked popcorn that has you exhaling smoke. Frozen caipirinhas are mixed with liquid nitrogen tableside, as fog billows out.

The boneless chicken wings topped with olive purée and the little translucent jicama-wrapped parcels of guacamole are good examples of how Andrés takes classic dishes and makes something new. Unlike most of the items on The Bazaar's menu, these can be made at home. No machines to compress watermelon or 63-degree water baths to cook eggs to the perfect custard; instead, you need a little bit of patience and a few simple ingredients.

Given how forward thinking Andrés is, I was pleased to learn that he loves to mine the past for his futuristic dishes. He is an avid collector of old cookbooks and gets more animated than usual, which is a lot, when I tell him about the 1894 book of recipes, *How We Cook in Los Angeles*. The chapter "Olive Culture in California" is of particular interest. "In Spain and Italy, where olive oil enters most generally into the cuisine of the people, it almost entirely replaces butter and lard. It is used for salads, for seasoning of all kinds of vegetables, and for frying vegetables, fish, and meat." Andres uses a lot of olives and olive oil in his cooking—he fries his chicken wings in olive oil and makes a purée out of olives to use as the sauce; he also adds olive oil to the lime dressing for his jicama guacamole wraps.

Avocados were introduced to California in the later part of the nineteenth century and prized for their rich, nutritious flesh. The Spanish, who had learned to mash avocado with finely chopped onion and chiles from the Aztecs, introduced America to the delights of guacamole. Andrés wraps his in a pickled jicama slice—giving this a delicious crunch.

Boneless Chicken Wings with Green-Olive Purée

These perfect little boneless chicken wings are first cooked and preserved in a confit to make the meat super-succulent, and then dipped in bread crumbs and fried to a golden crunch. They're topped with the taste of Jose Andrés' Spain—a bright green olive purée. The crispy chicken nuggets are a crowd-pleaser at The Bazaar and now you can make them and eat them in the quiet comfort of your own home.

½ cup Spanish extra-virgin olive oil

7 garlic cloves, 3 cloves peeled and minced

½ teaspoon sweet pimentón (Spanish smoked paprika)

1½ pounds chicken winglets (only the upper joint), about 12 pieces

¼ cup fresh flat-leaf parsley leaves

½ cup pitted green olives

¼ cup flat mineral or filtered water

4¼ cups blended olive or vegetable oil

3 sprigs fresh rosemary

3 sprigs fresh thyme

1 bay leaf

2 cups dry bread crumbs

Sea salt

SERVES 4

1. In a large mixing bowl, combine 2 tablespoons of the Spanish extra-virgin olive oil, the minced garlic, and pimentón. Add the chicken winglets, toss to coat, and season with salt. Cover the bowl with plastic wrap and refrigerate overnight.

2. In a blender, combine the parsley, olives, ¼ cup of the Spanish extra-virgin olive oil, and the mineral water, and blend until smooth. Set the olive purée aside.

3. In a large wide pot, heat 4 cups of the blended oil over low heat until it reaches 200°F on a candy thermometer. Add the remaining 4 whole garlic cloves, 2 sprigs of the rosemary, 2 sprigs of the thyme, and the bay leaf to the oil. Add the winglets, spreading them out in the pot so they cook evenly. Cook for 20 minutes, until the meat starts to separate from the bones. (You are going to preserve the winglets in a confit, so they should always be covered with oil while cooking.)

4. With a slotted spoon, transfer the winglets to a pape towel–lined plate to drain. When cool enough to handle, carefully debone the winglets with your fingers, trying to keep the shape of the winglet intact.

5. Remove the leaves from the remaining sprigs of rosemary and thyme and chop finely. In a large mixing bowl, combine the herbs with the bread crumbs. Add the winglets one at a time, patting them with the bread crumbs and making sure to coat them well.

6. Heat the remaining ¼ cup of blended olive oil in a 6-quart sauté pan (the oil should cover the bottom of the pan) over medium heat.

7. Working in batches, carefully add the breaded winglets to the pan and cook until golden brown on both sides, about 4 minutes total.

8. Transfer the breaded winglets to a paper towel–lined plate to drain.

9. To serve, divide the winglets among four plates. Put a teaspoon of the olive purée on top of each winglet and season with salt.

Jicama Guacamole Wraps

The delicate pickled jicama—cut so fine it becomes translucent—houses a lightly spiced guacamole. These easy-to-make bite-size pouches certainly pack a lot of punch in the flavor and texture departments, plus they are so pretty on the plate. The creamy guacamole pairs perfectly with the sweet pickled root vegetable. Crunchy and refreshing, this is a really innovative way to serve the green stuff we all love to dip into.

1 large jicama root, peeled

½ cup freshly squeezed lime juice

2 tablespoons honey

2 teaspoons kosher salt

½ teaspoon freshly ground white pepper

½ cup extra-virgin olive oil

2 ripe avocados

¼ cup chopped onion

7 tablespoons chopped fresh cilantro

7 tablespoons crumbled corn chips

MAKES 16 WRAPS

1. Using a mandoline, thinly slice the jicama root.

2. In a large bowl, combine the lime juice, honey, 1 teaspoon of the salt, and pepper. Gradually whisk in the olive oil to make the dressing.

3. In another bowl, mash together the avocados, onion, 3 tablespoons of the cilantro, and the remaining teaspoon of salt to make the guacamole.

4. Take one slice of the jicama and place a half teaspoon of the guacamole in the center. Gather the edges of the jicama slice into the center and press together to form a small pouch. Repeat until you have a total of 16 pouches.

5. Drizzle with 4 tablespoons of the lime dressing and garnish with the remaining 4 tablespoons of cilantro and the corn chips.

Chef Andrés' Tip

"The trickiest part is slicing the jicama very thin. Try having them slice it for you at the supermarket deli counter."

"If you don't have a mandoline large enough to make large, round, paper-thin slices of jicama, you can also place a small dollop of guacamole in the center and simply fold it in half to create a mini semicircular case."

Potato-Wrapped Oysters Rockefeller

ALEX SEIDEL [Fruition, *Denver, Colorado*]

THE BACK OF THE HOUSE AT ALEX SEIDEL'S RESTAURANT
Fruition is staffed by a crew of four or five people, including the chef, all working in very close quarters. On one side is the line for meat and fish, and across a narrow walkway is the tiny kitchen where all the desserts and appetizers are prepared. Seidel has built the restaurant up in baby steps without a lot of outside investors. This is proof that you don't need a lot of space to turn out food of an exceptionally high standard. Watching over the plates as they go out, I chat with Seidel about his vision for his restaurant. "I'd obviously like more space but I'm not looking to open a second restaurant at the moment because I'm enjoying building up the farm."

Seidel has taken farm-to-table cooking one stage further—not only is he a chef, but he's become a farmer, too. His ten-acre ranch, Fruition Farm, has crops of herbs, microgreens, fruit, leeks, onions, root vegetables, delicate pea tendrils and more, all grown for his restaurant. He also raises chickens "We go through a lot of eggs at the restaurant," he says. "The latest project is the sheep for making cheese, in particular the ricotta."

With his experienced partner, maître d' Paul Attardi, taking care of customers, Seidel is most comfortable creating memorable dishes in the kitchen. He describes his menu as "sophisticated comfort food" and the restaurant's atmosphere as having "the ambience of home."

A perfect example of Seidel's cooking is his Potato-Wrapped Oysters Rockefeller. The original Oysters Rockefeller was created at Antoine's restaurant in 1899, and was named after the wealthiest man in the world at the time for the richness of the dish. Seidel's riff on the New Orleans classic is even more decadent. A crunchy potato chip wrapped around an oyster, served over baby spinach, with lardons—what could be better than that?

2 leeks, cut into medium dice

$1/2$ yellow onion, cut into medium dice

$2 1/2$ large Russet potatoes, scrubbed

$1/4$ cup white wine

1 cup heavy cream

$1/4$ cup grated Parmigiano-Reggiano cheese

$1/4$ cup fresh flat-leaf parsley, finely chopped

20 large oysters, preferably Hama Hama

1 pound baby spinach

6 ounces naturally smoked bacon, cut into large dice

1 tablespoon sherry vinegar

Salt and freshly ground pepper

Peanut oil, for frying

SERVES 4

1. In a small sauté pan, sweat the leeks and onion until translucent. Peel the half potato and cut into large dice; add to the pan. Deglaze the pan with white wine and reduce until the wine has almost evaporated. Add the heavy cream and cook the potato in the liquid mixture until soft. Add the cheese, parsley, salt, and pepper. Puree the mixture in a blender, set aside, and keep warm.

2. Using a mandoline, slice the 2 remaining unpeeled potatoes lengthwise into very thin slices, about the thickness of a potato chip, making 20 slices. Reserve in cold water.

3. Blanch the potato slices in salted boiling water for 1 minute so the slices will roll without snapping. Shock the slices in an ice bath, drain, and pat dry. Arrange on a clean dry surface.

4. Shuck the oysters, checking for and removing any shell debris. Place an oyster on one end of a potato slice, roll up, and secure with a toothpick through the center of the oyster. Set aside.

5. Render the bacon in a sauté over medium heat. Pour off excess bacon fat and add the spinach leaves. Wilt the spinach and finish with the sherry vinegar, salt, and pepper. Set aside and keep warm.

6. Pour the peanut oil into a deep, heavy-bottomed pot to a depth of 2 inches. Heat the oil to 350°F over medium-high heat. Line a large plate with paper towels. Carefully lower the potato-wrapped oysters into the hot oil, a few at a time, and fry for about 2 minutes until golden and crispy. Remove from oil with a slotted spoon and transfer to the paper towels to drain off excess oil. Carefully remove the toothpicks.

7. On a warm rectangular plate, place a mound of wilted spinach at one end and build a tower out of five wrapped oysters on top. At the other end of the plate place a large spoonful of the leek and potato emulsion in a pile and spread it out in a teardrop shape using the back of the spoon. Repeat for the remaining three plates. Serve immediately.

Vietnamese Spring Rolls

CHARLES PHAN [The Slanted Door, *San Francisco, California*]

THE DAY WE MEET, CHARLES PHAN IS ON THE FRONT PAGE OF the *San Francisco Chronicle* for his stance on not eating shark fin soup. A couple stops him on the street to congratulate him for speaking out. "My Asian colleagues in Chinatown don't like what I've said," he says. "They think I'm messing with their culture. I say, 'I don't care what culture you are from, if you are burning my house down I've got to stop you. Sometimes it might be good for your tongue but it's not good for the environment.'"

Charles Phan came to America as a refugee, part of the boat people exodus from Vietnam. Of Chinese heritage, but born and raised in Vietnam, the family settled in San Francisco. "I learned how to bus tables at eight years old," he says, "at an English pub where my father was the janitor." After brief forays into architecture and the garment industry, he came back to cooking. "My job is to make good food—that's my calling. I wanted to be a potter and do something with my hands. But whether I make a pot of soup or the pot itself, it's all the same." He built his dream Vietnamese restaurant, helped along the way by countless brothers, sisters, cousins, and aunts—all working together. A strong sense of family pervades everything he does.

Over the years, the food at the restaurant has evolved because of the produce that Phan has been able to source. A new farm with a new breed of pig, for instance, will change certain things on the menu. With vegetables, sometimes he requests a certain size or sometimes the farmer hands him the seed book. "It's like picking out a pair of shoes on the Internet—next season they grow it for you." In China, he had a stir-fry that he loved with a particular pepper. "So I went through the catalogue and I found the Japanese *shoshito*. The farmer bought the seeds and the next season he had grown *shoshito* for me."

"It's about exploiting the local landscape and getting the best of the best from here in America and at the same time mining a piece of Asian history and culture and marrying those two things. That's my philosophy. One day I used Italian flour with very high gluten in my Shanghai dumplings and all of a sudden I have the best Shanghai dumplings. But at the end of the day you can't go too far away from the original," he says. "Ninety percent of it is still the same—the flavor, the texture."

Phan advises going out into the world to taste dishes before you try them at home. "Eat the food where it comes from and learn backwards how to make it." His words are echoed in the introduction to *Chinese-Japanese Cook Book* from 1914, which states: "The authors advise any one who intends to cook 'Chinese' to go to some Chinese restaurant and taste the various dishes he desires to cook. A good cook always should know what a dish tastes like before he tries to cook it."

Phan takes traditional culinary ideas and aesthetics from Vietnam and brings them back to America, where he reinterprets them, using local ingredients and sometimes the local aesthetic. "For instance in the spring roll we put miso paste inside the sauce—they weren't doing this in Vietnam.

Vietnamese Spring Rolls

Keeping it in the family, this is Charles Phan's mother's recipe. "The nuances are in the sauce, everything else is pretty straightforward. There is some technique—if the roll is the size of a burrito or like a cigar it's not going to work—it has to be somewhere in between." The spring rolls are light and fresh—shrimp, pork, lettuce, mint, and rice noodles all rolled up tight in rice paper with Mom Phan's mayonnaise, to be dipped in the spicy peanut sauce. I haven't yet managed to recreate exactly the ones Phan and I shared in his restaurant's kitchen, but I'm going to keep trying—they are pretty darn close—"it's all in the details," or so he kept saying.

Peanut Sauce

1/4 cup uncooked sweet rice (aka: glutinous rice)

3 tablespoons red miso paste

1/2 cup roasted peanuts

1 to 2 Thai chili peppers

2 cloves garlic

3 tablespoons ketchup

3 tablespoons sugar

2 tablespoons oyster sauce

1 tablespoon freshly squeezed lemon juice

1/2 teaspoon sesame oil

2 teaspoons chopped roasted peanuts, for garnish

Makes about 2 cups sauce

Spring Rolls

1 egg yolk

1/2 cup canola oil

1 (8-ounce) package thin rice noodles (rice vermicelli)

15 whole shrimp, shell on

1/2 pound lean pork

10 twelve-inch round sheets rice paper

15 sprigs spearmint, leaves picked, no stems

1 head red leaf lettuce, washed, leaves separated, and trimmed to 5 to 6 inches long

MAKES 10 SPRING ROLLS

To Make the Peanut Sauce

1. Prepare the sweet rice by washing it three times in cold water; drain. Add 3/4 cup water to a small saucepan, add the rice, bring to a boil, reduce the heat to low, and gently simmer for about 5 minutes. Turn off the heat and cover the saucepan; the rice will continue to cook.

2. Add all the ingredients to the bowl of a food processor and grind to a fine paste, adding a little water occasionally until the texture has a smooth and creamy consistency.

3. Refrigerate the sauce. Garnish with the chopped roasted peanuts when ready to use.

To Make the Spring Rolls

1. Beat the egg yolk. Slowly drizzle and whisk in the oil, a little at a time, to form the mayonnaise and set aside. (You can substitute store-bought mayonnaise.)

2. Prepare the mint and lettuce. Refrigerate until needed.

3. Bring three pots of water to a boil on the stovetop: one for the noodles (4 quarts), one for the shrimp (1 quart), and one for the pork (2 quarts).

4. Place the rice noodles in its pot of boiling water, reduce the heat to medium, and hard simmer 5 to 7 minutes, or until the noodles are soft. Drain the noodles; rinse with cold water, then rinse with very warm water. Cover with plastic wrap or a clean damp cloth. Set aside.

5. Place the shrimp in its pot of boiling water. Turn off the heat and let sit for 3 to 5 minutes, or until the shrimp are cooked through. Rinse with cold water. Remove the shell and vein. Slice the shrimp in half lengthwise. Rinse again and drain excess liquid.

6. Place the pork in its pot of boiling water, simmer for 10 to 12 minutes, or until cooked through; it will depend on the thickness of the meat. Remove the pork from the water and place in cold water to cool. When cooled thinly slice the pork.

7. To assemble the spring rolls, fill a large bowl of warm to very hot water or as directed by the package instructions, dip one sheet of rice paper to make it pliable. Remove and spread it out on a flat tabletop. The rice paper will absorb the moisture and become soft, thus ready for use. Do not prepare more than two wet rice papers at a time because the paper may dry out and be difficult to roll.

8. Lay one piece of lettuce over the bottom third of the rice paper and spread a thin layer of mayonnaise over the lettuce. Place a small amount of rice noodles on

top of the lettuce. Place 2 to 4 slices of pork and 3 to 6 mint leaves on top of the noodles, distributing them in even proportions.

9. Fold left and right sides over the filling to contain it. Roll up the rice paper halfway into a tight cylinder. Place 3 shrimp halves, orange side down, along the crease, then finish rolling the paper into a cylinder.

10. Place the spring rolls on a platter, covered with a lightly dampened towel so they will stay moist.

11. Cut the rolls into thirds, straight across the roll, and serve immediately with peanut dipping sauce.

Chef Phan's Tips

"Even something as simple as cutting the roll has to be done correctly. People have learned from somewhere that you cut Asian spring rolls diagonally, but if you do this everything falls out. You never see a Vietnamese person cut it on the diagonal."

"Don't make the spring rolls ahead of time, at home we make them at the table."

Green Corn Tamales

Mary Sue Milliken and Susan Feniger [Border Grill, *Los Angeles, California*]

PERHAPS BEST KNOWN FOR THEIR TV HIT SHOW *TOO HOT TAMALES*, Susan Feniger and Mary Sue Milliken are all about introducing Americans to authentic Latin cuisine, and have set the bar high for modern Mexican food over two-and-a-half decades. Talking to them, you forget that they have been doing this for a while. Back in the late '70s, Feniger worked for Wolfgang Puck at Ma Maision, and Milliken was the first female chef at Le Perroquet, in Chicago. They first decided to go into business together almost on a whim. Both were working in France—Milliken in Paris and Feniger in the South—and over a glass of wine one day, the decision was made to open their own restaurant in Los Angeles. First came City Café, in 1981, then CITY restaurant, and subsequently the Border Grill, born out of their desire to eat great Mexican food without needing to travel across Los Angeles to find it.

"We had no idea what we were doing," says Feniger, and Milliken laughs, nodding in agreement. "A hot plate and a hibachi grill in the alley—there's a film of us in that tiny kitchen in the opening week. We should find it and put it on the website. It was so hot."

Border Grill has grown into a brand, with restaurants in Santa Monica, Downtown Los Angeles, and Las Vegas, plus a food truck to follow on Twitter. Feniger also has her own restaurant, Street, fulfilling her dream to serve genuine street food from around the world, which takes up yet more of her time. Milliken is proud of her business partner's success at Street but says she prefers to devote any spare time to her family. They have long since given up hosting the radio show *Good Food*, but are often seen on television—most recently on the Bravo hit TV show *Top Chef Masters*, raising money for their respective charities, Scleroderma Research Foundation and Share Our Strength, No Kid Hungry.

How We Cook in Los Angeles contains an almost identical recipe to Milliken and Feniger's for "Green Corn Tamales." Published in 1894, the book came out just forty-six years after California was transferred to the United States as a result of the Treaty of Guadalupe Hidalgo, which ended the Mexican-American war. The population in Los Angeles at that time was rapidly expanding with the completion of the Transcontinental Railroad, growing from 50,000 to 1 million people between 1890 and 1900. Clearly, the Mexican heritage was not forgotten: the book contains a "Spanish Department," with many Latino dishes. The nineteenth-century recipe and the modern recipe show that very little has changed in the art of making tamales. Both call for steaming the corn filling inside the corn husks in a pot—the old recipe uses the cobs as a nest during cooking, while the modern recipe uses the additional corn husks. Both result in creamy corn in neat little portable parcels. The old recipe suggests serving hot with butter, while Milliken and Feniger put the butter (and cream) inside and suggest salsa fresca and sour cream.

> ### GREEN CORN TAMALES
> Maria de los Reyes Dominguez de Francis.
>
> Two dozen ears sweet corn; 1 tablespoon fresh lard; a little salt.
>
> Grate the corn, (saving the inside husks), beat it smooth with the lard, and salt. Put a tablespoon of the mixture into a husk and double it over. Put some of the cobs in a kettle with sufficient hot water to cover them. Lay the tamales on the cobs, with a plate on top to keep them in place. Cover the kettle, and steam them half an hour. Serve hot, with butter.

Maria de los Reyes Dominguez de Francis' recipe for "Green Corn Tamales" from How We Cook in Los Angeles*, published in 1894.*

Green Corn Tamales

I first ate these warm, filled parcels off the Border Grill Truck at a charity event, and I'm thrilled to learn from the "Too Hot Tamales," Mary Sue Milliken and Susan Feniger, what goes into making their tamales so delicious. Wrapping them up with the corn husks is a little tricky, but practice makes perfect.

10 ears of corn

2 tablespoons (1/4 stick) unsalted butter

1/2 teaspoon salt

1/4 teaspoon freshly ground pepper

Pinch of sugar, if necessary

1/2 cup heavy cream

1/2 teaspoon baking powder

1/2 cup hominy grits

Salsa fresca, for serving

Sour cream, for serving

SERVES 10 TO 12 TAMALES

1. Remove the corn husks by trimming off both ends of the cobs, trying to keep the husks whole as you peel them off.

2. Place the largest husks in a pot of hot water and set aside to soak.

3. Meanwhile, make the stuffing. Working over a bowl, run the point of a sharp knife down the center of each row of corn kernels on the cobs, then scrape with the dull side of the knife to remove the kernels.

4. In a large skillet, melt the butter over medium heat. Add the corn and its juices, the salt, pepper, the sugar if the corn isn't sweet, and the cream, and simmer until the mixture thickens, 5 to 8 minutes. Set aside to cool.

5. Then stir in the baking powder and grits and reserve in the refrigerator.

6. Drain the corn husks and dry them on paper towels. Make ties for the tamales by cutting a few of the husks into thin strips.

7. To stuff the tamales, overlap 2 or 3 husks and spread about 3 tablespoons of filling down the center. Fold over the sides and then the ends to enclose the filling. Tie with a corn husk string. Repeat with the remaining filling and corn husks.

8. In a steamer or pot fitted with a rack, make a bed for the tamales with the remaining corn husks. Add the tamales and steam over low heat for 1 hour, adding more water as necessary.

9. Remove from the steamer and let rest for 10 minutes. Serve hot in the husks with salsa fresca and sour cream.

Pretzel Rolls

ANDREW LITTLE [Sheppard Mansion, *Hanover, Pennsylvania*]

WHEN PROFESSIONAL TUBA PLAYING DIDN'T WORK OUT, ANDREW Little turned to cooking. He studied at the Culinary Institute of America, during which time he *staged* at some of New York's finest restaurants, and upon graduation he worked for Patrick O'Connell at the Inn at Little Washington in Virginia. In 2006, Little returned to his hometown, Hanover, to establish a restaurant at Sheppard Mansion. His love of homegrown and locally sourced produce was given full reign with the development of an herb and cutting garden, an extensive vegetable garden, the Sheppard Mansion's family farm, and a large network of local farmers in the region. "I'm really proud of our area," says Little. "I want the concept of the Dining Room at Sheppard Mansion to be a love letter to central Pennsylvania, showcasing the fruits of the land and the time-honored dishes people have traditionally enjoyed here, pretzels being a good example."

There's nothing new about pretzels, chewed on by Roman legions in the sixth century as they marched through Europe, and then brought to America centuries later by the Pennsylvania Dutch. The first pretzel bakery in the United States was founded in Lititz, Pennsylvania, in 1861. Pretzels have since become a national snack—crunchy or soft, smothered in mustard or rock salt, in numerous shapes and sizes.

Little gives us his recipe for salty chewy pretzel rolls. "Nothing says central Pennsylvania like soft pretzels," he says. "As a kid, I always got very excited at the prospect of a warm pretzel smeared with yellow mustard. These rolls are a way to bring everyone's favorite treat to the dinner table."

2 1/4 tablespoons (1 envelope) active dry yeast

1 tablespoon salt

1/2 cup packed dark brown sugar

3 cups bread flour

1 cup baking soda

Coarse sea salt, for garnish

MAKES 16 ROLLS

1. Combine the yeast, salt, and brown sugar in a mixing bowl. Pour 1 cup of warm water into the mixing bowl and allow the yeast to proof. Once the yeast is bubbly on top, add the flour and transfer to a stand mixer fitted with the dough hook. Mix on medium speed for 12 to 15 minutes, or until the dough cleans the sides of the bowl and is smooth and pliable.

2. Remove the dough from the bowl and place directly on a clean, floured countertop. Allow it to rest for 15 minutes.

3. Cut the dough into 16 pieces of equal size and roll them into rounds. Place on a baking sheet and refrigerate for 15 minutes.

4. While the rolls are resting in the refrigerator, pour 1 gallon of water into a stockpot, add the baking soda, and bring to a boil. Dunk the rolls in the boiling water for 30 seconds. Using a slotted spoon, remove the rolls and transfer to a baking sheet lined with a nonstick silicone mat. Sprinkle with the coarse sea salt.

5. Allow the rolls to proof in a warm location for about 2 hours, or until doubled in size.

6. Preheat the oven to 400°F. Score the rolls with a sharp knife and bake for 12 minutes. Transfer to a cooling rack.

7. Serve with butter, preferably homemade.

Keswick Cheese Fondue

JOSE GARCES [Amada and JG Domestic, *Philadelphia, Pennsylvania*]

LIKE MANY OF THE CHEFS I HAVE MET ON MY JOURNEY AROUND
America, Jose Garces credits his mother, Magdalena, as the person who taught him how to cook and inspired him at an early age. "We would make empanadas together and shrimp ceviche, and she would bake cheesecakes a lot and I would lick the bowl— many bellyaches! Now my kids eat the pancake batter." Garces has an eight-year-old daughter and a four-year-old son and they love to be a part of whatever is happening in the kitchen. "I went to culinary school in Chicago and worked in Spain and New York before coming to Philadelphia. It has been a great market for me. Before opening my own restaurant, Amada, I opened two restaurants for a restaurant group. At that time, I saw holes in the market—there wasn't a Spanish tapas restaurant so I did one and it was very well received." That was back in 2005 and he has subsequently added nine more restaurants and bars to his ever-growing roster.

Garces has recently purchased a farm about an hour outside of Philadelphia where he will be growing produce, such as herbs and microgreens, for the restaurants. "I've been a city boy my whole life so getting involved with the farm—it's very exciting for me to take a step back and see what it's all about." As he gets his boots muddy for the first time he's enjoying the freedom of being able to grow different heirloom varieties of vegetables for his menus. "It takes a lot of work to source, so to grow it myself now is great."

Garces named his latest restaurant "Domestic" because, he says, "it's anything American. I didn't want to limit myself just to ingredients from Pennsylvania, because in January and February it might be hard to put together a full menu, but we are as local as we can be."

Keswick Creamery, a small family run dairy located near Newburg, Pennsylvania has a herd of Jersey cows, a breed known for the particularly high-fat content of its milk. The Vermeer cheese from Keswick inspired Garces' fondue. If you can't get this local artisanal cheese, you can use a good aged cheddar. "It's a great appetizer," says Garces. "We pair it with a local beer."

The Swiss and the French both lay claim to inventing fondue—from the French *fondre* (to melt)—and early recipes included eggs, which suggests they were more soufflés than fondues. Fondue recipes do not appear in early American cookbooks, but Welsh rarebit does and it is made from a mixture of cheese, butter, seasoning, and ale that is melted in a pot, and then spread on toast. Mrs. Rorer, a formidable food personality of her time, who started the Philadelphia Cooking School, was a prolific writer of recipes and edited her own magazines *Table Talk* and the short-lived *Household News*, and was domestic editor of the *Ladies Home Journal* for fourteen years. She includes a recipe for

WELSH RARE-BIT

2 cups of grated cheese   ½ cup of milk
Yolks of two eggs   Salt and cayenne to taste

Toast carefully square slices of bread with the crusts removed; while hot, butter them, and then plunge in a bowl of hot water. Place on a heated dish and stand in the oven to keep warm while you make the rare-bit. Put the milk into a porcelain-lined or granite saucepan; stand it over a moderate fire; when boiling hot, add the cheese; stir *continually* until the cheese is melted; add the salt, cayenne and yolks, and pour it over the toasted bread.

If the rare-bit is stringy and tough, it is the fault of the cheese not being rich enough to melt.

Old English dairy cheese makes the best Welsh rare-bit.

A recipe for "Welsh Rare-Bit" from the Philadelphia Cook Book *by Mrs. S. T. Rorer, published in 1886.*

"Welsh Rare-Bit" in her *Philadelphia Cook Book* (1886) that does not include ale and uses eggs, but the "fondue" is there—spread on the bread rather than the bread dipped in it.

As with many dishes, it's hard to say who truly invented fondue, and it's probably more of an evolution—perhaps beginning as a way to put together a family meal by using up stale bread and old hard cheese. Welsh rarebit has disappeared from the tables of America—replaced by grilled cheese sandwiches, and, when ale or wine is added, cheese fondue. Americans loved their fondue parties in the '60s and '70s—every wedding registry seemed to include a fondue pot that would often sit unused in the back of the cupboard. Here Garces makes this "something old" new again.

2 tablespoons (¼ stick) unsalted butter

¼ cup minced Spanish onion

1 teaspoon minced fresh garlic

½ teaspoon dry mustard powder

1 tablespoon all-purpose flour

2 cups vegetable stock

2 cups Keswick Creamery Vermeer Cheese, or 1½ cups grated, aged cheddar cheese and ½ cup grated, smoked cheddar cheese

1 can American lager beer (about 12 fluid ounces)

Salt and freshly ground pepper

1 baguette, sliced and toasted

3 apples, cored and finely sliced

1 tablespoon chopped fresh herbs, for garnish

SERVES 4

1. Heat the butter in a stainless steel saucepan over medium heat, add the onion, and sweat until translucent, about 10 minutes.

2. Add the garlic, dry mustard powder, and flour and cook for 2 minutes, stirring constantly.

3. Slowly whisk in the vegetable stock and bring to a low boil.

4. Reduce the heat and add the cheese, a half cup at a time, until completely incorporated.

5. Cook until the cheese is melted and the fondue is smooth and creamy. Finish the fondue with the beer and cook for an additional 5 minutes.

6. Season to taste with salt and freshly ground pepper. Serve with the toasted baguette and fresh apple slices.

Greek Caviar Dip—Taramosalata

Erik A. Cosselmon [Kokkari, *San Francisco, California*]

A SHY, SOFT-SPOKEN MAN, ERIK A. COSSELMON MAKES THE rounds greeting regulars in Kokkari's dining room, but you get the sense he's most comfortable watching from behind the counter of the open kitchen or checking on the spit roast in the open fireplace. Before attending the Culinary Institute of America, he worked the line at Tavern on the Green, where his initiation test was to chop a huge bucket of onions. Upon graduation, he worked in many of New York's top restaurants, including Le Bernardin, Daniel, Montrachet, and Tribeca Grill. He is now using his vast culinary expertise to elevate Greek food from the expected feta salad to more sophisticated dishes fit for the gods—or at least San Francisco's cosmopolitan diners.

America loves dips of all varieties—sour cream, ranch dressing, salsa, guacamole, artichoke, cheese—or a mixture of any of these. Served with potato chips, corn chips, bread sticks, or crudités, dips are a party staple. Here we have a twist on the typical chip accompaniment with Greek Taramosalata. The Greeks are big on dips for their meze—tzatziki being perhaps the most well-known. A Greek *yia yia* (grandmother) would make this with a mortar and pestle; today being the era of the kitchen appliance, however, taramosalata is one for the food processor. Don't be put off by the *tarama* (salted carp roe): the resulting dip is lemony and fluffy rather than fishy; even though this is a caviar dish of sorts, the flavor is subtle—briny, creamy, and smooth.

---

3 slices day-old dense, non-sour French or Italian bread

2 tablespoons tarama (salted carp roe)

2 tablespoons freshly squeezed lemon juice

1 teaspoon finely grated white or yellow onion

1 teaspoon white wine vinegar

1/2 cup canola oil

1/4 cup extra-virgin olive oil

MAKES 1½ CUPS

1. Break or cut the bread into smaller chunks, remove the crusts, and put in a bowl.

2. Cover with cold water and let the bread soak until thoroughly moistened, about 15 minutes. Lift the bread out of the water and squeeze firmly to remove excess moisture. You should have about 1/2 cup.

3. Put the bread in a small food processor along with the tarama, lemon juice, onion, and vinegar. Process until smooth.

4. Combine the canola and olive oils, and with the food processor running, add them in a slow, steady stream, as if making mayonnaise. If the mixture gets too stiff, add a small amount of water; the consistency should be thick and spreadable.

5. Cover and refrigerate for at least 2 hours before serving. This spread tastes best the day it is made.

Brandade

KOREN GRIEVESON [avec, *Chicago, Illinois*]

KOREN GRIEVESON HAS WORKED WITH HER MENTOR, PAUL
Kahan, since 1998—starting as his sous chef for the launch of Blackbird, and moving next door as avec's chef de cuisine in 2003, winning praise and awards along the way. She describes her food as "simple Mediterranean, that works." Prior to graduating from the Culinary Institute of America, Grieveson served nine years in the United States Army. "The military definitely taught me discipline and attention to detail, "she says, "which I use everyday now in my kitchen."

When I ate at avec, the whipped garlicky salt cod brandade slathered on rustic garlic toast was a stand-out favorite. The velvety mixture of fish and potato, cream and garlic, olive oil and herbs was a comforting belly warming respite from the icy cold wind off Lake Michigan.

Mrs. Lincoln's Boston Cook Book (1891 edition) includes recipes for both "Salt Fish Balls"—where the mixture of fish and potato is made into little balls fried "in smoking-hot lard one minute"—and "Creamed Salt Fish:" "Serve one cup of the picked up fish in a rich cream sauce with potato border or on toast."

At home, make up a batch of Grieveson's rich, creamy brandade and eat on toast as an appetizer or snack.

1/2 pound salt cod, soaked for 24 to 48 hours in water to remove salt (change water at least 8 times)

2 cups whole milk

1 sprig thyme

1 bay leaf

4 cloves garlic

2 small Yukon Gold potatoes

2 tablespoons extra-virgin olive oil, or more as needed

3/4 cup heavy cream, warmed

Salt and freshly ground pepper

Chopped chives, for garnish

6 slices garlic bread or toast

MAKES 2 CUPS

1. In a small saucepan, simmer the pre-soaked salt cod in the milk with the thyme, bay leaf, and 3 of the garlic cloves until tender, about 10 minutes.

2. Simultaneously boil the potatoes until tender. Drain, peel, and rice or mash. Place in a mixing bowl.

3. Drain the salt cod. Discard the garlic, bay leaf, and thyme, and transfer the fish to a small food processor. Cover and blend. With the machine is running, pour in 2 tablespoons of the olive oil and 1/2 cup of the warmed heavy cream, and drop in the remaining clove of garlic. You may have to do this in batches, depending on the size of the machine. Stop occasionally to scrape down the sides.

4. Once the mixture is sufficiently puréed, fold it into the riced potato. Season with salt and pepper and adjust the consistency to that of a thick spread using the remaining 1/4 cup cream and some additional olive oil.

5. Sprinkle with the chopped chives and serve piping hot with garlic bread or toast.

Pork and Duck Rillettes with Italian Plum Conserve

PAUL KAHAN [The Publican, *Chicago, Illinois*]

CHEF AND RESTAURATEUR OF FOUR TOP CHICAGO RESTAU-
rants, Paul Kahan is the face of a new guard of American chefs, with a long list of accolades—Michelin stars, James Beard Awards, and *Chicago Tribune* stars. It seems strange that someone so forward thinking and likeable doesn't have a cookbook or even a TV show, but Kahan is happy to spend his time thinking up creative menu items, new ventures (a butcher's shop is next on the list), and helping grow the talent of younger chefs in his kitchens.

"I grew up around food," says Kahan. "My father owned a delicatessen and a smokehouse in Chicago. When I wanted to make a buck, I would help him take the fish out of the brine, hang them on the racks, and wheel them into the smokehouse."

Inspired by classical cuisine, particularly American, Kahan doesn't just cook seasonally, he's passionate about it. Long before it was fashionable, he developed friendships with local Midwestern farmers and created menu items around the produce he sourced from them. He's always looking to use the entire animal—not just the obvious cuts of meat. His pork rillettes, for instance, make use of fattier and tougher cuts that might be considered less desirable but are perfect when cooked at a low heat for a long time in their own fat.

The key to this recipe is to separate the fat from the meat by slow, careful cooking. More European than classically American, this traditional way of preserving meat and shrimp by setting it in a pot and sealing it with a layer of fat would have been common in the pantries of the late 1800s and was the precursor to industrial canned meat products.

For the conserve you can use whatever stone fruit happens to be in season. "At the Publican we like to change it up," says Kahan. "Apricots are another favorite." The conserve is also delicious without the rillettes on fresh crunchy bread with lots of butter—my idea of pure comfort.

Italian Plum Conserve

2 pounds Italian plums, washed, quartered, pitted, pits reserved

1 pound granulated sugar

1 tablespoon Colman's or other high-quality superfine dry mustard powder

1 1/4 tablespoons yellow mustard seeds, lightly toasted

1/2 teaspoon kosher salt

Makes 5 to 6 cups

Rillettes

1 pound duck legs

1/2 pound pork belly, cut into 1-inch cubes

1 pound pork shoulder, cut into 1-inch cubes

1 1/2 teaspoons salt

1/4 teaspoon frshly ground black pepper

1/2 teaspoon mixture of sage/thyme/bay

1 cup white wine

1 onion, studded with cloves

1 clove garlic

2 tablespoons cognac

1 loaf rustic bread, sliced and toasted

MAKES ABOUT 4 CUPS

To Make the Conserve

1. Crack reserved plum pits using the side of a knife, a meat tenderizer, or a nutcracker and place in a cheesecloth sachet.

2. In a 12-quart or larger nonreactive (not aluminum or copper) pot, bring the sachet of pits and all other ingredients to a boil over medium heat.

3. Once boiling, reduce the heat to medium-low, and stirring frequently with a wooden spoon, cook for 25 to 45 minutes, depending the fruit'd moisture level.

4. After 25 minutes, test every 5 minutes on a frozen plate for doneness. Drag a line through the plum mixture to see how dense it is—it should set up on the plate and not run into itself when it's done.

5. Remove the cheesecloth sachet of pits and discard. Cool the conserve in an ice bath, and refrigerate until ready to use.

To Make the Rillettes

1. Season meat with salt, pepper, and herbs. Let sit overnight.

2. In a heavy-bottomed Dutch oven, brown the duck legs on all sides, rendering off fat and reserving it. Remove the duck legs from the pan and repeat the process with the pork belly and pork shoulder, again removing the meat and pouring off and reserving the fat.

3. Return the duck and pork to the Dutch oven, along with the white wine, onion, and garlic. Cook, covered, for at least 1 1/2 and up to 2 1/2 hours over low heat, until the duck legs are tender. Remove the duck legs and carefully pick out all the bones. Return the meat to the pot, and add 1 tablespoon of the cognac.

4. Cook, uncovered, until all the moisture has cooked off, approximately 30 minutes; rillettes should remain moist and fatty; add some of the reserved fat if desired. For a finer texture, mash with the back of a wooden spoon. Taste and adjust the seasoning. Serve on crusty, toasted peasant bread with Italian plum conserve or sliced fresh fruit such as apple or pear.

Chef Kahan's Tips

"Rillettes can be stored, refrigerated, in a glass jar capped with reserved fat for many months."

"The conserve will last for 2 weeks if refrigerated. This recipe—minus the mustard powder, seeds, and salt—is an excellent way of preparing any stone fruit conserve."

Marrowbone, Caramelized Onions, and Chimichurri

VINNY DOTOLO AND JON SHOOK [Animal, *Los Angeles, California*]

ANIMAL GREW OUT OF A CATERING BUSINESS JON SHOOK AND
Vinny Dotolo started in Los Angeles. The two met in culinary school in Florida and
worked in restaurants around the country before settling in California. "The idea was to
make a restaurant where chefs would like to go to eat," says Shook. Jonathan Gold in the
LA Weekly claims it has "become the most influential restaurant in Los Angeles."

Three years in, they have finally grown into the concept that they initially thought
up. When they opened, serving pig's ear was considered crazy—now you can find it on
menus across the city. Dotolo and Shook have just opened their second restaurant, Son
of a Gun, which specializes in fish. It is already as popular, if not
more so, than Animal. Traditional and nontraditional items are
on both of their menus. "People like to write about the weird,
but we also do the normal," says Dotolo.

"I think a lot of the chefs like to come here because the
quality of the food is really good," says Shook. "It's not just about
the cuts, it's the preparation, the time, and the vibe." Dotolo follows up, "We really care about sourcing our ingredients, but
what does sustainable or organic actually mean anymore? We
don't advertise the food that way, but 95 percent of it is local and
organic. We feel quality is really important."

At home Shook cooks anything as long as it takes less
than an hour. "Last night I had grilled shrimp with caramelized
fennel and tomato, and oven-roasted spaghetti squash, simply
done," he says. "Nothing really special, and it took about thirty minutes, but it was good,
better than most restaurants. A lot of the food sucks in this city! I hate to say it."

I ask if they are surprised to learn there was a collection of recipes from Los Angeles in the late nineteenth century. "I respect that stuff, I love that," says Dotolo. "I
geek out on old things like that, and how they've been adapted and interpreted." Shook
agrees: "It's amazing how food is like fashion where
it comes back around. When you look at old menus
from the 1800s it's like the stuff we are doing now is
totally part of that. They ate the whole animal because of necessity and affordability."

Marrow Bones

Six marrow bones, one teaspoon salt, parsley.
Have your butcher cut the marrow bones three inches
thick and scrape the sides perfectly clean. Place in a
hot oven for six minutes. Salt and send to table at
once. Dress in a parsley bed and serve with toast
points.

*A recipe for "Morrow Bones"
from the* Neighborhood
Cook Book *by the Council
of Jewish Women, published
in 1914.*

Shook and Dotolo suitably choose to contribute a marrowbone dish. A similar recipe to theirs can
be found in *The Neighborhood Cook Book* (1914), by
the Council of Jewish Women, which calls for baking the bones in a hot oven and serving with parsley and toast. Shook and Dotolo use parsley but bump things up by making
it into chimichurri. The fatty marrow is cut by the vinegar and spice. "Drink beer with
this dish," advise Dotolo and Shook. "A dark rich beer goes perfectly with the richness of
the marrow."

Marrowbones

3 center-cut veal marrow bones, 6 inches long split down the middle (6 halves)

Kosher salt

Chimichurri Sauce

1 cup finely chopped fresh flat-leaf parsley

1/3 cup finely chopped fresh oregano

1 whole jalapeño (leave some seed and membrane for heat), worked to a paste

3/4 cup distilled vinegar

7 cloves garlic, worked to a paste

1 tablespoon hot red pepper flakes

3/4 cup extra-virgin olive oil or grapeseed oil

Salt

Caramelized Onions

1 1/2 tablespoons grapeseed oil

2 cups small diced white onions

To Serve

Chimichurri Sauce

4 tablespoons Caramelized Onions

6 pieces Marrowbone

6 slices pain de mie or good quality white bread

2 tablespoons (1/4 stick) unsalted butter

SERVES 6

To Prepare the Marrowbones

1. Heavily salt the marrowbones the day before and refrigerate for about 20 hours.

2. The next day, preheat the oven to 450°F.

3. Wash off the marrowbones and pat dry.

4. Place the marrowbone, uncovered and face up, on a sheet pan. Transfer to the oven for 4 to 6 minutes, depending on the size, until the internal temperature reaches 165°F all the way through.

To Make the Chimichurri Sauce

Combine all the ingredients in a nonreactive bowl, and set aside.

To Make the Onions

Heat a large sauté pan over medium-high heat and add the grapeseed oil; it should slide across the pan with ease. Add the onions. Cook, stirring, for about 5 minutes until the onions start to become translucent. Reduce the heat to medium-low and continue to cook until the onions are deeply caramelized, about 30 minutes. Remove from heat and cool to room temperature. Use immediately or refrigerate.

To Assemble and Serve

1. Heat the caramelized onions in a pan until hot.

2. Meanwhile, cut six 2-inch thick slices of pain de mie, butter both sides of the slices, and toast in a pan over medium heat. Remove the marrowbones and divide among six plates. Divide the carmelized onions equally among the six marrowbones and spoon on top of each. Spoon some chimichurri sauce on top of the caramelized onions. Cut the toasted pain di mie and in half diagonally and place to the side of the marrowbone.

Chef Dotolo and Chef Shook's Tips

"We use veal marrowbones split down the middle."

"Drink beer with the bone marrow. Stone brewery from San Diego do a seasonal brew that I like a lot. A dark rich beer is good with something that's fatty and rich."

Pasta
Pizza
&
Grains

Macaroni and Cheese in Parmesan Tuiles with Virginia Country Ham

PATRICK O'CONNELL [The Inn at Little Washington, *Washington, Virginia*]

THIS IS DEFINITELY NOT THE MAC AND CHEESE THAT PATRICK O'Connell's mother would cook for him as a child, using that very orange American processed cheese, but that's what inspired his dish. "I remember as a child lying in bed watching my grandfather, who was from Wisconsin and adored cheese, going to the refrigerator late at night, opening the door and the light flooding out into the kitchen as he'd stand there and slice himself Velveeta. It was the glow of the refrigerator and that iridescent orange of the cheese—even then it had a rather sci-fi aspect."

Every bit as comforting and soul satisfying as his mother's, this suave and sophisticated version of an old childhood favorite is easy to make. It can all be prepared in advance and finished just before serving. The recipe has many layers that can be included or left out. If you want a jiffy quick mac for the children, you can just cook the first part and still have a great meal, or follow the complete recipe for an elegant show-stopping dish.

O'Connell uses a well-aged Dutch Gouda cheese, which has the consistency of Parmesan when he makes this dish for his guests in the luxurious dining room at The Inn at Little Washington. "We serve the macaroni in individual Parmesan tuiles shaped

like a sleigh, with a tuffet of frisée, and fragrant black truffles shaved over the pasta at the table. It looks spectacular and yet it delivers the punch of the best macaroni and cheese you've ever had." If you wanted to keep it vegetarian you can leave out the ham. But as O'Connell explains, "We can't resist giving people a taste of our native Virginia ham. It's a nice surprise under there but not at all necessary."

Macaroni and cheese, usually baked, was the first and most popular pasta dish in the early 1800s in America. Thomas Jefferson is said to have served this comfort food staple at a state dinner in the newly finished White House in 1802. Over 200 years later President Obama and his young family still enjoy this American classic. In Mary Randolph's *Virginia House-wife* (1824), there is a recipe for a savory baked "Maccaroni Pudding" with Virginia ham, cheese, and eggs. She steams her pudding in a pan of boiling water and serves it "with rich gravy."

"It's a dish you don't get bored with after the second or third bite," says O'Connell of his refined take on mac and cheese. "It's unctuous and full of flavor, with the crunch of the Parmesan wafer and the bread crumbs on top full of texture."

> **MACCARONI PUDDING.**
> SIMMER half a pound of maccaroni in a plenty of water, with a table-spoonful of salt, till tender, but not broke—strain it, beat five yelks, two whites of eggs, half a pint of cream—mince white meat and boiled ham very fine, add three spoonsful of grated cheese, pepper and salt; mix these with the maccaroni; butter the mould, put it in, and steam it in a pan of boiling water for an hour—serve with rich gravy.

A recipe for "Maccaroni Pudding" from the Virginia House-wife *by Mary Randolph, published in 1824.*

Macaroni and Cheese in Parmesan Tuiles with Virginia Country Ham

Patrick O'Connell's flamboyant style can be seen in everything he touches. From the fabulous Inn at Little Washington, where every detail is exquisitely thought out, to reinventing something as simple as mac and cheese. The Parmesan baskets are filled with creamy noodles topped with crunchy garlicky breadcrumbs—an elegant presentation of a truly scrumptious dish.

Garlic Bread Crumbs

2 tablespoons (¼ stick) unsalted butter

½ teaspoon minced garlic

1 cup panko bread crumbs

1 teaspoon finely chopped fresh flat-leaf parsley

Parmesan Tuiles

1 cup freshly grated Parmigiano-Reggiano cheese (about 4 ounces)

Pasta and Sauce

¾ cup macaroni or your favorite tubular pasta

1 tablespoon olive oil

2 tablespoons (¼ stick) unsalted butter

2 cups heavy cream

½ cup freshly grated aged Gouda cheese (about 2 ounces)

¼ cup freshly grated Parmigiano-Reggiano cheese (about 1½ ounces)

Pinch of freshly grated nutmeg

Salt and freshly ground pepper

Assembly

4 Parmesan tuiles, shaped into baskets

2 slices Virginia country ham, cut into fine julienne (optional)

1 cup garlic bread crumbs

2 teaspoons finely chopped fresh chives

Black truffle (optional)

SERVES 4

To Make the Bread Crumbs

1. Warm an 8-inch sauté pan over medium heat. Add the butter and the minced garlic and cook until fragrant.

2. Add the bread crumbs and stir them into the butter for 5 to 6 minutes, or until golden and crunchy. Remove the pan from the heat.

3. Add the parsley and stir to incorporate. Pour the crumbs out into an even layer on a sheet pan and cool. Store the bread crumbs in an airtight container in the refrigerator until ready to use.

To Make the Parmesan Tuiles

1. Preheat the oven to 350°F.

2. On a nonstick baking sheet or on a baking sheet lined with a nonstick silicone baking mat, place ¼ cup of Parmigiano-Reggiano in a little mound. Using the back of a spoon, spread the mound out into a circle about 4 inches in diameter. Repeat, keeping about 1 inch between each circle.

3. Bake for 4 to 5 minutes, just until they turn crisp and golden brown.

4. Remove from the oven. Allow the wafers to cool for 1 minute. While they are still warm, remove them from the mat with a spatula, gently drape them over the back of a small bowl, and cool. This amount of cheese makes about 4 large wafers.

To Make the Pasta and Sauce

1. In a large pot, bring 4 quarts of salted water to a rapid boil. Add the macaroni and cook until the pasta is half done; the interior will be slightly raw. Drain the pasta and place it in a small bowl. Add the olive oil and toss to keep the macaroni from sticking together. Set aside and allow to cool. This can be done the day before and stored in the refrigerator until needed.

2. In a 4-quart saucepan over medium-low heat, melt the butter. Add the cream, bring to a rapid boil, then reduce the heat to a simmer. Cook, stirring, until the cream has reduced by one-fourth and coats the back of a spoon.

3. Whisk in the grated cheeses and cook for a minute or so until the cheese is melted and the mixture is smooth. Season with nutmeg and salt and pepper to taste. Remove from the heat and pass through a fine strainer (optional). At this point, the sauce can be refrigerated for a day or two.

4. Return the cheese sauce to the pan over low heat and add the partially cooked macaroni. Simmer for a minute or two to make sure the pasta is warmed through.

To Assemble and Serve

Place a Parmesan basket in the center of 4 warmed plates. Spoon about ¹/₂ cup of the pasta into each basket. Top each portion with the bread crumbs, Virgina ham, and chopped chives. If you like, the black truffle can be shaved on top at the table.

Chef O'Connell's Tip

"The delicate, crisp Parmesan tuiles are incredibly simple to make as little circles and perfect to nibble with a glass of champagne. They can be made in advance, stored in a sealed tin or airtight container, and offered as a gift during the holidays. Our guests love them."

Rigatoni Carbonara

BARBARA LYNCH [No. 9 Park, *Boston, Massachusetts*]

AMERICA HAS ADOPTED ITALY'S CARBONARA, A PASTA DISH PRE-
pared with typical breakfast ingredients—bacon, eggs, and cheese—and made it our own.
In the United States, this dish is commonly made with the addition of cream and more sauce
than the original Italian version. Barbara Lynch, renowned Boston chef and restaurateur,
keeps it Italian—no cream—and she adds the hot pasta to the raw eggs to cook them.

Lynch is the recipient of numerous accolades, including a James Beard award—she
is a major culinary force in Boston and beyond. Located in the historic neighborhood of
Beacon Hill, the first of her many restaurants, No. 9 Park, provides an intimate, European-
scale setting in which to enjoy her refined cuisine—an artful blend of regionally inspired
Italian and French dishes, with an emphasis on simplicity and flavor.

Another famous Bostonian, Mrs. Mary J. Lincoln, wrote *Mrs. Lincoln's Boston
Cook Book* and started the Boston Cooking School. Lincoln included recipes for macaroni,
spaghetti, and vermicelli in the vegetable section of her cookbook: "Vermicelli is used
in soup and puddings; macaroni and spaghetti as vegetables." Most of her pasta recipes
are variations of baked macaroni and cheese, but she does give detailed instructions on
cooking spaghetti: "Take a handful of the long sticks, plunge the ends into rapidly boiling
salted water—serve without cutting, if you are skilled in the art of winding it around your
fork, as the Italians do."

Lynch's carbonara is made with rigatoni, a large tube pasta, and seasoned with
three different kinds of peppercorns. The rich creamy sauce that coats the pasta, with lots
of pepper and the salty morsels of guanciali, is proof that simplicity is often the best way
of achieving the most satisfaction, both in the cooking and in the eating.

1 box (16 ounces) high-quality rigatoni

2 large eggs

4 large egg yolks

1/4 pound guanciale, diced small and rendered

1/4 cup grated pecorino Romano cheese, plus extra for serving

Salt

Peppercorns: Madagascar green peppercorns, French East Indies pink peppercorns, and Sarawak white peppercorns, freshly ground

SERVES 4

1. Bring a large pot of cold salted water to a rapid boil. Drop in the pasta and stir. Cook for about 15 minutes until al dente; reserve 1 cup of the cooking water and then drain.

2. Meanwhile, in a large mixing bowl, lightly whisk the eggs with a fork and add the cooked guanciale. Gradually add the drained hot pasta and then the cheese. Mix until the pasta is thoroughly coated with the creamy sauce. If necessary, add a little of the reserved cooking water to thin the sauce. Season with the salt and the freshly ground peppercorn mix.

3. Divide the pasta among four warm bowls, garnish with a bit more cheese.

Chef Lynch's Tips

"If you can't find the peppercorns in your local market, lots of freshly ground black pepper can be used instead."

"Reserve a cup of the pasta cooking water when you drain the pasta, and use a little of this water to thin the sauce if the pasta seems dry."

Pappardelle Bolognese

MARIO BATALI [Babbo, *New York, New York*]

NO ONE KNOWS THE PLEASURE AND DEEP COMFORT PROVIDED by a hearty, flavorful bowl of pasta better than America's reigning king of Italian cooking, Mario Batali. Needing little in the way of introduction, clad in orange Crocs, a sleeveless vest, and shorts, Batali is always first with a quip, a character trait he admires in others. With restaurants in New York, Los Angeles, Las Vegas, and now Singapore, an Italian vineyard, the phenomenon that is Eataly, and an ever burgeoning TV career—Batali is living large. What's this Iron Chef's favorite way to spend an evening? Cooking dinner at home with his wife Susi and his boys.

Pasta in all its many variations from simple spaghetti with olive oil and garlic to classic meaty lasagna is perhaps the ultimate comfort food. Macaroni has been in America since Thomas Jefferson fell in love with pasta in Paris and brought it back with him. The influx of Italian immigrants in the mid- to late-nineteenth century increased the popularity and variety of pasta from the usual baked macaroni and cheese to many more shapes and sizes. Adapted in the New World to please American tastes, the portion sizes increased, tomato became a standard for the sauce, and more meat was added to the dishes.

Here Batali offers us ribbons of homemade pappardelle covered in a thick staisfying Bolognese sauce. Batali uses white wine in this dish that is served at Babbo, which results in a bold orange sauce, not quite as vibrant as his signature Crocs, but definitely *molto* Mario.

Pasta Dough

3 1/2 cups all-purpose flour, plus extra for kneading

5 large eggs

Bolognese Sauce

1/4 cup extra-virgin olive oil

2 medium onions, finely chopped

4 celery stalks, finely chopped

2 large carrots, peeled and finely chopped

4 cloves garlic, thinly sliced

1 pound ground veal

1 pound ground pork

1/4 pound pancetta or slab bacon, ground

1 can tomato paste

1 cup whole milk

1 cup dry white wine

1 teaspoon chopped fresh thyme leaves

Kosher salt and freshly ground pepper

1 1/2 recipes basic pasta dough

Parmigiano-Reggiano cheese, for serving

SERVES 6 TO 8

To Make the Pasta Dough

1. Mound the flour in the center of a large wooden board. Make a well in the center of the flour and add the eggs.

2. Using a fork, beat the eggs together and then begin to incorporate the flour, starting with the inner rim of the well. As you expand the well, keep pushing the flour up to retain the well shape (do not worry if it looks messy). When half of the flour is incorporated, the dough will begin to come together.

3. Start kneading the dough, using primarily the palms of your hands. Once the dough is a cohesive mass, set the dough aside and scrape up and discard any dried bits of dough from the board.

4. Lightly flour the board with additional flour as necessary. The dough should be elastic and a little sticky. Wrap the dough in plastic wrap and allow it to rest for 30 minutes at room temperature before using.

To Make the Pappardelle and Bolognese Sauce

1. In a 6- to 8-quart, heavy-bottomed saucepan, heat the olive oil over medium heat. Add the onions, celery, carrots, and garlic and sweat the vegetables over medium heat until they are translucent but not browned, about 5 minutes.

2. Add the veal, pork, and pancetta and stir into the vegetables. Brown over high heat, stirring to prevent the meat from sticking.

3. Add the tomato paste, milk, wine, and thyme and bring just to a boil. Reduce the temperature and simmer over medium-low heat for 1 to 1 1/2 hours. Season with salt and pepper.

4. Meanwhile, roll the pasta dough to the thinnest setting on a pasta machine. Cut the pasta sheets crosswise into 1 1/2-inch-wide strips. Set aside on a baking tray, with the layers of pasta separated by wax or parchment paper.

5. Bring 6 quarts of water to a boil and add 2 tablespoons of salt.

6. Transfer 2 cups of the sauce to a 12- to 14-inch sauté pan and heat gently over medium heat.

7. Cook the pappardelle in the boiling water until tender, about 1 minute. Drain the pasta, add it to the pan with the sauce, and toss over medium heat until the pasta is coated and the sauce is dispersed, about 1 minute.

8. Divide evenly among six to eight warmed bowls. Grate Parmigiano-Reggiano over each bowl and serve immediately.

Arugula Risotto and Arancini

GIUSEPPE TENTORI [Boka and GT Fish & Oyster, *Chicago, Illinois*]

GIUSEPPE TENTORI RECENTLY GRACED THE COVER OF *TIME OUT* *Chicago* pictured in his chef's whites, with anonymous hands applying his makeup and adjusting his toque, under the headline, MAKING A CELEBRITY CHEF: IS GIUSEPPE TENTORI READY FOR HIS CLOSE-UP? One of the hottest chefs in Chicago, Tentori hasn't taken to his newfound fame as naturally as the other star chef of the Boka group, Goat girl Stephanie Izard, but he's being a good sport about it all. He sees the attention for what it is, a means to an end—ultimately, it's all about driving business into his two restaurants—Boka and the recently launched GT Fish & Oyster.

We meet at Boka and spend time in the bright, airy kitchen. A team, mostly young men, is prepping food and the atmosphere is relaxed but professional. Phil Vettel wrote in the *Chicago Tribune*: "New Chef Giuseppe Tentori transforms Boka into one of the city's best." Before Boka, Tentori worked in the kitchen at Charlie Trotter's for nine years, the last two as the chef de cuisine. There he learned classic technique, explored ideas, and made lifelong friends. He also improved his language skills—when he arrived in Chicago at the invitation of Gabriel Viti, he spoke absolutely no English. Today his English is excellent, spoken with a thick Italian accent.

If you are going to make a really good risotto, it's best to ask an Italian, particularly one like Tentori, who has memories of being in a farmhouse kitchen with his *Nonna* as she kneaded pasta dough and stirred pots of stocks. Tentori's risotto turns bright green through the addition of blended arugula, which adds a peppery depth of flavor without making it heavy. He likes to keep his cooking light and simple, using less butter and cream and staying true to the ingredients, never complicating a dish.

A RICE DISH (*Risotto à la Milanaise*).

Put one ounce of butter (size of a pigeon's egg) into a stew-pan, and when hot mix in a quarter of an onion (half an ounce), minced, and cook until it assumes a pale-yellow color; put in the washed rice (uncooked), and stir it over the fire until it has a yellow color also; then add a pint of stock. White stock is preferable, as it preserves the light color of the rice, yet any stock may be used. Boil slowly until the rice is tender (about half an hour), when the stock will be mostly absorbed. When about to serve, add one ounce of grated cheese, stirring for a few moments over the fire, without letting it boil; sprinkle a little grated cheese over the top.

This dish can be served alone as an *entremêt* or as a vegetable, with any kind of meat. A brown sauce may or may not be served around it.

A recipe for "A Rice Dish (Risotto à la Milanaise)" from Practical Cooking and Dinner Giving *by Mary Newton Foote Henderson, published in 1877.*

Mary Newton Foote Henderson includes the earliest American recipe for risotto I could find in her book *Practical Cooking and Dinner Giving* (1877). Having cooked on both sides of the Atlantic, Henderson brings a level of sophistication to her cookbook rarely found in other publications of this era. She adds the rice to the butter and cooks it a little before adding the stock but omits any instructions to stir the risotto or add the stock in batches like Tentori instructs in his recipe. Still, it's definitely a step up from the other American cookbooks that call for cooking the rice and then adding cheese and baking.

Not satisfied to stop at risotto, Tentori takes his recipe a step further. Rolling chilled risotto into little balls, he deep-fries them—perhaps not quite as healthy as his usual cooking—and with one bite you get to the surprise, the unexpected vibrant green middle hidden beneath the crispy golden-yellow breaded crust.

Arugula Risotto

4 cups arugula

2 tablespoons extra-virgin olive oil

1 cup Arborio rice

2 tablespoons shallots, minced

¼ cup white wine

4 cups vegetable stock

1 tablespoon mascarpone cheese

2 tablespoons grated Parmigiano-Reggiano cheese

Salt

SERVES 4

Arancini

1 recipe Arugula Risotto

½ cup all-purpose flour

1 cup panko bread crumbs, ground fine

2 large eggs

2 tablespoons whole milk

4 cups grape seed oil, for frying

MAKES 10 TO 12 BALLS

To Make the Arugula Risotto

1. Blanch the arugula in boiling salted water for 30 seconds, or until completely wilted. Immediately submerge the arugula in an ice-water bath to keep the nice green color. Blend in a blender until smooth.

2. Heat a sauté pan over medium heat and add the olive oil and rice. Stir for 30 seconds, or until you smell a nutty aroma from the rice; and then add the shallots.

3. Continue cooking for 1 minute more and add the white wine. When the wine has completely evaporated, add the vegetable stock, one ladleful at a time, stirring constantly, and allowing each ladleful to be fully absorbed before adding more. This should take about 20 minutes.

4. When all the vegetable stock has been added and the rice is al dente—soft but toothsome—remove from the heat and add the mascarpone, Parmigiano-Reggiano, and arugula. Season with salt and stir until fully incorporated.

5. Let the risotto sit for 2 minutes and serve.

To Make the Arancini

1. If you wish to make the risotto into *arancini*—risotto balls—place all of the cooked risotto on a sheet pan lined with parchment paper and refrigerate. Cool completely and then use an ice-cream scoop to form it into balls.

2. Place the flour and panko into two separate small bowls. Beat the eggs and milk together in a third small bowl.

3. Dip each risotto ball first in flour, then into the egg mixture, and then into the panko.

4. Heat the grape seed oil in a deep-fat fryer or large heavy pot over medium heat to 350°F. Working in batches, carefully lower the arancini into the fryer and cook until golden brown, 3 to 4 minutes, turning as required. Transfer to paper towels to drain off excess oil, let rest for 2 minutes, and then serve.

Gnocchi Gratinata Gorgonzola Cream Sauce

MICHAEL WHITE [Marea, Osteria Morini, and Ai Fiore, *New York, New York*]

MORE MIDWESTERNER THAN ITALIAN IN PERSON, AND YET more Italian than even the most Italian of Italians when it comes to cooking, Michael White's food is a true melting pot of cuisines. At twenty, he told his banker father that he wanted to be a chef. His father's main concern was how he could possibly make a living.

His New York restaurant Marea has earned countless awards, including three stars from the *New York Times*, two Michelin stars in 2011, and Best New Restaurant by the James Beard Foundation. Since then, he has added two more restaurants. Osteria Morini serves the bold flavors of the Emilia-Romagna region to a hip Soho crowd and is an ode to where White got his training in Italy. Most recently, he opened Ai Fiori in midtown Manhattan (also the recipient of three stars from the *New York Times*), which offers refined Mediterranean cuisine with more of a French than Italian influence.

I ask White to give me the secret to great gnocchi and making them as light as a feather. "It's all in the texture, using the right potatoes and cooking them with the skin on. It's all about how you dry them out—get the steam out, and work the potato with your hands to make it light and fluffy. The cheese adds the flavor and the lipid to bind it all together."

Long before Lidia Bastianich and Marcella Hazan were penning their Italian recipe books, there was Antonia Isola, the first person to publish an Italian cookbook in America, *Simple Italian Cookery*, in 1912. And long before White and Batali battled over who was more Italian, using time spent in Italy as verification, Isola, we are told, was "an American who has lived much in Rome." *Antonia Isola* was Miss Mabel Earl McGinnis's pseudonym—I suspect the publisher wanted to authenticate the author. White uses the name *Chef Blanco* on Twitter, a modern-day twist to make himself sound more Italian. Isola's book has a recipe for "Gnocchi of Potato." Like White, she boils the potatoes in their skins and then peels them before ricing them using a "fine colander" and mixing them with flour. Once the gnocchi are cooked, Isola covers them in gravy and cheese, to be served as a side "with meat, or as a first course."

Gnocchi of Potato

Take six medium-sized potatoes and put them on to boil in their skins. When they are done, peel them and pass them through a fine colander. Add a little salt. Take one cup of flour, and mix on the breadboard with the potatoes until they form a paste. Roll this paste with the hands into a sausage about the thickness of three fingers. Cut this roll across into pieces about an inch long. Press these pieces lightly with the finger or the handle of the knife, so they will take little cup-shaped forms. Leave these to one side, and put two quarts of salted water on to boil. When it boils add the gnocchi a few at a time, until all are in the water. When the gnocchi rise to the surface of the water, take them out with the skimmer. Put them into a platter a few at a time, adding each time gravy and cheese, and covering them well. Put a layer of grated cheese sprinkled on top. Serve with meat, or as a first course.

A recipe for "Gnocchi of Potato" from Simple Italian Cookery *by Mabel Earl McGinnis aka Antonia Isola, published in 1912.*

White has given us perhaps the most decadent, rich recipe ever for his light gnocchi: potatoes with eggs and cheese, with a sauce of cream with cheese that is then topped with more cream, cheese, and egg yolks—certainly comforting. Who knew potatoes from Idaho could reach such culinary heights?

Gnocchi Gratinata Gorgonzola Cream Sauce

If mac and cheese had a grown up cousin with a bold personality, this is it. It's so good it should come with a health warning, because you'll want to eat more than anyone in their right mind should.

Gnocchi

1¼ pounds Idaho or other baking potatoes

2 large eggs, beaten

1¾ cups all-purpose flour, plus extra for dusting

½ cup freshly grated Parmigiano-Reggiano cheese

2 teaspoons sea salt, or add according to preference

Pinch of freshly ground white pepper

Pinch of freshly grated nutmeg

Gorgonzola Cream Sauce

1 cup heavy cream

3 cups (about 13 ounces in weight) crumbled Gorgonzola cheese

1 tablespoon unsalted butter

Gratinata

½ cup heavy cream

2 large egg yolks

¼ cup Parmigiano-Reggiano cheese

2 tablespoons chopped fresh chives, for garnish

SERVES 6 TO 8

To Make the Gnocchi

1. In a large stockpot, cover the potatoes with cold water and bring to a boil. Cook until the potatoes are easily pierced with a knife, about 20 minutes, then drain. When cool enough to handle, peel the potatoes and pass them through a potato ricer onto a lightly floured work surface. Using a fork, spread the riced potatoes out into a 6-inch square to cool.

2. Make a well in the center of the potatoes. Pour in the eggs, sprinkle on 1½ cups of the flour, and add the cheese, salt, pepper, and nutmeg. Using your hands or two pastry scrapers and working from the outside edges, knead until the mixture is just evenly blended, adding the remaining ¼ cup of flour as needed, 3 to 4 minutes. Do not overmix, or the gnocchi will become tough and gluey.

3. Lightly dust your hands and the dough with flour. Form the dough into a log about 4 inches in diameter and sprinkle with flour. With a knife or dough scraper, divide the log into 6 equal pieces. Roll each piece into a cylinder about ½ inch in diameter. Cut into 1-inch pieces, put on a sheet pan lined with wax paper and dusted with flour, and set aside.

4. Bring a very large pot of salted water to a boil. Add the gnocchi, and when the water returns to a boil, cook until they rise to the surface, 2 to 3 minutes, plus 30 to 40 seconds, until tender. Remove the gnocchi with a slotted spoon and drain well. Place the gnocchi in a casserole dish and keep them warm.

To Make the Sauce

1. While the gnocchi are boiling, make the sauce. In a medium heavy-bottomed saucepan, bring the cream to a simmer. Add the Gorgonzola and whisk until melted. Finish with a knob of butter.

2. Spoon the sauce over gnocchi and toss.

To Make the Gratinata

Whip the cream to soft peaks and fold in the egg yolks and cheese. Spread over the top of the gnocchi. Broil in the oven until golden brown, 3 to 4 minutes. Serve with a sprinkling of chopped chives.

Chef White's Tip

"Be creative. Keep it simple. Use what you have. Stay in your comfort zone when cooking—don't overthink it—and you will have great success."

Pizza with Pancetta, Pecorino, Spinach, and Quail Eggs

ANDREA CAVALIERE [Cecconi's, *West Hollywood, California*]

I MEET ANDREA CAVALIERE AT CECCONI'S, THE ITALIAN HOT
spot at the corner of Melrose and Robertson in Los Angeles, on a busy Friday afternoon.
The sun shines through the tall hedge at the entrance, the terrace doors are open, and the
restaurant is winding down from lunch service. Cavaliere stops at a table of two ladies

and greets them in Italian. He later tells me they are food purveyors and sell good olive oil. As one might expect from an Italian chef, good-quality olive oil is Cavaliere's favorite ingredient and his menu at Cecconi's reflects this.

Born in Turin, in Northern Italy, Cavaliere started cooking at his family's tratorria. After culinary school and working in various European restaurants, he moved to London in 1998 to work at Neal Street Restaurant with Antonio Carluccio. It was there that he was approached by entrepreneur Nick Jones, founder of the Soho House Group, the hipper than hip members-only boîtes in London, Bath, New York, Miami, Berlin, and West Hollywood. Back in 2004 Jones had bought the original Cecconi's in London and was looking to transform it from a dowdy grande dame into a place to see and be seen. And, with Cavaliere, he did just that. In 2009, they worked their magic again, this time in Los Angeles, transforming one-time film industry favorite Mortons, home to the fabled *Vanity Fair* Oscar parties, into a new Cecconi's. The result is an ultracontemporary setting, sporting cerulean blue leather chairs, black-and-white tiled floors, and enormous glass jars filled with cherries, which provide an accent of color to the bar.

Cavaliere's signature dish? "Pappardelle with rabbit—my mother's recipe. We would have it a lot in Italy. But it's not on the menu at Cecconi's." I ask if he feels America is ready for rabbit? "America, yes, but I don't know about Beverly Hills. I did it in London. Maybe I shall try to do it here." When I am back at Cecconi's a week later, Cavaliere proudly presents me with a plate of thick melt-in-your-mouth ribbons of pasta covered in a meaty brown sauce with small delicate bites of white rabbit meat. "The rabbits came from a man in Sonoma," he tells me. "They arrived with the skin on so we had to take extra time to prepare them. I hope you like it. I'm putting it on the menu on Monday."

It's no secret that my favorite food in the whole world is pizza. Some of the best I've had is at Cecconi's. The simple margherita never fails to please the children—my daughter Minty likes to add capers, while my son Rémy prefers olives. Cavaliere always generously obliges their requests. I love to share the truffle pizza with girlfriends for lunch, best eaten outside on the patio with fingers and a glass of Prosecco.

The Neapolitan pizza of cheese, tomato, and basil (echoing the tricolor of the Italian flag) was served to Queen Margherita in 1889, who gave her name to this classic. Pizza arrived in the United States at around this time with the many Italian immigrants, and Gennaro Lombardi opened a pizzeria on Spring Street in New York in 1905, which is generally considered the first of many in America. By the early twentieth century, America had appropriated pizza as its own. Ingredients were substituted with what was available in various areas of the country, leading to a variety of differences in the flavor, size, and texture of the finished pies. Frozen pizzas were introduced in the 1950s for the convenience of popping a pizza in the oven at home. It wasn't until the 1980s, during the California cuisine revolution, that Alice Waters and Wolfgang Puck raised pizza to gourmet status when they put it on the menus at Chez Panisse and Spago.

Pizza with Pancetta, Pecorino, Spinach, and Quail Eggs

Cavaliere's menu balances Northern Italian comfort food with local healthy Californian fare. One bite of his pizza and I am transported back to a tiny pizzeria off St. Mark's Square in Venice. On top of a thin and crisp oven-baked crust, the tomato sauce is sweet and fresh, the slightly salty buffalo mozzarella is perfectly melted, there's pancetta, and quail eggs are nestled into spinach to beautifully round out the flavor and to add color.

Dough

3 1/2 cups Italian "00" flour

2 teaspoons salt

4 1/2 teaspoons (2 envelopes) active dry yeast

Pizza

1 tablespoon olive oil, plus more for drizzling

1/2 clove garlic, finely chopped

Pinch of hot red pepper flakes

1/4 pound fresh spinach leaves

4 tablespoons canned San Marzano tomato (pulp and juices blended together)

1/4 pound fresh mozzarella cheese (mozzarella di bufala), diced into 1/4-inch cubes

1/4 cup grated pecorino Toscano cheese (about 1/8 pound)

8 slices pancetta, finely sliced

16 quail eggs

MAKES 4 INDIVIDUAL SIZE PIZZAS

To Make the Dough

1. In the bowl of a stand mixer fitted with the dough hook, mix 3 1/4 cups of the flour, the salt, and yeast. Pour in 1 1/2 cups warm water (110°F) and combine.

2. Mix in the remaining 1/4 cup of flour a bit at a time, until the dough begins to pull away from the sides of the bowl. Knead for 7 1/2 minutes, checking periodically, and adding splashes of warm water as necessary to ensure the dough is elastic but not firm.

3. Form the dough into a ball and place in a bowl with the sides dusted with flour. Cover with plastic wrap and set aside in a warm draft-free place. (An ambient temperature of 75°F or so is preferred.) After the dough has doubled in size, about 1 1/2 hours, divide it into 4 balls and let rise again for another hour. Then let rest for several hours in the refrigerator.

To Make the Pizza

1. Preheat the oven to 500°F.

2. Heat the olive oil in a heavy skillet over medium heat. Add the garlic and pepper flakes and sauté for 1 minute. Add the spinach and cook to wilt the leaves, about 1 minute. Drain and set aside.

3. Press out a ball of dough on a lightly floured surface into an oval shape, about 9 x 5 inches. Press from the center outward, leaving the border untouched to create the best airy crust. Transfer the crust to a greased baking sheet.

4. Divide the topping ingredients equally into four portions; one-fourth for each pizza. Spread some tomato over the crust. Spread the spinach over the tomato, and then sprinkle the diced mozzarella on top. Add the sliced pancetta and break 4 quail eggs on top. Season with salt and freshly ground black pepper. Sprinkle with the grated pecorino cheese and drizzle with extra-virgin olive oil. Brush the border with olive oil for an extra crispy crust.

5. Bake the pizza for 10 to 12 minutes, or until crispy. Serve hot!

6. Repeat the procedure for the other 3 pizzas.

Melanzane alla Parmigiana

Jonathan Benno [Lincoln, *New York, New York*]

IN THE HEART OF LINCOLN CENTER IS THE RESTAURANT LINCOLN.
Glass and natural light dominate, with floor-to-ceiling windows on both sides that look out on the reflecting pool with the Henry Moore sculpture and the street overlooking Julliard. The enclosed, large, open kitchen in the middle of the dining room takes center stage. This truly is the theater of the kitchen, where chef Jonathan Benno, the former chef de cuisine at Per Se, steps out from the shadows of Keller and has his moment in the limelight.

"We have two performances a day, seven days a week," he says, referring to the afternoon lunch service and evening dinner service, which includes a pre- and post-theater rush.

"It's a very delicate balance," says Benno of creating a modern Italian menu in America. "You have to have a mixed green salad, you have to have a chicken and a salmon. It has to be accessible. But then we do a *testa di maiale* (pig's head) and a terrine of smoked eel and foie gras. That's the balance."

Another balance that all chefs must strike is the one between work and family. In Benno's case, it requires extra planning and effort because his wife is also a chef: she heads up Le Verdure, the vegetable restaurant at Eataly. "She's done very well there. We already have a three-year-old and she is pregnant again. It's challenging to see each other but we work it out."

"The pressure of keeping three stars once you've attained them is too much for many. I had a glimpse of that [in France] and it's insanity," says Benno. "Take for example the very sad story of Bernard Loiseau [the French chef who committed suicide in 2003]: he spent his whole life chasing this accolade of three stars and with that comes success and endorsements but also the stress of maintaining it. People who cook in America don't understand that mentality."

Like other Americans of Italian heritage, for modern inspiration Benno taps in to his memories of the food his grandparents cooked. "I remember the way my grandmother's eggplant parmigiana tasted," says Benno. "It's very similar to mine. She was of Italian heritage, from the South, where a lot of people emigrated. The eggplant parmigiana itself is simply tomato sauce; eggplant that has been thinly sliced, dusted in flour, and sautéed; mozzarella—we use a local mozzarella from New Jersey; and Parmigiano-Reggiano. That's really it."

Melanzane alla Parmigiana

My five-year-old niece, Elsie, insists she's a vegetarian but loves chicken. With her very English accent she says, "I only eat tomatoes on Wednesdays." I cooked this dish for her recently and the baked layers of eggplant, cheese, and tomatoes had even this quirkiest of eaters asking for more. It was a Friday.

Tomato Sauce

2 tablespoons extra-virgin olive oil

1 can (28 ounces) San Marzano tomatoes, passed through a food mill or food processor

1/2 red onion, minced

2 cloves garlic, minced

Kosher salt and freshly ground pepper

1 sprig basil

1 bay leaf

1 tablespoon red wine vinegar

Fried Eggplant

2 medium Italian eggplants

Salt

All-purpose flour, for dusting

Extra-virgin olive oil, for sautéing

Assembly

Tomato Sauce

Fried Eggplant

1 cup grated Parmigiano-Reggiano

1 ball fresh mozzarella, cut into 1/4-inch slices or pre-grated

1/2 bunch flat-leaf parsley, rinsed and coarsely chopped

SERVES 4

To Make the Tomato Sauce

1. Heat the olive oil in a 4-quart saucepan over medium-low heat. Add the onion and garlic; season with a pinch of salt and freshly ground black pepper. Sweat, stirring occasionally, until translucent.

2. Increase the heat to medium and add the remaining ingredients. Bring the sauce to a gentle simmer and reduce the heat to low. Let the tomato sauce cook for 1 hour, stirring occasionally.

3. Remove the sauce from the heat; taste and adjust seasoning with salt, pepper, or red wine vinegar. Set aside the sauce until needed.

To Make the Eggplant

1. Rinse the eggplant under cold water. Cut lengthwise into 1/4-inch slices. Lightly season the slices on both sides with salt and lay on a rack for 30 minutes to draw out some moisture.

2. Pat the slices dry with paper towels and dredge them in the flour to evenly coat each slice, shaking off the excess.

3. In a large sauté pan over medium-low heat, warm enough extra-virgin olive oil to cover the bottom. In separate batches, gently sauté the slices in a single layer, until they are a light golden brown on each side.

4. Upon removing the eggplant from the pan, lay them out to cool on the rack in a single layer and set aside until assembly.

To Assemble

1. Preheat the oven to 350°F.

2. Spread a thin layer of tomato sauce in the bottom of an 8 by 8-inch baking dish. Lay down one even layer of eggplant followed by another thin layer of tomato sauce and enough Parmigiano-Reggiano and chopped parsley to evenly cover the tomato sauce. Add another layer of eggplant, tomato sauce, the mozzarella, Parmigiano-Reggiano, and chopped parsley.

3. Follow with two more layers comprised of eggplant, tomato sauce, Parmigiano-Reggiano, and chopped parsley. The top layer should be tomato sauce, Parmigiano-Reggiano, and chopped parsley evenly distributed from edge to edge and corner to corner.

4. Bake in the oven for 30 minutes. The top should take on a light golden color, and when a knife tip is inserted into the the middle of the layers, it should come out hot to the touch. Remove from the oven and let stand at room temperature for at least 10 minutes before attempting to portion and serve. The longer it sits, the more stable it will be when portioned.

Italian-American Lasagna

L I D I A B A S T I A N I C H [Felidia, *New York, New York*]

THE MOTHER OF ITALIAN-AMERICAN CUISINE, LIDIA BASTIANICH, has done it all—restaurants and vineyards, cookbooks and television shows, cookware, and even pasta and jars of sauce—and all from less-than-easy beginnings. After World War II, her home in Istria, a region of northeastern Italy, was included into Yugoslavia and lost to Bastianich forever. Bastianich came to Queens, New York, with her family from an Italian refugee camp in 1958, when she was just eleven. Having left her beloved grandmother behind, this young girl cooked the daily family meal and through food kept the fond memories of their former days alive. She loved the newness of America but she missed Italy, especially when she discovered that the food Americans referred to as "Italian" was not at all what she had eaten back in her homeland.

Italian immigrants arriving more than sixty years before Bastianich had not been able to find the same ingredients they had in Italy, so they had to adjust and substitute as well as they could. Pasta was easy to make because they could find durum wheat flour here, and dried pasta was already being imported from Italy. Meat was abundant, so more than usual was incorporated into the dishes. "These are people who came to a new country and did their best with what was available. They found garlic here—and garlic is garlic—so they made the sauce with lots of garlic because it was the one flavor that really reminded them of home," says Bastianich. "But if you go to Italy you'll see we do not use all that garlic in one sauce." She has become an advocate for this "cuisine of adaptation," so much so that the *New York Times* named her the "Queen of Italian-American cuisine."

Most dishes in America have been brought here from elsewhere. Bastianich breaks down transporting an authentic dish into two elements: the product and how you cook it. The early immigrants didn't have the same ingredients so they based it all on the technique, "and the memories they had of those flavors." Bastianich shows the chefs in her restaurants her techniques and then gives them the freedom to use their talent and knowledge to make the dishes their own. "At Del Posto, Mark Ladner really respects the basic flavors and then goes off on tangents, but is true to form. I can see within his dishes traditional Italian flavors and techniques. He makes his 100-Layer Lasagna the day before and then sears pieces to heat it before serving it. He's so artistic."

For Bastianich, eating is at the heart of her family. "The table is the most important part of the whole household," says Bastianich firmly. "As a kid, everything happened in the kitchen. The table is where you connect and get the pleasures of food and each other. So Italians very rarely eat by themselves—it's always about who is coming to share your table—that is sacred."

When I ask Bastianich who has been her favorite person to cook for, she surprises me by answering, "Pope Benedict XVI." And what did this doyenne of Italian-American cuisine cook for His Holiness? The comforting Bavarian food of his childhood. "It was his birthday and also the anniversary of his third papacy. I did things that I thought he'd eaten as a boy—sauerkraut, goulash, and strudel. At the end of the meal I made him a cake. We cut it together and then I asked him, 'Did you enjoy?' He looked at me and said, 'These were the flavors of my mother.' I connected with him because instead of being an outsider feeding him, I became an insider."

Food and family define Bastianich, so it's not surprising that she's the matriarch of an expanding family-run enterprise. She still lives in Queens, in a large house with her mother. The large kitchen has served as the set for all her cooking shows, on which all four generations of the family are frequent guests. Her daughter, Tanya Bastianich Manuali, works with her on the various television series, as well as her cookbooks, culinary tours of Italy, housewares, and Nonna foods. With her son, Joe Bastianich, she owns a number of highly acclaimed restaurants in New York and beyond, and stores, including the recently opened 50,000-square-foot New York food emporium, Eataly. From her humble checkered-tablecloth restaurant, Buonavia, in Queens in the early '70s, to Eataly, forty years later, this powerhouse of a woman, who embodies the celebration of all things Italian in America, now has a bastion to match her lifelong passion. What would those early immigrants have thought of this temple to their homeland?

Italian-American Lasagna

After all this time, Lidia Bastianich is still doing what she loves and does best: nourishing people and sharing her wisdom and recipes with future generations. "Deep within me is the great satisfaction that someone will cook my food in their home for their family in their setting—it's like they are inviting me to their table, and I am always so thankful for that. I just love it." Here is her recipe for a classic Italian-American lasagna, easy to make and hugely satisfying.

Ricotta

2 pounds fresh or packaged whole-milk ricotta cheese

Italian-American Meat Sauce

2 (35-ounce) cans Italian plum tomatoes (preferably San Marzano)

1/4 cup extra-virgin olive oil

2 medium yellow onions, diced (about 2 cups)

6 to 8 cloves garlic, peeled and finely chopped

5 or 6 meaty pork neck bones (about 3/4 pound)

1 pound ground beef

1 pound ground pork

Salt

4 bay leaves

1 1/2 teaspoons dried oregano, preferably the Sicilian or Greek type dried on the branch, crumbled

3/4 cup dry white wine

1/3 cup tomato paste

3 to 4 cups hot water

Lasagna

1 recipe Italian-American Meat Sauce

2 pounds lasagna noodles

2 tablespoons olive oil

2 large eggs

Pinch of salt

3 cups freshly grated Grana Pardano cheese

1 pound mozzarella cheese, preferably fresh, thinly sliced

SERVES 12, PLUS LEFTOVERS

To Drain the Ricotta

Line a sieve with a double thickness of cheesecloth or a basket-type coffee filter. Place the ricotta over the cheesecloth and set the sieve over a bowl. Cover with plastic wrap and refrigerate overnight or up to 1 day. Discard the liquid that drains into the bowl.

To Make the Meat Sauce

1. Pass the tomatoes and their liquid through a food mill fitted with the fine blade. Set aside.

2. Heat the olive oil in a heavy-bottomed, 4- to 5-quart pot over medium heat. Add the onions and cook, stirring occasionally, until golden, about 8 minutes. Make a little room in the center of the pot, dump in the garlic, and cook, stirring, until the garlic is lightly browned, about 2 minutes.

3. Add the pork bones and cook, turning, until lightly browned on all sides, about 5 minutes. Add the ground beef and pork and season lightly with salt. Cook, stirring to break up the meat, until the meat changes color and the water it gives off is boiled away, about 10 minutes. Continue cooking until the meat is browned, about 5 minutes.

4. Add the bay leaves and oregano, then pour in the wine. Bring to a boil and cook, scraping up the brown bits that cling to the bottom of the pot, until the wine is almost completely evaporated.

5. Pour in the tomatoes and the tomato paste and stir until the paste is dissolved. Season lightly with salt. Bring to a boil, adjust the heat to a lively simmer, and cook, uncovered, stirring often, until the sauce takes on a deep, brick-red color, 2 to 3 hours. Add the hot water, 1/2 cup at a time, as necessary to maintain the level of liquid for the length of time the sauce cooks.

6. Skim off any fat that floats to the surface and remove the bones from the sauce. Taste and adjust the seasoning as necessary. The sauce can be prepared entirely in advance and refrigerated for up to 5 days, or frozen for up to 3 months.

To Make the Lasagna

1. Bring 6 quarts of salted water and the olive oil to a boil in an 8-quart pot over high heat. Stir about one-third of the lasagna noodles into the boiling water. Return to a boil, stirring frequently. While the pasta is cooking, set a large bowl of ice water next to the stove. Cook the pasta, semi-covered, stirring occasionally, until al dente, 8 to 10 minutes.

2. When the lasagna noodles are al dente, remove them with a wire skimmer and transfer them to the ice water. Let them stand until completely chilled. Repeat the cooking and cooling with the remaining 2 batches of lasagna noodles. When the cooked noodles are chilled, remove them from the ice bath and stack them on a baking sheet, separating each layer with a clean, damp kitchen towel.

3. Beat the eggs with the salt in a mixing bowl until foamy. Add the drained ricotta and stir until thoroughly blended.

4. Preheat the oven to 375°F.

5. Ladle about $3/4$ cup of the meat sauce over the bottom of a 15 x 10-inch baking dish.

6. Arrange the noodles lengthwise, side by side, so as to cover the bottom of the baking dish and overhang the short ends of the dish by about 2 inches.

7. Spoon enough meat sauce, about 2 cups, to cover the noodles in an even layer. Sprinkle the sauce with $1/2$ cup of the grated cheese.

8. Arrange a single layer of noodles crosswise over the cheese so they overhang the long sides of the baking dish by about 2 inches, again trimming the noodles and overlapping them as necessary.

9. Spread the ricotta mixture evenly over the noodles and arrange a single layer of noodles lengthwise over the ricotta, trimming the noodles as necessary.

10. Arrange the sliced mozzarella in an even layer over the noodles. Spread 1 cup of the meat sauce over the cheese and sprinkle 1 cup of grated cheese over the sauce. Cover with a layer of noodles, arranged lengthwise.

11. Spoon enough meat sauce, about 2 cups, to cover the noodles in an even layer and sprinkle the sauce with 1 cup of the grated cheese. Turn the noodles overhanging the sides and ends of the dish over the lasagna, leaving a rectangular uncovered space in the middle. Spread a thin layer of meat sauce over the top layer of noodles. Sprinkle with the remaining grated cheese. Cover loosely with aluminum foil and bake for 45 minutes.

12. Uncover the lasagna and continue baking until the top is crusty around the edges, about 20 minutes.

13. Remove the lasagna from the oven and let rest at least 30 minutes, or up to 3 hours before serving. (If you need to reheat the lasagna before serving, cover it loosely with foil and place in a 325°F oven until heated through, 15 to 45 minutes, depending on how long it has been standing.)

Seafood

Day-Boat Pacific Halibut, with Onions Cooked with Dry Vermouth, Tomatoes, and Basil

MICHAEL CIMARUSTI [Providence, *Los Angeles, California*]

WATCHING MICHAEL CIMARUSTI FILLETING FISH IN THE COLD room at Providence is thrilling and chilling—it's so cold that I have been known to borrow his chef's jacket to stay warm.

With extreme tenderness he strokes a thirty-one-pound halibut as he cuts down the central line. "He's in good hands," says Cimarusti. "The quality of the fish is just perfect; he was line caught just yesterday by a small fishing cooperative of Native Americans (Quinault Indian Nation) in Washington who have fished the same grounds for generations." Cimarusti knows his fish. One of his favorite fish to cook is cod, but you won't find it on the menu at Providence: "Cod is not sustainable in the United States. Pacific cod from Alaska can be an exception—there's a sustainable area there—but none from the North Atlantic; it's been decimated. That's why we don't serve it here."

How did he learn how to fillet fish? "Time! I've been cutting fish since I was nine years old. The first time I went fishing with my dad in Maine, we came in after a long day fishing. He just handed me the stringer of fish and said, 'Okay, go clean them,' and that's how you learn. I am going back there this summer with my son and my father. It's freshwater, smallmouth bass. I can't wait."

I first met Cimarusti when I took him fishing for a story; we have subsequently been fishing together many times. Dining at Providence is always a treat—one of Los Angeles's most sophisticated restaurants, with two Michelin stars and numerous awards and nominations. At the end of the day it's all about the fish—I believe in his heart he's a fisherman first and a chef second.

Cimarusti takes a recipe for baked halibut with onions, garlic, tomatoes, and bread crumbs from 1894's *How We Cook in Los Angeles* and modernizes it for the home cook. He cooks the fish separately from the onions and tomatoes and adds basil to the bread crumbs for flavor and the brilliant green color. "The term *halibut* in the 1890s would have included any flatfish," he says. The old recipe calls for "a palatable seasoning of salt and pepper." Cimarusti uses salt and espelette, a refined pepper from France that has A.O.C. status.

> **BAKED HALIBUT**
> Juliet Corson.
>
> A halibut, weighing three or four pounds; 1 quart of tomatoes; 1 medium-sized onion; garlic, size of a dried pea; salt, pepper, butter, bread crumbs.
>
> The fish is to be cleaned and washed; the fins and tail trimmed; then laid in a baking dish in which it can be sent to the table; or in a pan from which it can be removed without breaking. The tomatoes and onion are to be peeled, sliced and placed in the pan with the fish, also the garlic—minced very fine, and a palatable seasoning of salt and pepper. The fish is to be dusted with fine sifted crumbs and dotted with butter. Bake half an hour in a moderate oven. Either fresh or canned tomatoes may be used.

Juliet Corson's recipe for "Baked Halibut" from How We Cook in Los Angeles, *published in 1894.*

Day-Boat Pacific Halibut, with Onions Cooked with Dry Vermouth, Tomatoes, and Basil

You have to catch a fish before you can put it in a dish, and no one knows this better than Michael Cimarusti. Always be mindful of where your fish is from, best case scenario, take a trip out to sea and wet a line. This easy to make baked halibut dish is a modern remake of an 1894 recipe from Miss Corson—little did she know her recipe was going to be so beautifully remastered.

Bread Crumbs

1 large loaf French country bread, crust removed

Salt and freshly ground pepper

2 cloves garlic

1/4 cup extra-virgin olive oil

Vegetable oil for frying

One bunch (1/2 pound) of green basil (smallest leaves reserved for garnish, largest leaves reserved for the onion-tomato mixture)

Halibut, Onions, and Tomatoes

4 halibut fillets (about 5 ounces each)

Salt and espelette or cayenne pepper for seasoning

1/2 cup-virgin olive oil, plus extra for drizzling

1 large Idaho potato, cut into 1/4-inch-thick slices

1 clove garlic

Bouquet garni of 1 bay leaf and 3 stems thyme

2 medium onions, cut into 1/8-inch-thick slices

1 cup dry vermouth

Salt

2 vine-ripened tomatoes, peeled, halved, seeded, and cut into 1-inch cubes

1/2 cup rich chicken stock

Basil leaves

Freshly ground pepper

1 lemon, peeled and segmented, juice reserved for sauce

Tiny purple basil leaves for for garnish (optional)

SERVES 4

To Make the Bread Crumbs

1. Preheat the oven to 275°F.

2. Cut the bread into 1-inch cubes and place them in a large bowl. Season with salt and pepper. Slice two cloves of garlic and add it to the bread. Toss the bread with 1/4 cup of the olive oil. Place bread cubes on a sheet pan and toast them in the oven until dry, about 1 hour.

3. Process the dried bread in a food processor to fine crumbs; leave in the processor while you prepare the basil.

4. Pour vegetable oil into deep, heavy-bottomed pot to a depth of 2 inches. Heat the oil to 350°F over medium-high heat. Prepare a large plate with paper towels. Pick through the bunch of basil; reserve the largest leaves for the tomato-onion mixture and the smallest leaves for garnish. Carefully lower the rest of the leaves into the hot oil, a few at a time, and fry for about two minutes, until crisp. Remove from oil with a slotted spoon and transfer to the paper towels to drain.

5. Add the fried basil leaves to the bread crumbs and process until the crumbs take on the color and flavor of basil. Season to taste. Store the extra bread crumbs in an airtight container. If refrigerated the crumbs will last for at least a week.

To Make the Halibut, Onions, and Tomatoes

1. Preheat the oven to 200°F.

2. Season the fillets on both sides with salt and espelette pepper.

3. Place 4 potato slices in a shallow baking dish with the fillets of fish resting on top. Add 1/4 cup of water to the dish and drizzle the fish liberally with extra-virgin olive oil. Cover the dish with plastic wrap and place in the preheated oven. (Using a potato under the fish insulates the fish from excessive heat and stops it from burning on the bottom. Discard the potato when the fish is cooked.)

4. Due to the low temperature, the fish may take up to 30 minutes to cook. Check for doneness after 10 minutes and every 5 minutes thereafter. (A cake tester is the best way to test for doneness. When the fish is properly cooked, the cake tester will pass through the fillet with very little resistance.) When the fish is done, turn off the oven and hold it there with the door ajar until the garnish is ready.

5. Meanwhile, cook the onion-tomato mixture by heating a straight-sided nonreactive saucepan over medium heat. Add 1/4 cup of the olive oil to pan and then add the garlic, the bouquet garni, and the onions. Cook for several minutes, stirring. Add the vermouth and season with a pinch of salt. Cover the pan and cook over low heat for 15 minutes.

6. Add the tomatoes, another pinch of salt, and the chicken stock. Do not stir the pot, so as not to break up the tomatoes. Place the lid on the pan, leaving a gap for steam to escape; cook until the tomatoes are warmed thoroughly. The juices will reduce to a near glaze. Remove the bouquet garni and clove of garlic. Add the remaining $1/4$ cup of olive oil to the pan and increase the temperature to a rapid boil to emulsify the olive oil and create a light sauce. Cut the large basil leaves into chiffonade and add to the pan. Adjust the seasoning with salt, pepper, and lemon juice, and divide the onion-tomato mixture among four warmed dinner plates.

7. Place a knife halfway across the filet, and sprinkle bread crumbs on top of fish; when you remove the knife, the edge of the blade will have acted as a stencil for a perfect straight line of bread crumbs. Garnish with lemon segments and tiny purple and green basil leaves. Serve immediately.

Grilled Organic Miso-Marinated Scottish Salmon, Yellow Pepper Mustard Sauce, and Steamed Baby Bok Choy

DAVID BOULEY [Bouley, *New York, New York*]

DAVID BOULEY KEEPS ME WAITING. I'VE BEEN WARNED THAT this might happen by his wife, Nicole—she refers to it as "Bouley time." He's juggling a lot of projects, not least the opening of his Japanese restaurant Brushstroke in Tribeca. The minutes go by fast as I wait with Gillian Lowe, his trusted eyes in the kitchen at Bouley, watching an efficient team prep for the evening service. Bouley is one of a small number of chefs in New York who are still going strong after many years of cooking elegant French-inspired food at restaurants that have received four stars in the *New York Times*. How did he manage it? He evolved. He has embraced other cultures, in particular those from Japan, and put them on his pretty plates. He has also scaled back, closing his bakery and shop to focus more on being in the kitchen at his gorgeous flagship restaurant, Bouley. The ultimate for Bouley is to be able to seek out the finest ingredients and then have his guests trust him to create the menu for them.

Finally, I am summoned to the Bouley test kitchen a couple of blocks south of the restaurant to meet him. I travel up in an old-fashioned elevator and the doors open into an office. Worker bees tap away on their computers, someone confirms dinner reservations for the restaurant, and an accountant-type seems to be crunching numbers, all in an

atmosphere that is calm and quiet. Bouley apologizes profusely—something about a bad drive in from the country—and we get down to discussing recipes. He wants to do fish and chooses salmon. "When it's marinated in miso and sake, it's actually quite hard for someone to overcook and dry out the fish."

He has fond memories of great home-cooked meals on his grandparents' farm and says it's all about making something simple but really well, and that begins with the ingredients. Chefs have access to the best of the best from their produce purveyors, and Bouley advises the home cook to "make sure that you purchase the fish from a trusted market. Freshness is the key." For his miso salmon dish, he strongly suggests using wild salmon, if available. He also advocates adapting: "If you go to the market and another fish looks fresher, buy that one instead and experiment." He adds that often the fishmonger can give you valuable advice on how best to cook the fish.

Salmon has been a favorite fish in America for centuries—the American Indians of the Northwest fished the Pacific with care and respect for this king of fishes. Esther Allen Howland included a recipe for broiled salmon in her book the *New England Economical Housekeeper* (1845). The salmon is broiled on a gridiron and then served with sweet cream or a little butter.

Bouley has moved away from sauces with lots of heavy cream and butter, instead relying upon other techniques, using vegetables, spices, and herbs for getting the most texture and flavor out of his ingredients. He serves his salmon with baby bok choy and a light, yellow pepper-mustard sauce that includes coconut milk and French tarragon.

Timing is everything when it comes to cooking a delicate piece of fish. "For the best outcome, make sure you have all the other components of the dish warm and ready to serve before grilling the salmon," advises Bouley. To cook his salmon, he uses a Japanese grill with Binchotan white charcoal. Binchotan is oak wood that is charred in a kiln initially at a relatively low temperature and then raised to about 1,000 degrees. The wood is then smothered in ash to cool. The charcoal is very hard and yields a smokeless long burn.

This is one of those recipes that can be stripped back to the very basics—a simple grilled, marinated salmon with bok choy, or taken to a fancier level with the addition of the special charcoal and a bright flavorful sauce. A celery root purée (page 238) would also makes an excellent addition to the plate.

Yellow Pepper Sauce

1/4 cup diced celery root

1/4 cup diced fennel

1/4 cup diced shallot

1/8 cup diced green celery

1/8 cup minced garlic

1/2 cup roasted yellow bell peppers

1/2 cup white wine

4 cups freshly squeezed orange juice

2 cups coconut milk

Yellow Pepper-Mustard Sauce

1 cup Yellow Pepper Sauce

1 tablespoon grainy mustard

Chopped fresh tarragon leaves

Miso-Marinated Salmon and Bok Choy

1 cup sweet white miso

1/2 cup mirin

1/2 cup sake

6 salmon fillets (4 to 6 ounces each)

6 pieces baby bok choy, steamed

Japanese charcoal grill with Binchotan white charcoal (optional)

SERVES 6

To Make the Yellow Pepper Sauce

1. Sweat the mirepoix (the diced vegetables and minced garlic) until soft. Add the roasted peppers and the wine and reduce by half.

2. Add the orange juice and coconut milk. Simmer for about 45 minutes. Puree and strain.

To Make the Yellow Pepper-Mustard Sauce

Reheat 1 cup of the yellow pepper sauce with the mustard. Taste and adjust the seasoning if necessary. Finish with the chopped fresh tarragon.

To Make the Salmon and Serve

1. Mix the miso, mirin, and sake together to make the marinade. Store in the refrigerator, covered, until ready to use. (This mix can be made in advance and will last for weeks.)

2. In a nonreactive container, cover the fish with the marinade and set aside for about 30 minutes. Before grilling, wipe off any excess marinade with paper towels, or rinse off the fish with white wine or sake.

3. Light and heat the Binchotan charcoal outside the grill before using, for approximately 20 minutes, turning and heating on all sides. When the charcoal turns bright red, you are ready to put it in the grill and start cooking. If you don't have access to this type of speciality wood and grill, pan sear the fish over medium-high heat indoors, or cook on a regular outdoor grill.

4. Reheat the baby bok choy and the yellow pepper-mustard sauce.

5. Brush the grill with oil to prevent the salmon from sticking. Place the marinated fillets on the grill; watch carefully, they will cook quickly, about 2 minutes on each side.

6. Place some bok choy on each plate and place the salmon on top. Spoon the yellow pepper-mustard sauce over the fish.

Poached Halibut with Potato Purée and Pickled Baby Turnips

MICHAEL ANTHONY [Gramercy Tavern, *New York, New York*]

FOR FIVE YEARS NOW, MICHAEL ANTHONY HAS BEEN THE CHEF at Gramercy Tavern, serving up refined contemporary American cuisine of the highest standard. I am struck by Anthony's exquisite use of color and the artistry he brings to every plate. Anthony came to Gramercy Tavern from Blue Hill Stone Barns and has spent time cooking in France. His background is steeped in farm-to-table—forging relationships with those who make his food better. When I am in the kitchen at Gramercy Tavern, we stop to taste artisan pickles that a colleague is making—he can't wait to get them on the menu, perhaps as a garnish to a dish, to add color and depth of flavor.

A large party all needs to be served at the same time. Twenty plates are laid out and four or five people all work to get the food arranged perfectly. Crabmeat, greens, and dressing made into beautiful towers of seafood salad. The waiters impatiently chomp at the bit wanting to get the dishes to the guests, but must wait until every last microgreen is placed with the precision of a surgeon. Tweezers are the tool of choice. "Not only can we get everything down on the plate," says Anthony, "but because the food isn't touched, it doesn't heat up."

Anthony has a young loyal team working under him in the kitchen. He makes it all look so easy—trust me, it's not. The food has a simplicity to it but the dish—from the selection of the local seasonal ingredients to the innovative cooking techniques to the plating—is carefully orchestrated. During my visit, Anthony is testing a new halibut dish. The fish is plated, and then, without any invitation, everyone seems to know to wander over, pick up a fork, taste, and comment. There's some discussion with the team before they all return to their various stations.

Fish was generally overcooked back in the nineteenth century. *How to Cook Fish* (1908), by Olive Green aka Myrtle Reed, includes eighty ways to cook halibut—nearly all are baked, boiled, or fried. (Reed was better known as a novelist but wrote about food and housekeeping using a pseudonym—just three years after publishing this book she committed suicide.)

Anthony uses the technique of slow-poaching the fish at a very low temperature in olive oil. He serves it with potatoes two ways, puréed and whole baby fingerlings, and for that precise final touch, some sunny yellow baby turnips and bright green chervil.

Poached Halibut with Potato Purée and Pickled Baby Turnips

Michael Anthony plays with extremes in this fish dish, hot and cold, spicy and bland, until they all come together in perfect harmony. However, if you want to pare back the recipe and just make a fillet of fish with potato purée, that would work wonderfully, too.

Pickled Baby Turnips

2 1/2 cups baby turnips, sliced

1 1/2 cups rice wine vinegar

1/2 cup sugar

1 1/2 teaspoons salt

1/2 piece star anise

Small pinch of coriander seeds

Small pinch of whole black peppercorns

Small pinch of mustard seeds

Small pinch of saffron

Zest of 1/2 lemon

Halibut

3 cups olive oil

1/2 vanilla bean, scraped

Zest of 1/2 orange, removed with a peeler

Zest of 1/2 lemon, removed with a peeler

Zest of 1/2 lime, removed with a peeler

4 fillets of halibut (2 1/2 to 3 ounces each)

Fresh chervil, for garnish

Fingerling Potatoes

20 small fingerling potatoes

1 teaspoon whole black peppercorns

2 tablespoons pickling liquid

Salt

Potato Purée

5 medium Yukon Gold potatoes, peeled and quartered

1 clove garlic

4 tablespoons unsalted butter, cubed and cold

1/2 cup heavy cream, warmed

Salt and freshly ground pepper

SERVES 4

To Make the Pickled Turnips

Combine all the ingredients except for the turnips in a small saucepan with 1/2 cup of water and bring to a boil. Pour the hot liquid over the turnips and let cool in the liquid. Refrigerate until needed.

To Make the Halibut

1. In a small pan over medium heat, combine the olive oil, vanilla, orange, lemon, and lime zest. Heat to 165°F and infuse the oil for 5 minutes.

2. Remove from the heat and cool to room temperature, 30 to 45 minutes.

3. Strain through a fine-mesh sieve and discard the aromatics.

4. Bring the oil to 128°F, add the halibut fillets, and cook for 10 minutes.

To Make the Fingerling Potatoes

1. Add the fingerling potatoes, whole peppercorns, and pickling liquid to a small saucepan and cover with 1/2 inch water. Season with salt.

2. Cook slowly at a gentle simmer until tender, about 10 minutes.

3. Let cool in the liquid for 20 minutes. Strain, reserving the solids, the potatoes, and the aromatics.

To Make the Potato Purée

1. Cover the potatoes with cold water. Add the garlic, season with salt, and bring to a simmer. Cook for 20 minutes, or until the potatoes are tender.

2. Strain the potatoes, discard the garlic and pass through a food mill or potato ricer.

3. Put the pureed potatoes in medium pan and place over low heat. Stir in the heavy cream and butter. Season with salt and pepper and set aside.

To Serve

In the center of each of 4 large dinner plates, place a mound of potato purée and place a halibut fillet on top. Scatter 5 fingerling potatoes around the fish, with about 6 slices of turnip. Top with chervil leaves and serve.

Chef Anthony's Tip

"When poaching fish in olive oil, the texture of the fish is best when the temperature of the oil is kept steady, not rising or falling."

Jumbo Louisiana Shrimp with Jacob's Andouille and Organic White Grits

JOHN BESH [August, *New Orleans, Louisiana*]

"HUNT, FISH, SHOP, AND EAT LOCAL"—THIS COULD very well be John Besh's mantra. Dinner at Besh's flagship restaurant, August, was a highlight of my visit to New Orleans, and one of my best meals ever. It was a mixture of delicious, perfectly executed dishes—a light but flavorful soup, a delicate trout, foie gras, and to finish, a beautiful soft rum cake, encased in layers of white chocolate like the petals of a classic tea rose. Octavio Mantilla, Besh's business partner and co-owner of August, was as charming as he was generous. I left the restaurant at one o'clock in the morning, full, happy, and more than a little bit tipsy—I blame Southern hospitality. Sadly, Besh wasn't able to join us at this memorable dinner. Where was he? Quail hunting.

Besh grew up in Louisiana and is no stranger to its bounty. Whether it's shrimping in Lake Pontchartrain, fly-fishing with his father for speckled trout in the local streams, or hunting quail, this outdoorsman has many memories connecting food with where it comes from. As a boy, Besh dreamed of running away to join the Foreign Legion; instead he joined the Marines to see the world. Returning from the first Gulf War, he decided to enroll at the Culinary Institute of America. Besh came home to New Orleans where he now has six restaurants, and another one in San Antonio. In the aftermath of hurricane Katrina, Besh fed those in need rice and beans from a friend's boat. He tells the story of the first person he served turning to him and saying, "Now what kind of rice and beans are those? My mother's red beans are much better." But that's New Orleans for you—a giant gumbo pot of cultures, recipes, and stories all mixed together to create an amazingly diverse and vibrant food scene that is steeped in history.

Shrimps a la Creole

Stew a few tomatoes, a small green pepper and a small clove of garlic together. Make a poulette sauce of the following: Small piece of butter, one tablespoon of flour, add one pint cream or milk; when done strain tomatoes into sauce. Then let shrimps cook a few minutes and serve hot in ramekins or on buttered toast.

A recipe for "Shrimps a la Creole" from the Neighborhood Cook Book *by the Council of Jewish Women, published in 1914.*

Everyone is passionate and opinionated about cooking in the "Big Easy," and that's what has helped them overcome Katrina and more recently the BP oil spill. Besh invited chefs from around the country, including White House chef Cristeta Comerford, to go fishing with him in the Gulf to show the world the seafood was safe to eat.

Published in 1914, the *Neighborhood Cook Book* by the Council of Jewish Women, includes a recipe for "Shrimps a la Creole."

No thickening of the sauce with flour for Besh, who makes his shrimp like his grandmother might have done—using fresh local produce cooked up in a spicy sauce and served over another Southern favorite, cheesy white grits.

Shrimp Stock

1 celery stalk, quartered

1 carrot, peeled and quartered

1 onion, peeled and quartered

1 sprig thyme

1 head garlic, split in half horizontally

2 pounds shrimp shells

White Grits

1 teaspoon salt

1 cup white stone-ground organic grits

2 tablespoons (1/4 stick) unsalted butter

1/2 cup mascarpone cheese

Sautéed Louisiana Shrimp

30 jumbo Louisiana shrimp

1/2 teaspoon Creole spice

Pinch of salt

2 tablespoons extra-virgin olive oil

6 tablespoons minced Jacob's Andouille sausage

1 tablespoon minced shallot

1 tablespoon minced garlic

2 tablespoons minced piquillo peppers

1 tablespoon chopped fresh thyme leaves

3 3/4 cups shrimp stock (about 30 ounces)

2 tablespoons (1/4 stick) unsalted butter

1 teaspoon freshly squeezed lemon juice

2 cups diced tomatoes

1 tablespoon chopped fresh chives

1/2 cup picked fresh chervil pluches

SERVES 6

To Make the Shrimp Stock

1. Place all the ingredients for the stock in a large pot, cover with 1 gallon of water, and simmer for 1 hour over low heat, skimming the fat the whole time.

2. Strain, cool, and reserve the stock.

To Make the Grits

1. Bring 4 cups water to a rapid boil and lightly season with salt.

2. Add the grits while stirring rapidly, then reduce to a simmer.

3. Simmer the grits over low heat for about 20 minutes, stirring all the time to prevent the grits from sticking to the bottom of the pot.

4. To finish, stir the butter and mascarpone into the grits.

To Make the Shrimp

1. In a small bowl, mix the shrimp with the Creole spice and salt.

2. Heat a large pan over medium heat and add the olive oil. Add the shrimp and sauté until they start to brown and turn pink but are not cooked all the way through. Remove the shrimp and set aside.

3. Add the andouille, shallot, garlic, piquillo peppers, and thyme to the pan and sauté until they become aromatic, about 2 minutes.

4. Add in the reserved shrimp stock and bring to a low simmer. Stir in the butter and reduce until nice and thick, about 5 minutes.

5. Return the shrimp to the pan and cook through. Finish with the lemon juice, diced tomatoes, and chopped chives.

To Serve

Place 4 generous tablespoons of the grits in the middle of each of six large serving bowls and arrange the shrimp in a circle on top, tails facing in. Spoon the sauce around to fill the negative space and garnish with the fresh chervil pluches.

Maine Lobster and Black Truffle Potpie

Jared Wentworth [Longman & Eagle, *Chicago, Illinois*]

THE BEST TYPES OF INTRODUCTIONS ARE FROM PEERS, AND when one chef recommends another, you know you should listen. Giuseppe Tentori is so keen for me to meet Jared Wentworth and to visit his restaurant Longman and Eagle, he drops everything in his kitchen at Boka and we hop in his car for what he tells me is a shortish ride over to Logan Square (we get a little lost—the scenic route around snowy Chicago means bonus time with Tentori).

Longman & Eagle has just been awarded a coveted star in the Chicago edition of *The Michelin Guide* when I visit—however unexpected, it was not undeserved. Wentworth's cooking is refined within a pleasant gastropub setting—a long bar dominates the room, and wood is everywhere—including the ceiling. The menu bursts with flavorful American fare and has a balance of various price points. Wentworth loves cooking with luxury ingredients, but always uses what's seasonal and sustainable as the starting point—think nose to tail and farm to table done right, not just because it's fashionable. I instantly warm to the way Wentworth is so serious about his cooking but never takes himself too seriously. An example of this is a postcard he has made up using his worst Yelp review, which not only complains about the "dark, gloomy, and noisy atmosphere" but also the food: "Who eats that kind of food? Bone marrow & wild boar? Yucky!" With lines out the door, a Michelin star, and high praise in the press, Wentworth knows he's getting it right.

Potpie, a savory meal of meat and vegetables wrapped in pastry, was once the choice of Tudor pastry cooks to kings in Europe to showcase their skills, and is immortalized in the nursery rhyme "Four-and-Twenty Blackbirds." Less-dainty dishes of savory pies have been popular as a way of stretching the food available since ancient times. Meat, vegetables, and sometimes cheese were cooked in pastry, often as individual portable pies to be eaten the following day: Spanish empanadas, Cornish pasties, Russian pierogi, English pork pies, Arabic sanbusak, Italian calzones, and Indian samosas are all examples of savory portable pies from around the world. Early American settlers would have turned to pie because pastry uses less flour than bread, and when food is scarce, pies are a good way to use up scraps of meat to make another meal to feed hungry mouths. By the middle of the eighteenth century, the term "potpie" was being used in America for the technique of putting pastry on top of a mixture of ingredients in a deep pot, for both sweet and

savory pies. Mrs. Lettice Bryan, in *The Kentucky Housewife* (1839), marks one of the earliest records of potpie being used in the title of the recipe—"A Chicken Pot-Pie" and "An Apple Pot-Pie." The latter is sweeter and closer to a modern cobbler. Almost forty years later, in 1877, Estelle Woods Wilcox published a recipe for "Chicken Pot-pie" in *Buckeye Cookery* and states: "Veal and Lamb may be used in the same way." Potpie today is an Americanism, a savory casserole dish of chicken, beef, or turkey topped with flaky pastry.

Wentworth gives us a decadent potpie of truffles and lobster in a rich brandy cream sauce tucked under a flaky puff pastry crust fit for a king. A nice way to prepare this dish is in individual ramekins with a square of puff pastry resting on top instead of one large pie.

2 Maine lobsters (1 pound each)

2 tablespoons butter (1/4 stick), plus extra for greasing dish

1 leek, white part only, cut into rounds

1 carrot, diced small

1 bulb fennel, diced small

3 ribs celery, small diced

2 yellow potatoes, peeled, and diced small

1 cup good-quality brandy

3 ounces tomato paste

1 1/2 pints heavy cream

1 Périgord black truffle, shaved

Salt and freshly ground pepper

1 sheet puff pastry

1 large egg, beaten

SERVES 4 TO 6

1. Kill the lobsters with a knife to the head. Separate the claws and tails from the bodies and reserve.

2. Blanch the tails and claws in lightly simmering water for about 2 minutes. Plunge in ice water and when chilled, separate the meat from the shell and chop into large chunks.

3. In a 3- to 4-quart saucepan or soup pot, heat the butter and sauté the reserved lobster bodies and vegetables. When the vegetables are just turning translucent, about 10 minutes, deglaze with the brandy and burn off alcohol. Add the tomato paste and heavy cream and simmer for 20 to 30 minutes over low heat. Remove the lobster bodies from the pot.

4. Preheat the oven to 375°F.

5. Grease a ceramic ovenproof dish with butter. Add the vegetable mixture, lobster meat, and shaved truffle. Stir to incorporate the ingredients and season with salt and pepper.

6. Dock a sheet of puff pastry with a fork, pricking it all over to allow the steam to escape while it's baking. Place on top and trim the edges, leaving a 1/2-inch overhang. Crimp it tightly to the dish and brush with egg wash.

7. Bake till the pastry is golden brown and the filling is piping hot, about 15 minutes. Remove from the oven and cool for 5 minutes before serving.

Chef Wentworth's Tips

"Oregon black truffles would totally work with the dish. When buying them, a reputable forager or dealer is important because many come to market unripe or past their prime—mushy and smelly."

"It is important not to boil the lobster bodies initially because you want the flavors to infuse into the cream and vegetables as they cook."

"I usually cut the lobster right between the eyes for a quick kill."

Jumbo Lump Crab Cake with Tomato, Cauliflower, and Golden Raisin Chutney

S TEPHEN L EWANDOWSKI [Tribeca Grill, *New York, New York*]

LUNCH SERVICE IS WINDING DOWN AT TRIBECA GRILL WHEN I arrive to meet Stephen Lewandowski. On my way to the kitchen, I pass a couple of tables, mainly businessmen and women in suits, gathered to dine on contemporary American over a deal or two. No recognizable faces to spot today, but as the *New York Times* says, "there's an almost constant flow of celebrity guests." Opened in 1990 by co-owners and friends restaurateur Drew Nieporent and Academy Award-winning actor-restaurateur Robert De Niro, Tribeca Grill has become a downtown Manhattan treasure, and many claim it helped put the neighborhood of Tribeca on the map.

The young fresh-faced Lewandowski reviews orders on the yellow tickets and calmly surveys the grill to make sure that the burgers will be perfectly broiled to order. One ticket calls for two patties, no bun, and he's off to the dining room to check that a waiter hasn't gotten this wrong—the patties are extremely large to begin with, and he's shocked someone would want two!

Lewandowski's classic American menu of farmers' market–driven dishes delivers bold flavors and not-so-diminutive portions—all beautifully prepared in the kitchen before being whisked to the table by highly trained staff. His tall crab cakes sit on a bed of tomato, cauliflower, and raisin chutney. The presentation of the dish and the accompaniments change seasonally.

Early crab cake recipes are called "crab croquettes," and essentially use the same technique of binding the crabmeat into a patty and frying it in a pan. In her book *What Mrs. Fisher Knows About Old Southern Cooking* (1881), Mrs. Abby Fisher uses finely powdered cracker crumbs in her recipe for "Crab Croquettes;" Lewandowski uses Japanese panko bread crumbs. Both have onion, herbs, and seasoning—Fisher writes, "Season with salt and pepper, also the least bit of fine red pepper, as crabs have to be seasoned high to be nice." Mirroring this call for high seasoning, Lewandowski's combination of delicately flavored crabmeat with a spicy-sweet chutney is beyond "nice"—it's a fresh and exciting twist on a traditional favorite.

Chutney

4 cloves garlic, thinly sliced

2 shallots, thinly sliced

Extra-virgin olive oil

1 cup tomato paste

4 anchovy fillets

2 tablespoons sugar

Pinch of hot red pepper flakes

16 plum tomatoes, quartered

1/2 cup white wine

1 teaspoon capers

1 cup cauliflower, sautéed
until caramelized

3/4 cup golden raisins

Crab Cakes

1 pound jumbo lump
crabmeat

2 tablespoons red bell
pepper, finely diced

2 tablespoons yellow bell
pepper, finely diced

2 tablespoons red onion,
finely diced

2 tablespoons Old Bay
Seasoning

1/4 cup mayonnaise

2 tablespoons mustard

2 large eggs

1 cup panko bread crumbs

2 teaspoons minced fresh
flat-leaf parsley

2 teaspoons minced fresh
chives

Vegetable oil, for sautéing

SERVES 8

To Make the Chutney

1. In a saucepan over medium heat, sauté the garlic and shallots in the extra-virgin olive oil for 2 minutes.

2. Add the tomato paste, anchovies, sugar, and pepper flakes and sauté for an additional 2 minutes.

3. Add the tomatoes, white wine, and capers and let simmer for 15 minutes; do not overcook or reduce the mixture. Taste and adjust the seasoning.

4. Fold in the cauliflower and golden raisins and cook for 3 minutes longer.

To Make the Crab Cakes

1. To a large mixing bowl, add the crabmeat, bell peppers, onion, seasoning, mayonnaise, mustard, eggs, and bread crumbs, reserving 1/4 cup of the bread crumbs. Mix well, but gently, taking care not to break up all the crabmeat. Fill a medium ring mold with the crab mixture, then remove the mold. Roll the crab cake in the remaining bread crumbs and set aside. Repeat this procedure until all the crabmeat mixture is used. Refrigerate the molded cakes for approximately 20 minutes before cooking.

2. Heat some vegetable oil in a nonstick sauté pan over medium-high heat. Once the oil is hot, add the crab cakes and sauté, in batches if necessary, until golden brown and heated through, about 5 minutes on each side.

To Serve

Spoon the chutney into the bottom of eight shallow bowls, distributing it equally. Top with a crab cake and garnish with the parsley and chives.

Fish and Chips, Long Island Style

DAVID PASTERNACK [Esca and Eataly, *New York, New York*]

AT THE FISH COUNTER OF EATALY YOU WILL OFTEN FIND THE
fisherman made famous by a 2005 profile called "Gone Fishing" in the *New Yorker* magazine—David Pasternack. Pasternack is an old-school chef with no desire to be a celebrity chef. If he doesn't have a rod in his hand, he wants to be working—filleting fish, revising the menu, placing orders, and answering the phone, "Kitchen." When he's not running the show at his Italian fish restaurant Esca in the theatre district, or watching over the crudo counter at Eataly, he's fishing with salty sea dogs who he's fished with for years. These men are hardcore—tattoos, Vietnam vets, and union men, all with stories to tell.

For his Fish and Chips recipe, he looks back to his paternal grandmother Gertrude from Brighton, England. She would use cod and make a mixture called meal, made from finely ground hard biscuits. She would dip the fish in milk and then in the meal and fry it in a cast-iron skillet in which she had already fried some onions to infuse the oil with flavor. "She would do fries and none of them were ever the same shape. They were never crispy but they were always delicious. She would then turn off the heat and leave the fish on the stove to cool down, and serve it at room temperature with the fried onions. She never ate it hot. This made the dish much more flavorful. If fried food is served hot you can't taste anything."

Gertrude Pasternack came to America in the early 1900s on a boat where she scrubbed potatoes to pay her way to Coney Island, New York. "She was one of the first women ever allowed in the Brighton Beach Baths, which was all men. There was an exercise club, and they would swim and play in the water whatever the season. She was a polar bear and swam all year." Sadly Gertrude was killed in her eighties, hit by a drunk driver on Coney Avenue.

"She was a good cook, a one-pot cook, always on a top stove broiler—she never turned her oven on because one time it exploded on her." Gertrude had one cast-iron skillet and she would cook everything in it. "They were poor."

"The next day she'd make her famous fish head soup. She would take the cod head, tail, collar, and scraps, she would split the fish head open, and add potatoes, carrots, celery, onion, and dill—no water. She put it all in a pot with a heavy lid over a very low flame and all the juices from the fish and the vegetables would come out."

Pasternack is much more comfortable telling me the story of his grandmother but when I ask him about how he became a chef he doesn't answer the question and comes back to Gertrude with another story about how great her cooking was. I guess she inspired him in many ways he doesn't talk about.

In *How to Cook Fish* (1908), there are recipes for tartar sauce and pan-fried codfish. Many of the recipes call for cornmeal, dredging, lemon juice, and serving the fillets or steaks with tartar sauce. Interestingly, one recipe for "Fried Fillets of Codfish" calls for soaking the fillets in a mixture of olive oil, two tablespoonfuls of lemon juice, and salt, grated onion, and paprika. This marinade sounds awfully close to something Pasternack might serve as crudo. His crudo dishes, developed in the kitchen after a trip to Italy with his partners at Esca, Joe Bastianich and Mario Batali, introduced America to this Italian technique. Funny how if Olive Green had not cooked her cod fillet but instead thinly sliced it, and then added a red peppercorn or two, black lava sea salt, and a touch of tangerine juice, she could have put it on the tasting menu at Esca.

A recipe for "Tartar Sauce" from How to Cook Fish *by Olive Green, aka Myrtle Reed, published in 1908.*

TARTAR SAUCE—I

Chop together capers, olives, parsley, and pickles. Add one half cupful of the mixture to a cupful of Mayonnaise.

FRIED FILLETS OF CODFISH

Mix together one tablespoonful of olive-oil, two tablespoonfuls of lemon-juice, and salt, grated onion, and paprika to season. Soak fillets of codfish in this for an hour, then drain, dip into beaten egg, then into crumbs, and fry in deep fat. Drain on brown paper and serve with Tartar Sauce.

A recipe for "Fried Fillets of Codfish" from How to Cook Fish *by Olive Green, aka Myrtle Reed, published in 1908.*

Fish and Chips, Long Island Style

"Cod is God," Pasternack tells me as he races off down a staircase to get one from a walk-in refrigerator somewhere below the food halls of Eataly. Pasternack cooks up this God of fish in a truly authentic rendition of fish and chips, served with tartar sauce and malt vinegar, using his grandmother Gertie's "one skillet cooking" recipe.

Tartar Sauce

3/4 cup plus 1 tablespoon canola oil

1/4 cup plus 1 tablespoon olive oil

3 large egg yolks

Freshly squeezed juice of 2 lemons

2 teaspoons Dijon mustard

1 tablespoon small diced cornichons (or any pickle variety)

1 tablespoon salted capers, soaked overnight in water, rinsed, and chopped

2 teaspoons finely diced shallot

1 tablespoon chopped fresh tarragon

2 tablespoons chopped fresh flat-leaf parsley

Sea salt

Freshly ground pepper

Pinch of cayenne pepper

Italian-style Bread Crumbs

1 loaf Italian bread

1 1/2 tablespoons extra-virgin olive oil

1 teaspoon finely diced garlic

1 tablespoon finely grated lemon zest

1 1/2 tablespoons chopped fresh flat-leaf parsley

2 teaspoons sea salt

1 teaspoon freshly ground pepper

To Make the Tartar Sauce

1. Prepare the tartar sauce early on the day of serving or the day before.

2. Make a mayonnaise base, whisking the oils slowly into the egg yolks in a large bowl with a fine wire whisk.

3. Add the lemon juice, mustard, cornichons, capers, shallots, and herbs. Season with salt, freshly ground pepper, and cayenne, and set aside.

To Make the Bread Crumbs

1. Preheat the oven to 350°F.

2. Tear the loaf of bread into 2-inch chunks. Place them on a baking sheet and bake until the bread is dry and crunchy, about 15 minutes.

3. Put the chunks in a food processor and pulse to a fine crumb. Set aside.

4. Heat 1 tablespoon of the olive oil in a small sauté pan. Add the garlic and cook, stirring, until it begins to brown, about 3 minutes. Add the lemon zest and cook for 30 seconds until fragrant.

5. Add the bread crumbs, parsley, and the remaining 1/2 tablespoon olive oil and stir well. Season with salt and pepper and remove from the heat. Makes about 2 cups bread crumbs. The bread crumbs can be stored in a covered container until ready to use.

To Make the Chips

1. In a large cast-iron pan, add the olive oil to a depth of 3/4 inch, and place over low to medium heat, allowing the entire pot to preheat with the oil. When the oil is shimmering, but not smoking, add the onion slices and gently fry until golden brown. This will soften and sweeten the flavor of the oil. Remove the onion, season, and enjoy.

2. You have two options for the chips: you can par-boil the potatoes first, cool, and fry twice, or you can cook them just by frying once. By par-boiling and frying them twice, they will end up crispier with a fluffy interior. For this you need to bring a large pot of salted water to a boil, add potatoes, return to boil, and then reduce heat to a gentle simmer for 10 minutes. Strain, cool on a wire rack, and refrigerate for at least 30 minutes. In the cast iron pan, with the onion-infused oil, fry the chilled chips at 270°F for 9 minutes, until lightly golden. Then spread loosely on a wire rack, and cool in the refrigerator for 1 hour. Raise the temperature of the oil to 375°F and fry again for 2 to 3 minutes until crisp and golden. Season and serve. If you decide to fry the chips once, you will still have a perfectly tasty chip with less hassle. In this case, fry the chips 10 to 12 minutes at 275°F until golden.

Chips

3 cups olive oil

1 Vidalia onion, cut into ¼-inch slices

2 pounds large Idaho potatoes, cut into roughly ¼ inch x ¼ inch x 3-inch bâtons

Sea salt and freshly ground pepper

Fish

4 local flounder or cod fillets (6–8 ounces each)

2 cups instant flour (Wondra)

Sea salt

Freshly ground pepper

3 large eggs

1 cup whole milk

2 cups Bread Crumbs

3 tablespoons olive oil

SERVES 4

To Make the Fish

1. In selecting your fish, ask your fishmonger to choose whichever is fresher, and have him fillet it for you, removing all skin and bones.

2. Prepare the dredge. You will need three pans large enough to fit the fillets and allow a little extra room to move them around to coat thoroughly. Add the instant flour seasoned with a good amount of salt and pepper to the first pan. In a small bowl, beat the eggs, combine with the milk, and pour into the second pan. Put the bread crumbs into the third pan.

3. Remove the fillets from the refrigerator, pat them dry with a paper towel, and allow to come up to room temperature.

4. Season the fillets well with salt and pepper on both sides. One by one, drop a fillet into the flour, then into the egg mixture, then into the bread crumbs. At each stage, shake off all excess dredge.

5. To cook, in a large cast iron pan, heat the oil until shimmering, but not smoking. Place the fillets in the skillet and cook until golden brown, 4 to 5 minutes. Flip and cook an additional 2 to 3 minutes. Transfer to a wire rack or paper towels, season immediately with additional salt and pepper. Serve with chips and tartar sauce—newspaper is optional!

Chef Pasternak's Tips

"In place of, or in addition to, tartar sauce, malt vinegar is an excellent complement to fish and chips."

"When cutting the potatoes, don't worry about perfect cuts—my grandmother never did."

Poultry
&
Meat

Duck Fat–Fried Chicken with Piquillo Ketchup

Ludo Lefebvre [LudoBites, *Los Angeles, California*]

NAMED CHEF OF THE FUTURE BY *TIME* MAGAZINE IN 2010 AND on many "Best Things I Ate" lists from coast to coast, including those by Sam Sifton for the *New York Times* and Pulitzer Prize–winning *LA Weekly* critic Jonathon Gold, Ludo Lefebvre has conquered not only classic French cuisine, modern cooking techniques, and American food culture, but also a whole new business model with his daring pop-up venture. Together with his wife, Krissy, they have invaded bakeries, cafés, art galleries, a disused restaurant space, and even the latest hot dining trend of L.A.—the food truck. Most recently, they have traveled around the country for his new television show *Ludo Bites America*.

Whatever the kitchen, however large or small, Lefebvre brings affordable high-end French food to those lucky enough to get a table. Within an hour of releasing reservations, LudoBites fans have snapped them all up. The system usually crashes from sheer numbers—35,000 people all trying to jump on the limited run. This is more like trying to get a ticket to a rock concert than a dinner reservation. Then again, Lefebvre seems more rock star than chef in pictures and on television: there's a particular shot of him lifting a striped bass out of the surf in jeans and nothing else. In the kitchen, however, there's no denying he's a chef first and foremost. When I visit him he is playing classical music "to calm my prep cooks," he jokes as he slices up a large slab of foie gras. The menu at Ludo-Bites features an abundance of truffles, oysters, foie gras, and caviar at surprisingly low prices. He tells me he'd like to have a restaurant devoted entirely to foie gras—he has been known to incorporate it into the frosting for a cupcake!

"I can cook anything," says Lefebvre. "Michelin-star-quality cuisine is what I like to do, and yet what does everyone ask for? Not classic French dishes mixed with modern techniques, but fried chicken!" So what if the food ran out when critic Gold arrived for his reservation—Lefebvre made fried chicken, in the spirit of "The show must go on." Gold went so far as to say it was one of the best meals he had that year. Fried chicken is also the signature dish on Lefebvre's food truck, wrapped in the bright red LudoBites rooster logo.

Mrs. W. H. Pendleton's recipe for "Fried Young Chicken" from How We Cook in Los Angeles, *published in 1894.*

Like many American dishes, fried chicken didn't originate here in the United States; it came to the South via African slaves and Scottish immigrants, who had a history of frying chicken in lard. When I sent Lefebvre a recipe for "Fried Young Chicken" from *How We Cook in Los Angeles* (1894), he asked me if it was a joke, because of the brevity of the instructions. Mrs. W. H. Pendleton's recipe calls for only flour, butter, lard, salt, and chicken. Yet Lefebvre's recipe hasn't changed so dramatically from the original. Instead of lard and butter we have rendered duck fat, and for flour there is the light touch of cornstarch. With the addition of a few flavors from around the world, Lefebvre's fried chicken is finger-lickin' fantastic.

> **FRIED YOUNG CHICKEN**
> Mrs. W. H. Pendleton.
>
> Flour, butter, lard, salt, chicken.
>
> Cut the chicken in pieces; salt, roll in flour and fry slowly in equal quantities of hot butter and lard, until of a fine brown.

LEFT: *LudoBites's distinctive tattooed rooster logo.*

MIDDLE AND RIGHT: *Lefebvre's own artwork.*

Duck Fat–Fried Chicken with Piquillos Ketchup

Ludo has turned to Asian ingredients to marinate the meat and infuse it with a depth of flavor that elevates this American classic to a gourmet marriage with the chef's French heritage and culinary traditions from farther afield. The resulting golden, crisp coated, succulent pieces of white and brown meat are served simply with a sprinkling of herbes de Provence and a spicy red dipping sauce.

Piquillo Ketchup

1 cup drained piquillo peppers (del destino)

2 cups raspberry vinegar

1/2 cup sugar

Kosher salt

1 tablespoon Tabasco sauce

Freshly ground white pepper

Fried Chicken

3 cups light soy sauce

1 cup sesame oil

1/2 cup chili oil, no seeds

3 tablespoons chopped fresh ginger

2 tablespoons chopped garlic

1 whole chicken (3 pounds)

6 cups duck fat

1 pound cornstarch

1/4 cup herbes de Provence

Salt and freshly ground pepper

SERVES 4

To Make the Ketchup

1. In a large saucepan, combine the piquillo with the raspberry vinegar, sugar, and a pinch of salt. Add 4 cups of water. Bring the mixture to a boil, then reduce to a low simmer.

2. Cover and cook for 1 hour, stirring every 10 minutes. The liquids will reduce to a syrupy consistency.

3. Carefully blend the piquillo mix in the blender until it is completely smooth, adding water as necessary.

4. Once the mix is completely puréed, gently stir in the Tabasco and white pepper by hand.

5. Set aside and reserve in refrigerator.

To Make the Chicken

1. In a bowl, combine the soy sauce, sesame oil, chili oil, ginger, and garlic; mix with a whisk and set aside.

2. Clean the chicken. Cut the chicken breasts in half, leaving the skin on.

3. Cut each chicken leg into two pieces at the joint, leaving the skin on.

4. Put the cut chicken pieces in a big bowl, add the marinade, and toss to coat. Let the chicken marinate overnight in the refrigerator.

5. On the next day, remove all the chicken meat from the marinade.

6. In a saucepan, heat the duck fat slowly over medium heat to 320°F.

7. Place the chicken legs in a bowl and toss them lightly with half the cornstarch.

8. Place the coated chicken legs in the duck fat, and let cook about 12 minutes (check temperature of meat with meat thermometer to ensure the interior is cooked to 160°F). Remove the legs from the duck fat and place on paper towels to drain. Season with herbes de Provence, salt, and pepper.

9. Repeat Steps 7 and 8 for the breast pieces with the remaining cornstarch.

10. Serve chicken hot, with the piquillo ketchup as a dipping sauce.

Chicken Paillard with Parmesan Bread Crumbs, Escarole, Capers, and Rosemary

SUZANNE GOIN [Lucques, *Los Angeles, California*]

SO POISED IN HER LONG-SLEEVED BLACK T-SHIRT, WHITE APRON,
and pulled back hair, Suzanne Goin greets me warmly at her restaurant Lucques, and leads me straight back to the kitchen. All the ingredients for her chicken paillard are laid out in little white dishes, a perfect example of excellent mise en place: always have everything well prepared before you start to cook. Goin proudly shows me a large colander of freshly washed escarole that she picked from her garden in the Hollywood Hills that morning. It's early February and most of America is under snow. I am jealous because anything that I grow in my garden in the hills is eaten by rabbits, squirrels, or deer. "I have a very big fence," she says. "And lots of wire was put in underground to stop the gophers."

As well as running Lucques, AOC, and Tavern with her business partner Caroline Styne, Goin also co-owns the Hungry Cat with her husband, David Lentz, in Hollywood, Santa Barbara, and Santa Monica. As if this workload isn't enough, she somehow manages to do it all while raising three young children. She explains that two of them are very open to food and love everything. "My four-year-old daughter even loves spicy food," she says, "My older boy, however, is my nemesis; he's the one who always wants french fries, juice, and chicken nuggets, so the chicken paillard is my answer to him and the dreaded chicken nuggets. It's crunchy, juicy, and cheesy. I can slice it for him and he loves it. All my kids love the capers. I'm not sure what it is with kids and sour things, but all three of my kids eat lemons and *love* pickles!"

Early American recipes for chicken fall into three main categories: roasted, fried, or minced and then rolled into a ball, dipped in flour, and fried. Goin's recipe for chicken paillard calls for pounding the chicken breast rather than mincing the meat. It is almost a cross between the fried chicken and the chicken croquettes—which if you think about it, is what a good chicken nugget is, as opposed to the fast-food variety, which is made from processed meat shaped to look like little legs.

Chicken Paillard with Parmesan Bread Crumbs, Escarole, Capers, and Rosemary

This dish hits all the right notes for me—there are no fancy ingredients and it's easy to prepare. The finished chicken is seriously juicy with just the right amount of spice, cheese, and crunch.

6 boneless, skinless organic chicken breasts

3/4 cup all-purpose flour

2 extra-large eggs

4 1/2 cups fresh bread crumbs

1 cup grated Parmigiano-Reggiano

6 tablespoons chopped fresh flat-leaf parsley

Kosher salt and freshly ground pepper

6 tablespoons extra-virgin olive oil

8 tablespoons (1 stick) unsalted butter

1 rosemary sprig, broken in half

1 dried chili d'arbol, broken in half

2 cloves garlic, sliced

2 heads escarole, cored, leaves separated and cleaned

2 tablespoons chopped capers

Finely grated zest of 1 lemon, plus juice

SERVES 6

1. Place the chicken breasts between two pieces of plastic wrap and pound them to an even 1/3-inch thickness.

2. Place the flour on a plate or in a pie pan. Beat the eggs in a shallow bowl. Combine the bread crumbs, Parmigiano-Reggiano, and half of the parsley in a shallow dish.

3. Season the chicken breasts with salt and pepper. Dredge the chicken in the flour, then the egg, and then the bread crumbs, using your hands to help fully coat the chicken.

4. Heat two sauté pans over high heat for 2 minutes. Swirl 2 tablespoons of olive oil into each pan and wait 1 minute. Carefully place 3 chicken breasts in each pan.

5. Cook 3 minutes and then add 1 tablespoon of butter to each pan. Cook another minute, and when the crumbs are golden brown, carefully turn them over. Reduce the heat to medium and cook a few more minutes, until the second side is golden brown and the chicken is just cooked through. Transfer the chicken to a sheet pan.

6. Return the pans to medium heat and swirl 1 tablespoon of olive oil into each pan. Divide the rosemary and chili between the two pans and let sizzle 30 seconds. Add half the garlic to each pan, stir a few seconds and then add the escarole to the pans. Season with salt and pepper and sauté gently 2 to 3 minutes, until the greens have just wilted.

7. Season the escarole with a squeeze of lemon and transfer to a large platter. Place the chicken on top.

8. Wipe out one of the pans and return it to the stove over medium heat. Add the remaining 6 tablespoons of butter and cook until it's brown and smells nutty. Remove from the heat and wait a few seconds. Add the capers, lemon zest, a generous squeeze of lemon juice, and the remaining 3 tablespoons of parsley. Taste for balance and seasoning.

9. Spoon the caper brown butter over the chicken and around the greens.

Chef Goin's Tips

"When you have leftover bread, grind it into bread crumbs and freeze it so you have it on hand to make this and other dishes. I love toasted bread crumbs sprinkled over pasta, for instance."

"Feel free to use other greens, like Swiss chard or spinach, besides escarole for this dish."

Lemon-Garlic Roasted Chicken with Twice-Fried French Fries

Michel Richard [Citronelle, *Washington, D.C.*]

RICHARD REMINDS ME OF SANTA CLAUS IN HIS BLACK CHEF'S jacket—with his *joie de vivre*, round jolly face, and trademark white beard.

"The white hats, aprons, and all of the food—I fell in love," Michel Richard says of the moment, upon peeking into a restaurant kitchen in France at the age of eight, when he knew he wanted to be a chef. His childhood dream became a reality, and after rising from apprentice to the top pastry position for Gaston Lenôtre in Paris, he was given a chance to come to America in 1974 when Lenôtre sent him to New York to open Chateau. The patisserie was short lived but Richard stayed on and has lived and cooked in the United States for more than thirty-five years.

It was his restaurant Citrus in Los Angeles that first put him on the culinary map, adapting French techniques to the tastes of California. He expanded with restaurants in Santa Barbara, San Francisco, Baltimore, and Tokyo before opening Citronelle in Washington, D.C. and making his permanent home there. His achievements are many, starting with being inducted into the James Beard Who's Who back in 1988, a *Gourmet* cover in 2004, James Beard Outstanding Chef 2007, and Best New Restaurant for his second restaurant in D.C., Central Michel Richard, in 2008. Most recently, he has opened Michel: "Traditional American cuisine with a special French flair."

"I love that America is a melting pot," he says. "Always close to world cuisine, I think America has embraced, adapted, and made French food to their own liking. It's great. *Trés bien!*"

America has taught Richard about texture. "Texture is very important," he says. "At the time I first came to America, we didn't do texture in France. I learned about texture here. Also the generosity in food, here the portions are so big. When I first got here I fell in love with a grand serving of prime rib."

A good steak ("but not filet mignon, it's boring") is Richard's dish of choice if he's cooking for himself. He also likes to eat classic American comfort food: fried chicken, carrot cake, white clam chowder, warm chocolate brownies, mac and cheese, and cheesecake.

Growing up in Ardennes, France, Richard's mother raised chickens and would often roast and serve them for dinner. "I probably use a little more garlic than she did," says Richard, "and the recipe has changed slightly over the years from her original." The chicken is cooked with tons of garlic and lemons, served with a gravy made from the juices and Richard's twice-fried french fries.

Recipes for roast chicken today haven't changed that much from early American times. I presume roasting a chicken was so commonplace that it didn't seem necessary to include a lot of recipes. There are old recipes for roast turkey, roast wild duck, and roast goose, and although roast chicken was often listed as a menu item, recipes are few and far between. In *The Virginia House-wife* (1824), Mary Randolph gives instruction on how to roast a chicken: "they will take a quarter of an hour in roasting; froth them up, lay them on the dish, pour butter and parsley on, and serve them up hot." The cooking time of fifteen minutes is due mostly to the young age and low weight of the bird (no supersized chickens in 1824), and the fact that it's spit roasted. Certainly though, the meat would have been much more rare than we'd find acceptable today.

> ## TO ROAST YOUNG CHICKENS.
> When you kill young chickens, pluck them very carefully, truss and put them down to a good fire, dredge and baste them with lard; they will take a quarter of an hour in roasting; froth them up, lay them on the dish, pour butter and parsley on, and serve them up hot.

Instructions "To Roast Young Chickens" from The Virginia House-wife *by Mary Randolph, published in 1824.*

Lemon-Garlic Roasted Chicken with Twice-Fried French Fries

Perhaps the best thing about this recipe, apart from the succulent chicken, is the way the house is filled with the most delicious aromas as it cooks. This is a supereasy, satisfying family dinner. Richard suggests being very American and serving the roast chicken with his twice-fried french fries.

Lemon-Garlic Roasted Chicken

2 onions, sliced

20 cloves garlic, unpeeled

One free-range chicken (about 4 pounds)

Salt and freshly ground pepper

2 lemons, cut in half, plus an additional 1/2 lemon

1 branch fresh thyme

4 tablespoons olive oil

2 tablespoons chopped fresh flat-leaf parsley

Twice-Fried French Fries

4 to 6 large baking potatoes (12 ounces each), peeled

Peanut or canola oil for deep-frying

Fleur de sel

SERVES 4 TO 6

To Make the Roasted Chicken

1. Place a rack in the middle of the oven and preheat the oven to 300°F.

2. Cover the bottom of a roasting pan with the onion slices and garlic cloves.

3. Rinse the chicken under cold running water inside and out, drain, and thoroughly pat dry with paper towels. Lightly season the cavity with salt and pepper and stuff with 4 of the lemon halves and the thyme. Place the chicken in the roasting pan, season with salt and pepper, and sprinkle with olive oil.

4. Roast in the middle of the oven for 1 hour. After an hour, remove the chicken from the oven and increase the heat to 450°F. When this temperature is reached, return the chicken to the oven and roast until golden and crisp. The chicken is cooked when a fork inserted into the thigh releases clear juices.

5. Remove the chicken from the oven and let it rest for 10 minutes. Remove the lemon halves from the cavity. Squeeze the juice of the remaining 1/2 lemon over the chicken and sprinkle with the chopped parsley.

6. Transfer the onion, garlic, and liquid from the roasting pan to a sauté pan and bring to a boil. Add 1/2 cup of water to the pan, mix well, and return to a boil. Strain and serve as a gravy with the chicken.

To Make the French Fries

1. Fill a large bowl with ice. Trim each potato into a 3- to 4-inch-long smooth-sided block, then cut lengthwise into 1/2-inch slices. Cut each slice lengthwise into 1/2-inch wide strips. Trim the fries to 3 to 4 inches long by 1/2 inch square. As you work, drop the potatoes into the ice water for at least a few minutes to rinse off the starch; they can be refrigerated in the water for up to a day.

2. For the first frying, heat the oil to 325°F in a deep fryer or a deep, heavy pot. If using a pot, you will need a fry basket. Remove the fries from the water and dry well on paper towels. (If the potatoes are not well dried, the oil will bubble up—be careful.) Place a handful of potatoes in the fryer basket and carefully lower it into the oil; do not crowd the potatoes. If the oil bubbles excessively, lift up the basket for a few seconds, then return the potatoes to the oil. Repeat if necessary; the bubbles should diminish. Cook for 4 to 5 minutes, or until the potatoes are cooked through and just lightly colored. Drain on paper towels and repeat with the remaining potatoes.

3. For the second frying, heat the oil to 325°F. Working a batch at a time as before, lower the fries in the basket into the oil and fry for 4 to 5 minutes, or until crisp and evenly browned. Drain on paper towels, sprinkle with fleur de sel, and serve hot.

Confit of Turkey, Roasted Breast of Turkey with Clam and Sausage Stuffing, and Olive Gravy

TODD ENGLISH [Olives, *New York, New York*]

WHILE STILL A STUDENT AT THE CULINARY INSTITUTE OF America, Todd English landed a job that would be integral to his early education as a chef. "I'm in the dorm, the phone rings, and a thick French accent at the other end asks for Todd English and says to me, 'Okay, you start on Monday'—click." The following week, he began working at La Côte Basque. It is here that he perfected the French technique of *confit*, cooking the duck that was to go into the cassoulet. "I feel like I got my bachelor's degree at the Culinary Institute of America," says English. "And then I went out into the world and got my master's, and I'm still working on my PhD—it will never end for me because there's always something to learn about food around the world." He's currently fascinated with spice.

English's "master's" involved building a giant multimillion-dollar brand. He has opened a long string of restaurants around the country and beyond, beginning in 1989 with Olives in Charlestown, Massachusetts, and has broadened his empire to include airline and cruise-ship foods, books, television shows, nonstick cookware, and even a line of frozen pizzas. Interestingly, it's this success that has led some to publicly question whether he's "sold out." English's answer to this is quite clear: he doesn't want to end up burnt out by the drudgery of working in a restaurant kitchen turning out haute cuisine day and night. He's seen it happen to too many chefs of the previous generation who taught him. The lesson he learned from them might well have been something they didn't realize they were teaching. It wasn't that he couldn't stand the heat but that he saw a niche to do so much more if he got out of the kitchen.

When I ask English to come up with a Thanksgiving turkey dinner that is comforting, not too challenging, and a little different, he gives me a dish that taps into many aspects of who he is as a chef. "I like to layer simple components to make intense and interesting flavor," he says. "Like in music, you may not hear the cello but it's there. It's the same with food, you may not taste the garlic but you'd taste its absence."

Known across the country as the centerpiece of the Thanksgiving table, roast turkey is as close to a national dish as America gets. The early settlers discovered and cooked up the bounty of the New World—wild turkey, venison, fish, clams, lobster, pumpkins, blueberries, nuts, corn (as meal in cakes), and cranberries—but it's unlikely that they enjoyed the bird as we know it today at the first Thanksgiving feast. For one thing, they didn't have ovens; the turkey would have been spit roasted—if it was eaten at all. The pilgrims referred to any wild fowl as "turkey," so they could have dined on duck or goose and still called it turkey. Last year when it was just four of us for Thanksgiving, I cooked up an organic roast chicken and convinced the children it was a small turkey. I had no idea how close I was to the pilgrims.

English breaks his turkey down and cooks the dark and light meat separately, stuffing and roasting the breast and slow-cooking the legs and thighs in fat to make a confit. Though there's no whole bird to present to the table, this method ensures that both the light and dark meats are perfectly cooked, and the slices of breast are so elegant with the stuffing at the center that no one will complain. English's stuffing includes clams—a nod to New England—and is served with lots of rich brown gravy. We used to say "swimming in gravy" when I was younger, and his olive gravy is just divine over the crispy golden stuffing and juicy meat.

By using the technique of confit to cook the turkey legs, the brown meat turns out moist and succulent. Don't be put off by this fancy-sounding technique or the fact that the meat is cooked in fat—it's relatively easy and the finished meat isn't greasy or laden with fat. The confit is then baked in the oven to crisp up the skin. The hardest part is probably learning how to truss the meat with butcher's twine—it takes a little practice, but you'll be so pleased with the results. Then there's that all-important question of oven space and timing. Plan ahead and you will be fine. The confit can be cooked a day or two in advance.

Although we can't be sure that turkey was part of the original Thanksgiving feast, clams, lobster, and fish most definitely were. Oysters were first added into sauces and stuffings in the late-eighteenth and early nineteenth century. Originating in the South, probably stemming from the French influences in New Orleans, oyster sauce spread up the eastern seaboard to New England. Amelia Simmons has two recipes for stuffing turkey in *American Cookery* (1798), but no mention of seafood. By 1824, Mrs. Randolph in *The Virginia House-wife* includes a recipe to boil a turkey with oyster sauce. Estelle Woods Wilcox includes a recipe for "English Roast Turkey" in *Buckeye Cookery* (1877), and includes a garnish of fried oysters.

We've come a long way with English's recipe for roast turkey with confit legs, clam stuffing, and olive gravy.

> ### ENGLISH ROAST TURKEY.
> Kill several days before cooking, prepare in the usual manner, stuff with bread-crumbs (not using the crusts) rubbed fine, moistened with butter and two eggs, seasoned with salt, pepper, parsley, sage, thyme or sweet marjoram; sew up, skewer, and place to roast in a rack within a dripping-pan; spread with bits of butter, turn and baste frequently with butter, pepper, salt and water; a few minutes before it is done glaze with the white of an egg; dish the turkey, pour off most of the fat, add the chopped giblets and the water in which they were boiled, thicken with flour and butter rubbed together, stir in the dripping-pan, let boil thoroughly and serve in a gravy-boat. Garnish with fried oysters, and serve with celery-sauce and stewed gooseberries. Choose a turkey weighing from eight to ten pounds. If it becomes too brown, cover with buttered paper.—*Mrs. C. T. Carson.*

Mrs. C. T. Carson's recipe for "English Roast Turkey" from Buckeye Cookery *by Estelle Woods Wilcox, published in 1877.*

Confit of Turkey, Roasted Breast of Turkey with Clam and Sausage Stuffing, and Olive Gravy

Part of the trial of cooking a large turkey is getting the white meat and the brown meat to be cooked and ready at the same time. English breaks down the bird and cooks the legs confit. Once you have tasted how succulent and juicy it is, you will never roast the whole bird again. The breast is rolled up with the stuffing in the middle, which keeps the meat moist, and it's so pretty on the plate once sliced.

It's not a true Thanksgiving without all the extra familiar flavors. We've added Stephanie Izard's sweet potato gratin and Daniel Boulud's celery root purée to the mix because everyone wants turkey with all the trimmings. For dessert, I would suggest Richard Ruskell's pumpkin pie or Alex Seidel's bourbon pecan pie with butterscotch sauce drizzled liberally on top, or both! As we toast in our house on Thanksgiving, "Let's give thanks for the giving and the giving of thanks!"

1 turkey (15 to 18 pounds), broken down: legs detached, thighs attached, breast split, ribs removed, first joint of wing bone intact ("airline style")

Turkey Confit

2 turkey legs, thighs attached

2 to 2 1/2 quarts duck fat

4 cloves garlic, smashed

1/2 red onion, roughly chopped

6 sprigs thyme

2 bay leaves

1 lemon, halved

1 carrot, roughly chopped

Salt and coarsely ground pepper

2 cups olive oil

Clam and Sausage Stuffing

3/4 pound loaves of day-old country bread, cut into 3/4-inch cubes (about 6 cups)

1 pound Italian sausage, casings removed

1 tablespoon minced garlic

2 cups finely chopped onion

1 1/2 cups chopped celery

3 tablespoons minced fresh thyme leaves

1 tablespoon minced fresh sage leaves

2 tablespoons Dijon mustard

2/3 cup finely chopped fresh flat-leaf parsley

To Make the Turkey Confit

1. Preheat the oven to 275°F.

2. In a medium saucepan, melt the duck fat.

3. In a skillet over medium heat, heat 2 tablespoons of the duck fat. In a medium bowl, toss the turkey legs with the garlic, onion, herbs, lemon, carrot, and salt and pepper and transfer to the skillet. Sweat the vegetables and turkey legs for 4 to 5 minutes. Place the turkey legs in a single snug layer in a high-sided baking dish or ovenproof saucepan. Pour the melted fat over the legs, then the olive oil, and place in the oven.

4. Cook slowly at a very slow simmer, with just an occasional bubble, until the legs are tender and can be easily pulled from the bone, 2 to 3 hours.

5. Remove the confit from the oven and let cool to room temperature in the pan.

To Make the Clam and Sausage Stuffing

1. Preheat oven to 325°F.

2. Arrange the bread cubes in one layer in shallow baking pans. Bake in the oven for 10 to 15 minutes, or until they are golden. Transfer them to a large bowl.

3. In a large skillet over medium-high heat, sauté the sausage, breaking it apart with a fork as it cooks. Remove with a slotted spoon and discard all but 2 tablespoons of the fat. Add the garlic, onion, celery, thyme, and sage over moderately low heat, stirring, until the vegetables are softened. Transfer the mixture to the bowl with the bread. Add the mustard, parsley, melted butter, littleneck clams, sausage, and salt and pepper to taste. Toss the stuffing well and let it cool completely.

To Make the Stuffed Breasts and Gravy

1. Butterfly each breast and season each with salt and pepper. Stuff each with 2 cups of the stuffing and roll up. Seal the edges with metal skewers, or tie with butcher's twine.

2. Preheat the oven to 375°F.

8 tablespoons (1 stick) unsalted butter, melted

2 dozen shucked littleneck clams, liquor reserved

Salt and freshly ground pepper

Stuffed Breasts and Gravy

1 turkey breast split, ribs removed, first joint of wing bone intact ("airline style")

Salt and freshly ground pepper

1 onion, roughly chopped

2 carrots, roughly chopped

2 celery stalks, roughly chopped

8 quahog clams, well scrubbed

2 cups turkey or chicken broth

2 cups white wine

1/3 cup maple syrup

1/2 cup chopped black olives

1 tablespoon roughly chopped fresh rosemary leaves

SERVES 6 TO 8

3. Place the onions, carrots, and celery in the bottom of a medium roasting pan. Nest the clams in the vegetables. Add the stock and 1 cup of the white wine. Lay the stuffed turkey breasts on top of the vegetables and quahog clams and cook 1 to 1 1/2 hours, or until an internal temperature of 155° to 160°F.

4. Remove the breasts and set aside to rest. Pour any liquid from the clams back into the pan and discard the clams. Drain excess liquid through a chinois or fine-mesh sieve and set aside.

5. Add the maple syrup to the vegetables in the pan and mash.

6. Deglaze the roasting pan with the remaining 1 cup white wine and reduce by half. Remove the fat from the reserved liquid, add it back to the pan with the roasted vegetables, and simmer for about 2 minutes.

7. Finish the gravy with the olives and rosemary. Season with salt and pepper to taste.

To Serve

1. Preheat the oven to 375°F.

2. Discard the vegetables, bay leaves, and excess fat from the turkey confit.

3. Place the remaining 4 cups of the stuffing in a shallow baking dish, top with the confit legs, and bake for 30 minutes, or until the confit is golden brown and the stuffing is crisp.

4. Carve the turkey breasts into 1/2-inch-thick slices and serve the confit and stuffing alongside.

5. To finish the plating, sauce the breasts with the olive and rosemary gravy.

Short Ribs Braised in Red Wine

DANIEL BOULUD [Daniel, *New York, New York*]

"THE BEST IN NEW YORK, IT'S TRUE," SAYS JEAN-JACQUES Rachou, my father-in-law, about Daniel Boulud, when we are recipe testing together in my little kitchen in Los Angeles. Rachou looks over the stack of recipes I have for us to test, and his eyes light up when he gets to Boulud. "This is a good recipe because it's the old-fashioned way, very easy, and, besides, it's French." Ruth Reichl is quoted as saying that Boulud has taken "everything that's so good about being French and everything that's good about being American and combined them" at his restaurant Daniel. I feel that the same is true of his short ribs recipe; it's derived from a classic French beef bordelaise.

Boulud has cooked his way up from his family farm in France, where they grew produce and raised livestock to sell at markets, to become one of Manhattan's top restaurateurs, all the time with grace and diplomacy. Daniel is one of only a handful of restaurants to ever receive the highest rating of four stars from the *New York Times*, and in 2010 he finally attained his lifelong dream when he was awarded three Michelin stars. He can work the dining room with smiles and small talk (perhaps learned from his ten years as the chef at Le Cirque working for the charismatic master of the front of house Sirio Maccioni). And then, like many chefs as they return to their kitchen, he's back to all business—relentless, demanding, and fastidious, but always fair.

In Miss Corson's *Practical American Cookery and Household Management* (1886), the author describes the rib cut as "the favorite roasting-piece of beef in America." She includes a picture of the ribs, cut short, trimmed or with the bones removed, rolled and ready to "be roasted, baked or braised, according to the general directions for such operations, and served with any chosen gravy or garnish, or with a plain green salad."

Instead of roasting the ribs, Boulud taps into his French heritage and braises them in a bordelaise sauce—lots of red wine, celery, onions, and beef stock. This classic French technique extracts the most flavor and brings out the best of the ingredients. When the ribs come out of the oven and are plated, the results are beyond delicious. This is one of the tastiest, most satisfying dishes I've ever had. "Now this is cooking!" says Rachou proudly, as we tuck into Boulud's short ribs for supper.

REMOVES (RELEVÉS). 313

ready for roasting. The third is a number of ribs boned and rolled by the butcher. All the trimmings should be sent home with the boned ribs, to be used for soups or

Ribs of Beef, Trimmed.

sauces; sometimes the ends of the ribs only are sawed off and removed. When all the bones are taken out, and the roll of meat is tied very tight, it will remain in place after cooking, and can be carved more easily and economically

Ribs of Beef, Boned and Rolled.

than when the bones remain. The rolled ribs may be roasted, baked, or braised, according to the general directions for such operations, and served with any chosen gravy or garnish, or with a plain green salad.

A section entitled "Removes (Relevés)" from Miss Corson's Practical American Cookery and Household Management *by Miss Juliet Corson, published in 1886.*

Short Ribs Braised in Red Wine

The depth of flavor from the meat and the wine is like a thousand flavors of France all packed into one American short rib. This is one of those dishes that has you still thinking about it days and weeks later—until the next time you pull out your Le Creuset!

Short Ribs

3 bottles dry red wine

8 short ribs, trimmed of excess fat

2 tablespoons vegetable oil

Salt

1 teaspoon whole black peppercorns, crushed

Flour, for dredging

10 cloves garlic, peeled

8 large shallots, peeled, trimmed, and split

2 medium carrots, peeled, trimmed, and cut into 1-inch lengths

2 celery stalks, peeled, trimmed, and cut into 1-inch lengths

1 medium leek, white and light green parts only, trimmed, coarsely chopped, washed, and dried

6 sprigs fresh flat-leaf parsley

2 sprigs thyme

2 bay leaves

2 tablespoons tomato paste

3 quarts unsalted beef stock or store-bought low-sodium beef broth

Freshly ground white pepper

Celery Root

1 quart whole milk

2 tablespoons coarse salt

2 pounds celery root, peeled and cut into 8 pieces

1 pound Yukon gold potatoes, peeled and halved

8 tablespoons (1 stick) unsalted butter, at room temperature, cut into 8 pieces

Salt and freshly ground white pepper

SERVES 8

1. Pour the wine into a large saucepan set over medium heat. When the wine is hot, carefully set it aflame, let the flames die out, then increase the heat so that the wine boils. Allow it to boil until it is reduced by half, then remove from the heat.

2. Center a rack in the oven and preheat the oven to 350°F.

3. Warm the oil in a Dutch oven or large casserole over medium-high heat. Season the ribs all over with salt and the crushed black pepper. Dust half the ribs with about 1 tablespoon flour and then, when the oil is hot, slip the ribs into the pot and sear 4 to 5 minutes on each side, until the ribs are well browned. Transfer the browned ribs to a plate, dust the remaining ribs with flour, and sear in the same manner. Remove all but 1 tablespoon of fat from the pot, lower the heat to medium, and toss in the vegetables and herbs. Brown the vegetables lightly, for 5 to 7 minutes, then stir in the tomato paste and cook for 1 minute to blend.

4. Add the reduced wine, browned ribs, and stock to the pot. Bring to a boil, cover the pot tightly, and slide it into the oven to braise for 2 1/2 hours, or until the ribs are tender enough to be easily pierced with a fork. Every 30 minutes or so, lift the lid and skim and discard whatever fat may have bubbled up to the surface. (Note: Not only can you make this a day in advance, it's best to make the recipe up to this point, cool and chill the ribs and stock in the pan. On the next day, scrape off and discard the fat that has solidified at the top. Rewarm until heated through.)

5. Carefully (the tender meat falls apart easily) transfer the meat to a heated serving platter with raised rims and keep warm. Boil the pan liquids until they thicken and reduce to approximately 1 quart. Season with salt and pepper and pass through a fine-mesh sieve; discard the solids.

6. To serve, plate the ribs on top of the celery root purée and pour the sauce over the meat.

To Make the Celery Root Purée

1. Put the milk, 4 cups water, the coarse salt, celery root, and potatoes in a medium saucepan and bring to a boil over medium heat. Lower the heat and cook at a simmer until the vegetables can be easily pierced with the point of a knife, 20 to 25 minutes. Drain the vegetables and return them to the pan. Return the pot to the stovetop over low heat and toss the vegetables around in the pot just long enough to cook off the excess moisture.

2. Transfer the vegetables to the work bowl of a food processor. Add the butter and process—taking care not to overwork the mixture—but just until the purée is smooth and creamy. Season with salt and white pepper. Keep the purée warm in the top of a double boiler over simmering water until ready to plate.

Grilled Flatiron Steak with Truffled Creamed Spinach and Pickled Onion Rings

GABRIEL RUCKER [Le Pigeon, *Portland, Oregon*]

IN RESTAURANT KITCHENS IN FRANCE, *LE PIGEON* IS THE person who has to do all the dirty jobs. Gabriel Rucker's Portland restaurant Le Pigeon is small, and as a result, all the employees, including the chef, muck in and do a bit of everything. Chef, or Gabe as everyone calls him, still has to peel garlic, chop onions, and wash and pick spinach, if that's what the menu items require. Rucker jokes that unlike celebrity chefs, he actually cooks in his kitchen most nights.

Le Pigeon sums up Portland dining—independent, intimate, irreverent, and incredibly serious about serving good full-flavored food. The little open kitchen dominates the 35-seat dining room, which consists of three communal tables. From a chair at the counter, you are so close to the action you can feel the heat from the stove and the chef. Don't ask for substitutions—there are none: it's "Gabe's way" or no way.

Beyond the tattoos and meteoric rise to national recognition is a serious chef who knows how to cook, twist, and play with his food. He's keen on putting offal and the less well-known cuts of meat on his menu, often prepared in unexpected and whimsical ways—foie gras jelly doughnuts; Cheek to Cheek, a dish made with one beef cheek and one halibut cheek; or his signature dish of squab served with the deep-fried pigeon's legs draped over the edge of the bowl. Taking something simple and elevating it is Rucker's forte. He will visit the farmers' market and change the menu according to what he finds. He gives this dish of steak and onions with creamed spinach a gourmet twist on the usual nutmeg, with a local favorite: black Oregon truffle.

The flatiron is a relatively new, less expensive cut of beef that is taken from a part of the animal that was once rarely used. Its name comes from the fact that its shape resembles an old-fashioned iron. In the *Neighborhood Cook Book* by the Council of Jewish Women (1914), there is a recipe for fried "Beefsteak and Onions." Rucker broils his steak and pickles his onions before frying them, which gives them an extra zing. If you can't find rib eyes at your local butcher, flank steaks work very well with this recipe, too.

Pickled Onion Rings

³/₄ cup white wine vinegar

¹/₄ cup sugar

3 tablespoons kosher salt

1 red onion, cut into 4 slices 1 inch thick

¹/₂ cup semolina flour

¹/₂ cup all-purpose flour

1¹/₂ cups light beer

Oil for frying

Steaks and Spinach

4 flatiron steaks (7 ounces each)

Kosher salt

2 cloves garlic, sliced

1 tablespoon unsalted butter

1 pound spinach, washed and picked

1 tablespoon truffle oil

4 tablespoons crème fraîche

Sea salt

Aged balsamic syrup, to finish

1 small black Oregon truffle, finely sliced

SERVES 4

To Make the Pickled Onion Rings

1. In a medium saucepan, combine the white wine vinegar, sugar, salt, and ¹/₄ cup water; bring to a boil. Cool and pour over the onion. Let stand for 2 hours.

2. In a large bowl, combine semolina and all-purpose flour with the beer to make the batter. Place the pickled onions in the batter and coat each one.

3. Pour oil into a large, heavy cast iron pot or 5-quart or larger sauté pan to a depth of 3 inches. Heat over medium-high heat to 350°F. Fry the onion rings until deep golden brown, adjusting heat as necessary for each batch to maintain temperature at 350°F, about 2 minutes. Transfer onion rings to paper towels to drain.

To Make the Steaks and Spinach

1. Season the steaks with kosher salt and grill to desired doneness. Remove from the heat and let rest.

2. In a large pot, sweat the garlic in the butter. Add the spinach and season with salt, stirring constantly until wilted. Finish with truffle oil and crème fraîche.

3. Mound portions of spinach on four large plates. Slice the steaks and place on top of the spinach mounds. Sprinkle the steaks with sea salt and top each one with three onion rings. Drizzle the plate with balsamic syrup and finish with a few slices of the black Oregon truffle.

Chef Rucker's Tip

"Rare does not work well for the flatiron steak; medium rare is the preferred doneness."

Kalbi Ribs with Macadamia Nut Rice

PETER MERRIMAN [Merriman's, *Waimea, Hawaii*]

MERRIMAN'S HAS BEEN THE DESTINATION RESTAURANT IN Waimea on the Big Island since it opened in 1988. The *Los Angeles Times* named chef and owner Peter Merriman "The Pied Piper of Hawaii Regional Cuisine," and he's proud of showcasing local ingredients on his menu. There are toasted Hawaiian macadamia nuts in the jasmine rice for extra texture and flavor, a good example of how he integrates ingredients to present them at their best. Originally, he sourced local produce simply because it tasted better, encouraging farmers to cultivate varieties never before grown on the island. With the creation of Hawaii Regional Cuisine, many local farmers and ranchers are now providing Merriman with a vast array of ingredients—from fresh organic mushrooms and greens to award-winning goat cheese and range-raised, hormone-free lamb and beef. All find their way onto Merriman's extensive menu with 90 percent of the ingredients from Hawaii.

Merriman also grows a lot of his own herbs, fruits, and vegetables for the restaurant in a little kitchen garden that the dining room overlooks. A couple of tomatoes cling to a dying vine from a season long since over in the rest of America; a large bunch of bananas are about to ripen; black sugarcane stands tall; and tiny, bright, super hot red peppers dot a low bush. Merriman shows off the abundance, bending to smell an herb and happy to share his stories. "These are all canoe crops," he tells me. "Brought to Hawaii hundreds of years ago. The only indigenous species are coconuts and kukui nuts [their oil is used as the fuel in tiki lamps]."

"This Korean twist on the American classic comfort food, short ribs, is supereasy and quick," says Merriman. "It's also a guys' recipe. It should be cooked outside on the grill. It goes great with a beer."

---

1 jumbo onion

6 cloves garlic

1/4 cup finely chopped fresh ginger

2 cups low-sodium soy sauce

1/4 cup brown sugar

5 pounds 1/2-inch-cut beef short ribs, use prime or choice corn-fed beef (you need the fat)

12 ounces jasmine rice

2 tablespoons garlic butter

1/2 cup chopped toasted macadamia nuts

1/2 cup chopped scallions

SERVES 4

---

1. Purée the onion, garlic, ginger, soy sauce, and brown sugar in a food processor. Pour over ribs and marinate for 8 hours.

2. Rinse the rice in a sieve under cold water, place in a small saucepan, and pour in enough water to cover rice and come to 1 inch above it. Bring to a boil and then reduce the heat and simmer for 15 minutes. Turn off the heat and let the rice rest for 15 minutes without opening the lid.

3. Grill the ribs over charcoal until medium rare.

4. Serve on jasmine rice tossed with garlic butter, toasted macadamia nuts, and chopped scallions.

Chef Merriman's Tip

"Half-inch pieces of beef absorb the marinade better, stay more tender, and cook more evenly—so have your butcher cut them down."

Mesquite-Grilled Prime Cut Rib Eye with West Texas Mop Sauce, Mango Coleslaw and Cornbread Pudding

DEAN FEARING [Fearing's Restaurant, *Dallas, Texas*]

THERE AREN'T MANY GRADUATES OF THE CULINARY INSTITUTE of America and winners of the James Beard Best Chef Award who go to work dressed in a chef's jacket, blue jeans, and brightly colored, custom-tooled Lucchese cowboy boots. Dean Fearing does. We are introduced by Peter Merriman, who highly recommends him as *the* BBQ guy. Dubbed the "Father of Southwestern Cuisine," Fearing is all about cooking highly flavorful food; his catch phrase is "Bold Flavors, No Borders." This he tells me doesn't just refer to the Mexican border. "We have a lot of different influences, from Asian to Indian to Southern comfort foods—we don't limit our cuisine to anything—hence no borders." Growing up in Kentucky, the son of an innkeeper, he learned to appreciate the subtleties of authentic Southern food and barbecue from his grandmothers, and he still uses these treasured original recipes today.

Fearing's rib-eye steaks are glazed in his special mop sauce, inspired by a true nineteenth-century recipe from West Texas. Cattle ranching has long been a central part of Texan culture—think Stetson hat, cowboy boots, and the long cattle drives loved by Hollywood at the end of the 1800s.

Immigrants were encouraged to come to Texas in the early days of the state, including Germans, who developed ways to tenderize brisket, a tougher cut of beef, using Dutch ovens and, later, smokers. Barbecue has come to mean different things to different folks. In Texas it's usually beef, and in particular brisket, whereas in the rest of the South it's all about pork shoulder roasts and Boston buts. "Barbecue" is also used to describe two different cooking techniques: firing up the grill and fast-cooking meat, and smoking—slow-cooking the meat at a low temperature over a long period of time, as one does in Texas pit roasting. Both include that all-important element of cooking outdoors for a gathering of friends. When grilling, barbecue sauce is mopped on top of steaks, as in Fearing's recipe, but when Texas pit roasting, the sauce is always served on the side.

I grew up on my family farm in Devon where my father still raises a rare breed of cattle called White Park. These beautiful white animals with long horns and black noses and ears were used by the Celts for sacrificial purposes and have been prized for their meat for more than two thousand years. During the Second World War, Winston Churchill commanded that a trio of breeding White Park be transported to America for their safekeeping in the event of an invasion, such was his appreciation of the meat. This beef is considered so delicious and supreme that King James I of England in 1617 called for his sword and knighted his supper—"Sir Loin." Whenever I eat steak, regardless of the particular cut, I think of this apocryphal tale.

Fearing's recipe for rib-eye steak will cure even the toughest cowboy's craving for a big juicy hunk of meat. The dark mop sauce, made with lots of molasses, chile, and balsamic vinegar, is sweet and spicy and tart—just what you need to glaze the steaks. To serve alongside are two barbecue favorites—fresh mango coleslaw with a Thousand

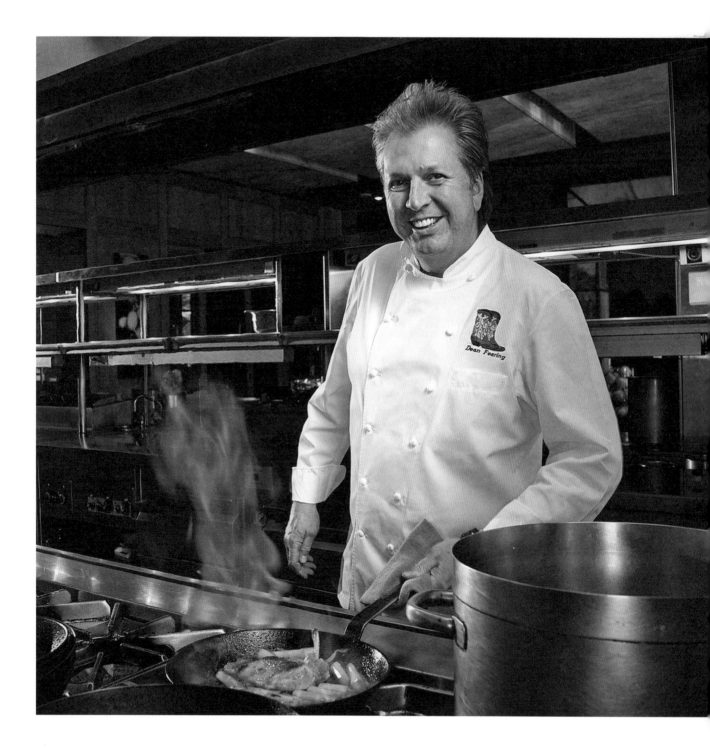

Island dressing and a cornbread pudding. The orange of the mango, bright pink of the pickled red onion, and the yellow of the cornbread pudding are almost as vivid as the embroidered boots on Fearing's chef jacket. With all the mighty flavors he packs into one plate, this makes for some fierce barbecue. I can't wait to serve this up at my Fourth-of-July party—and once you realize how straightforward it all is I'm sure you'll do the same. Plus, this is what real men eat—you know they'll thank you.

Mesquite-Grilled Prime Cut Rib Eye with West Texas Mop Sauce, Mango Coleslaw, and Cornbread Pudding

Dallas has always just been a TV show to me, until I ate "Chef in Boots" Dan Fearing's perfectly grilled steak with all the colorful sides. Now it will forever mean West Texas Mop Sauce, which I confess to eating straight from the pot with a spoon—it's so good.

West Texas Mop Sauce

1 tablespoon olive oil

1 cup chopped onion

2 tablespoons chopped shallots

1 tablespoon chopped garlic

1 tablespoon cracked black peppercorns

1 bottle Shiner Bock beer

2 cups molasses

1 cup Worcestershire sauce

1/2 cup balsamic vinegar

2 teaspoons Dijon mustard

1 teaspoon ground arbol chile

1/4 cup cornstarch

Salt

Fresh lime juice

Rib-Eye Steaks

4 center-cut rib eye fillets (about 12 ounces each), cleaned of all fat and silver skin

Salt and freshly ground pepper

1 recipe West Texas Mop Sauce

Barbecue Thousand Island Dressing

1/2 cup mayonnaise

1 tablespoon ketchup

2 tablespoons barbecue sauce (the smokier the better)

1 1/2 teaspoons white vinegar

1/2 hard-boiled egg, finely chopped

1 teaspoon sweet pickle relish

1/2 teaspoon minced white onion

1/2 teaspoon dry mustard powder

1 1/2 teaspoons capers, minced

To Make the Mop Sauce

1. Set a large saucepan over medium-high heat and add the oil. Add the onions and sauté for 3 minutes, or until lightly brown. Add the shallots, garlic, and black peppercorns and sauté for an additional 2 minutes, or until lightly brown.

2. Add the beer and deglaze the pan, then reduce by half, about 2 minutes.

3. Add the molasses, Worcestershire, balsamic, mustard, and arbol chile. Bring the mixture to a boil, reduce to a simmer, and cook for 5 minutes. In a small bowl, mix the cornstarch and 1/4 cup water to combine thoroughly. Slowly pour the slurry in a small stream while stirring into the molasses mixture until thick. Add salt and lime juice to taste.

To Make the Rib-Eye Steaks

1. Fire up the grill; the chef recommends using mesquite wood.

2. Season the rib-eye fillets with salt and pepper to taste.

3. Place as many fillets as you can on the hot grill without crowding. Cook the fillets for 4 minutes on each side; the meat should be medium-rare. Repeat if cooking in batches.

4. A minute before the fillets have finished cooking, brush on a generous amount of the mop sauce to glaze. Turn each fillet and cook until the glaze thickens, about 1 minute.

5. Remove the fillets from the grill and keep warm.

To Make the Dressing

Combine all of the ingredients in a small bowl and stir well to combine. Place the dressing in a covered container and refrigerate until ready to use.

To Make the Pickled Red Onions

1. Peel the onion and cut in half. Slice into very thin half-moon shapes, put in a small bowl, and set aside.

2. Heat the vinegar and sugar in a small saucepan over medium heat, stirring constantly. When the sugar has dissolved, remove the pan from the heat. Add a pinch of salt, and pour the mixture over the onion in the bowl. Cover with plastic wrap, place in the refrigerator, and allow to stand overnight and pickle, 8 to 12 hours. When cool, drain the onions and use for the coleslaw.

½ teaspoon minced garlic

½ teaspoon Worcestershire sauce

½ teaspoon chopped fresh flat-leaf parsley

½ teaspoon snipped fresh chives

1½ tablespoon freshly squeezed lemon juice

Salt and freshly ground pepper

Pickled Red Onions

1 red onion

½ cup white wine vinegar

½ cup sugar

Pinch of salt

Mango Coleslaw

2 ripe mangos, peeled and julienned

3 cups green cabbage, julienned

1 each red bell pepper, thin julienned

1 cup small diced jicama

¼ cup finely sliced fresh cilantro

1 recipe Pickled Red Onions

Barbecue Thousand Island Dressing, as needed

Salt

Cornbread Pudding

4 cups crumbled cornbread,

1 tablespoon olive oil

2 cups fresh corn kernels

1 shallot, minced

2 cups heavy cream

¼ cup scallions, minced

1 teaspoon chopped fresh thyme

1 tablespoon mashed roasted garlic

1 teaspoon chipotle Tabasco sauce

1 tablespoon maple syrup

Salt and freshly ground pepper

SERVES 4

To Make the Coleslaw

Place the first six ingredients into a large bowl. Add the dressing a small amount at a time until the salad is lightly coated. Season with salt and serve immediately.

To Make the Cornbread Pudding

1. Preheat the oven to 350°F.

2. In a medium sauté pan placed over medium-high heat, add the olive oil and the fresh corn kernels. Sauté the corn for 3 minutes.

3. Place the crumbled cornbread in a baking dish. Add the shallot, cream, scallion, thyme, garlic, Tabasco sauce, and maple syrup and fold in the sautéed corn. Season with salt and pepper.

4. Bake in the oven for 10 minutes, or until golden brown, and serve.

Grilled Colorado Lamb T-Bones with Pine Nut and Sage Bread Pudding

JENNIFER JASINSKI [Rioja, *Denver, Colorado*]

RIOJA IS SO PACKED THAT MY COLLEAGUES AND I FROM THE *MasterChef* casting can't get a table for love or money. Reality television usually opens doors around America, but given the small size of the dining rooms in the restaurants up and down Larimer Square, when a restaurant is full, it's full.

Jennifer Jasinski looks younger than her years and when we meet back of the house I tell her this. She laughs. She's finishing up a busy Saturday night and her efficient team is still at the stoves in the open kitchen. A graduate of the Culinary Institute of America before she turned twenty-one, Jasinski went on to work at the Rainbow Room in New York City where a chance encounter with Wolfgang Puck led him to suggest that if she were ever in Los Angeles she should "look him up." She did. He's been her "mentor and culinary role model" ever since. This high achiever worked with Puck for ten years before moving to Denver in 2003 and opening her own restaurant, Rioja. She has subsequently opened two other restaurants, Bistro Vendôme, across the street, and most recently Euclid Hall, around the corner in an historic 1883 building.

Given her geography, I ask Jasinski for a Colorado lamb dish. She opts for T-bones for her lamb chops. "T-bones are fabulous cuts of meat," she says. "Not only do you get the added bonus of flavor from the bone, but you also get the best of two other cuts: the strip and the tenderloin."

There are many recipes for lamb chops in early American cookbooks—usually grilled and served with a vegetable or two. In *Favorite Dishes* (1893), Mrs. Hester A. Hanback of Kansas, suggests trimming the chops and then rolling them in cracker crumbs before frying them and serving with peas. Jasinski serves her marinated grilled lamb chops with spinach and a savory pine nut and sage bread pudding. "The bread pudding recipe can be made a day in advance and baked when you are ready to serve," says Jasinski. "Just refrigerate the raw bread puddings in their molds and cover. They will take a little longer in the oven, but they'll bake the same way."

Lamb Chops.

From MRS. HESTER A. HANBACK, of Kansas, Lady Manager.

Trim neatly and hack with sharp knife until tender; dip each piece in beaten egg and roll in cracker crumbs; place in pan equal quantities of butter and lard very hot; fry until nicely browned and serve with green peas.

Mrs Hester A Hanback

Mrs. Hester A. Hanback's recipe for "Lamb Chops" from Favorite Dishes *by Carrie V. Shuman, published in 1893.*

Marinated Lamb

1/4 cup pure olive oil

2 tablespoons chopped fresh rosemary

2 tablespoons chopped garlic

16 Colorado lamb T-bones (about 5-ounces each)

Pine Nut Sage Bread Pudding

2 tablespoons (1/4 stick) unsalted butter

1 cup diced white onion

2 tablespoons chopped garlic

1/4 cup chopped fresh sage

4 cups heavy cream

Kosher salt and freshly ground pepper

3 large eggs

9 cups diced sourdough bread (a boule is preferable)

1 cup pine nuts, toasted

Olive Sauce

1 cup sliced shallots

1/4 cup roughly chopped garlic

1/4 cup pure olive oil

2 plum tomatoes, diced

1/2 cup julienned sun-dried tomatoes

2 sprigs thyme

1 teaspoon whole black peppercorns

2 cups red wine

1/2 cup balsamic vinegar

4 cups veal demi-glace

4 tablespoons (1/2 stick) unsalted butter

1/4 cup Niçoise olives, pitted and chopped

1 tablespoon chopped fresh rosemary

Kosher salt and freshly ground pepper

To Assemble and Plate

Kosher salt and freshly ground pepper

1/4 cup extra-virgin olive oil

4 bunches red chard, cleaned and stemmed

SERVES 8

To Marinate the Lamb

Rub the oil, rosemary, and garlic into the lamb and let the meat marinate at least 1 hour, up to overnight.

To Make the Pine Nut–Sage Bread Pudding

1. In a large sauté pan, melt the butter, add the onion, and sauté until translucent. Add the garlic and cook about 1 minute to release the flavor; do not brown. Add the sage and cook briefly to bloom the flavors. Pour in the cream and bring to a boil. Reduce the heat and let simmer for 5 to 10 minutes to reduce the liquid by one-fourth. Serve with salt and pepper.

2. While the cream is reducing, put the diced bread into a large mixing bowl, crack the eggs over the bread, season with salt and pepper, and mix very well so no large pieces of raw egg are evident. Add the toasted pine nuts to the bread mixture. Add the reduced cream to the bread mixture, stirring quickly so the warm cream does not cook the eggs. Taste and adjust the seasoning, as needed.

3. Preheat the oven to 350°F.

4. Spray eight 8-ounce molds with nonstick cooking spray and line the bottom of each with a parchment paper circle. Fill the molds past the top so that they are brimming. Place on a baking sheet and bake until the puddings are brown on top. An internal temperature of 135°F will ensure that the eggs are cooked. Remove the bread puddings from the oven and let them cool slightly before unmolding them.

To Make the Olive Sauce

1. Sauté the shallots and garlic in the olive oil in a heavy-bottomed saucepan over medium-high heat until they are a deep golden brown. Add the plum and sun-dried tomatoes, thyme, and peppercorns, and cook long enough to break down the tomato.

2. Deglaze the pan with the wine and vinegar, and reduce the liquid until syrupy. Stir in the demi-glace and bring to a boil. Reduce the heat to a simmer and cook, about 45 minutes, skimming as needed, until the flavors have combined and the sauce is nappé (that is, to a consistency that will coat the back of a spoon). Strain the sauce through a fine chinois. When you are ready to serve, finish the sauce by reheating in a small saucepan. Whisk in the butter, olives, and rosemary. Season to taste with salt and pepper.

To Assemble and Serve

1. Preheat a grill to high heat.

2. Season the marinated lamb with salt and freshly ground pepper. Grill the lamb to your liking; the chef suggests medium rare.

3. While the lamb is cooking, add the olive oil to a large pot over medium-high heat, add the red chard, and stir the greens quickly so that they wilt thoroughly. Place the wilted greens in a colander and drain off the excess liquid. Season to taste with salt and pepper.

4. Place bread pudding, chard, and 2 lamb T-bones on each plate and drizzle with the olive sauce.

Shepherd's Pie with Buttered Baby Vegetables

BRENDAN COLLINS [Waterloo & City, *Los Angeles, California*]

I HAPPEN TO VISIT BRENDAN COLLINS IN THE KITCHEN OF HIS restaurant Waterloo & City on the day he's expecting Gordon Ramsay in for dinner. It's not Ramsay's first time. "He always insists on coming into the kitchen in the middle of service," says Collins. "I've got work to do and can't stand around chatting." No kitchen nightmares here—having worked as Marco Pierre White's sous-chef at Quo Vardis in London, he can handle anyone, both in and out of the kitchen. Collins's butchering skills are put to daily use, breaking down the whole animal to make headcheese, charcuterie, and the more well-known cuts of meat. He proudly shows off his walk-in refrigerator—packed from floor to ceiling with items commonly found in a three-star Michelin restaurant.

The Shepherd's Pie is one of the most traditional dishes on the menu at Waterloo & City—"This is a true gastropub, we serve high-level gastronomic food in a relaxed bar setting." You can imagine Collins popping down to the pub for a quick pint and a round of darts back in his hometown of Nottingham, England. There's a dartboard in the private room—all that's missing are skittles (a type of bowling found in pubs back home).

Meat pies, and in particular mutton pies, topped with pastry, can be traced back to medieval England and probably earlier. However, it wasn't until the eighteenth century that potatoes were used; potatoes being a relatively new food in Europe, introduced by the Spanish from the New World. Late nineteenth-century American cooks were making shepherd's pie and even calling it such. Mrs. Rorer in her *Philadelphia Cook Book* (1886) has a recipe for a rather bland version. Interestingly, she adds flour to her mashed potatoes and makes a type of potato pastry to use as the crust. Since the flour isn't listed in the ingredients, I wonder if she added this at the last minute thinking that it wouldn't be a proper pie without a pastry crust?

Collins, being a Brit, understands that a true shepherd's pie uses lamb or mutton; if you use beef it's a cottage pie. He tops his meat with mashed potatoes and parsnips, mixed with horseradish, giving a nice unexpected bite to the dish. He then carefully balances a selection of glistening buttered baby vegetables, which he has cooked in an emulsion, on top of his piping hot pie. Shepherd's pie has never looked so pretty or tasted so good.

SHEPHERD'S PIE

1 pound of cold mutton	1 tablespoonful of butter
1 pint of cold boiled potatoes	½ cup of stock or water
	Salt and pepper to taste

THE CRUST
4 good-sized potatoes
¼ cup of cream
Salt and pepper to taste

Cut the mutton and boiled potatoes into pieces about one inch square; put them in a deep pie or baking-dish, add the stock or water, salt, pepper, and half the butter cut into small bits. Then make the crust as follows: Pare and boil the potatoes, then mash them, add the cream, the remainder of the butter, salt and pepper, beat until light. Now add flour enough to make a soft dough—about one cupful. Roll it out into a sheet, make a hole in the centre of the crust, to allow the escape of steam. Bake in a moderate oven one hour, serve in the same dish.

A recipe for "Shepherd's Pie" from the Philadelphia Cook Book *by Mrs. S.T. Rorer, published in 1886.*

Shepherd's Pie with Buttered Baby Vegetables

Shepherd's pie is one of my favorite dishes, and this tasty recipe is the crème de la creme. The parsnips and horseradish in the potato are exceptional, as are the baby veggies balanced on top.

Shepherd's Pie

1 tablespoon olive oil

1 large onion, chopped

1 leek, white part only, chopped

4 celery stalks, chopped

2 medium carrots, chopped

1¼ pounds ground lamb shoulder

¼ cup all-purpose flour

1 can (14-ounces) San Marzano plum tomatoes

2 tablespoons tomato purée

1¼ cups lamb or beef stock

1 bay leaf

1 teaspoon chopped fresh rosemary

½ teaspoon chopped fresh thyme leaves

2 tablespoons best-quality tomato purée

1 teaspoon Worcestershire sauce, or to taste

Salt and freshly ground pepper

1½ pounds potatoes, peeled and chopped

½ pound parsnips, peeled and chopped

9 tablespoons unsalted butter

¼ cup milk

2 teaspoons creamed horseradish

¾ cup bread crumbs

¼ cup grated Parmesan cheese

Buttered Baby Vegetables

6 baby carrots, peeled

3 baby turnips, peeled and quartered

6 cauliflower florets

6 baby zucchini

¼ cup English peas

8 tablespoons unsalted butter

SERVES 4 TO 6

To Make the Shepherd's Pie

1. Preheat the oven to 375°F.

2. In a large sauté pan, heat the oil over medium heat and add the onion, leek, celery, and carrots. Cook until soft, about 5 minutes.

3. Add the ground lamb and brown, about 8 minutes.

4. Add the flour to make a roux, and cook for 5 minutes, stirring constantly.

5. Add the canned tomatoes, tomato purée, beef stock, bay leaf, rosemary, and thyme. Cover and simmer for 30 minutes. Season the mixture with Worcestershire sauce and salt and pepper to taste.

6. Meanwhile, make the topping. Boil the potatoes and parsnips in water until soft. Drain and mash with the butter and milk. Stir in the horseradish and season with salt and pepper.

7. Spoon the meat mixture into an ovenproof dish. Top with the mashed potatoes, then sprinkle the bread crumbs and cheese on top.

8. Bake the pie in oven until golden brown, 20 to 25 minutes.

To Make the Baby Vegetables

1. Meanwhile, blanch the carrots, turnips, cauliflower, zucchini, and English peas in separate pans of boiling water to retain the individual flavors until al dente. Drain and refresh in iced water. Drain again and set aside.

2. In a small saucepan over medium heat, melt the butter and add ½ cup water to make an emulsion. Reheat the blanched vegetables in the emulsion, season with salt and pepper to taste, and drain.

3. Arrange the buttered baby vegetables on top of the pie and serve.

Chef Collins's Tips

"For a special presentation, bake in individually sized oven proof dishes, as Collins does at Waterloo & City."

"Serve the Shepherd's Pie with extra Worcestershire or HP Sauce to spice things up a bit."

Uptown Texas Chili

RICK BAYLESS [Frontera Grill, *Chicago, Illinois*]

THE MISCONCEPTION ABOUT CHILI IN THE UNITED STATES IS that it's from Mexico—any chili found in Mexico is served to American tourists to satiate expectations. It may well have originated from the Spanish who brought chiles with them to Texas and cooked them up with onions and tomatoes to stretch what little meat they had. Chili was popularized by the cowboys of the nineteenth century—dried and then rehydrated, they cooked it in a pot over the campfire during the long hard cattle drives for a taste of home.

Strange, then, to get a recipe for this non-Mexican dish from Rick Bayless, the top American chef who specializes in traditional Mexican cuisine with a modern approach, a man who grew up in Oklahoma City with his barbecue-chef parents. Since opening Frontera Grill back in 1987 with his wife Deann Bayless, he has furthered haute-Mex food during his illustrious career, winning the James Beard Best Restaurant in America award in 1997, beating his peers to win Bravo's *Top Chef Masters*, authoring many cook books, and conquering television with his own series on PBS. Many speculated that he would be the White House chef when the Obamas moved in from Chicago, instead he was invited to cook the State dinner for Mexican President Felipe Calderón—I wonder, did he dare to serve them chili?

Served with beans and various toppings—cheese, scallions, white onions, avocado, crushed tortilla chips, or sour cream—this is one dish that everyone loves. Eleanor Roosevelt apparently asked Chasen's in Los Angeles, who served perhaps one of the most famous chilis, for their recipe—they gracefully declined and sent her chili instead. Elizabeth Taylor would order chili from Chasen's to be delivered to her on the set of *Cleopatra* in Rome.

At the end of the nineteenth century, recipes for chili con carne began appearing in American cookbooks. In *Favorite Dishes* by Carrie V. Shuman, compiled for the World's Columbian Exposition in 1893, the most regional recipes are those from Señora Don Manuel Chaves of New Mexico, written in Spanish. She includes a recipe for "*Tamales de Chile*"—which calls for "carne con chile".

Bayless's rich, meaty chili, made with white runner beans, is served at Frontera Grill topped with finely shredded dry Jack cheese, white onion, and chopped fresh cilantro. This is a great way to feed a large group—one-pot cooking that can be made up the day before. Not only does this help ease prep time but it also improves the flavor of the chili. I like to put out a selection of toppings so that people can add as little or as much as they desire.

Ancho Seasoning Base

8 large cloves garlic, unpeeled

8 medium dried ancho chiles (about 4 ounces total)

1 1/2 teaspoons dried oregano, preferably Mexican

1/2 teaspoon black pepper, whole or freshly ground

1/8 teaspoon cumin seeds, whole or freshly ground

A scant 1/4 teaspoon cloves, whole or freshly ground

2/3 cup beef broth

Salt (about 1 teaspoon)

Chili

1 tablespoon oil or bacon drippings

2 pounds pork and lamb, cut into 1/2-inch cubes

1 large white onion, chopped

2 to 3 cups beef broth

Salt

Sugar

1 to 2 cups canned tomatoes (optional)

Masa harina (optional)

About 2 cups of your favorite cooked beans, either homemade or canned

Shredded dry Jack cheese, chopped white onion, and chopped fresh cilantro, for topping

SERVES 6

To Make the Ancho Seasoning Base

1. Set a heavy, ungreased skillet or griddle over medium heat. Lay the unpeeled garlic on the hot surface and let it roast to a sweet mellowness, turning occasionally, until soft when pressed between your fingers (you'll notice it has blackened in a few small spots), about 15 minutes. Cool, then slip off the papery skins and roughly chop.

2. While the garlic is roasting, break off the stems of the chiles, tear the chiles open and shake and/or pick out all the seeds. For the mildest sauce, be careful to remove all the stringy, light-colored veins. To give them a richer flavor, toast the chiles a few at a time on your medium-hot skillet or griddle: open them out flat, lay them on the hot surface skin side up, press flat for a few seconds with a metal spatula (if the temperature is right you'll hear a faint crackle), then flip them. (If you pressed them just long enough, they'll have changed to a mottled tan underneath. If you see a slight wisp of smoke, it's okay, but any more than that will mean burned chiles and bitter taste.) Now press down again to toast the other side (you won't notice as much change in color on the skin side). Transfer the toasted chiles to a bowl, cover with hot water, and let rehydrate for 30 minutes, stirring regularly to ensure even soaking. Pour off all the water and discard.

3. If using whole spices, pulverize the oregano, pepper, cumin, and cloves in a spice grinder or with a mortar and pestle, then transfer the ground spices to a food processor or blender, along with the drained chiles and the garlic. Measure in the broth and process to a smooth puree, scraping and stirring every few seconds. (If you're using a blender, and the mixture just won't move through the blades, add more broth, a little at a time, until everything is moving but still as thick as possible. Not only is a watery marinade uninteresting, but the puréeing capabilities of the blender are much reduced when too much liquid is added.) With a spatula, work the purée through a medium-mesh strainer into a bowl; discard the skins and seeds that remain behind in the strainer. Taste (it'll have a rough, raw edge to it), then season with salt.

To Make the Chili

1. In a large, heavy skillet or Dutch oven filmed with oil or bacon drippings, fry the meat and onions over medium-high heat, until nicely browned; drain off most of the fat.

2. Add the full recipe of the ancho seasoning, stir for several minutes to temper the raw flavor, then stir in enough water or beef broth so that everything's floating freely. Cover partially and simmer gently for 1 hour, or until it looks like chili. Season with salt and a touch of sugar. If you like a less intense flavor, add 1 cup or so of blended canned tomato along with the broth or water.

3. For a thicker chili, mix together a little masa harina and water, then whisk it into the chili during the last few minutes of simmering.

4. Just before serving, stir in the beans and continue cooking until warmed through. Serve topped with shredded cheese, white onion, and cilantro.

Crispy Pork Cheeks with Creole Dirty Rice

EMERIL LAGASSE [Emeril's Delmonico, *New Orleans, Louisiana*]

CREOLE JAMBALAYA AND CAJUN dirty rice share certain techniques and key ingredients—rice and the "holy trinity," a base of green peppers, onions, and garlic. Their history in Louisiana is intertwined, particularly in and around New Orleans.

Creole cuisine originated from African cultures. Many of the cooks working in the restaurants and kitchens of city homes and the grand plantations in the South, were of African descent. Their cuisine, Creole, evolved into the high-end haute cuisine served in restaurants and wealthy homes of New Orleans. Jambalaya is typically defined as a Creole rice dish, which utilizes meat or seafood, stock, and tomato. *La Cuisine Creole* (1885) contains a recipe for "Jambalaya of Fowls and Rice"—made with chicken, minced ham, and rice and includes the note: "Southern children are extremely fond of this. It is said to be an Indian dish and very wholesome as well as palatable; it can be made of many things."

Cajun cooking, on the other hand, is based on French-Acadian customs and stems from the Bayou country and smaller communities of southern Louisiana. Cajun is usually the domain of the home cook and includes a lot of cast-iron-pot dishes. Dirty rice is traditionally considered a Cajun rice dish using duck, chicken, or turkey livers and giblets, and ground pork or chicken.

Just when I'm beginning to think I've understood the various definitions and differences, along comes Emeril Lagasse and "Bam!" he gives me *Creole* dirty rice. But I thought dirty rice was Cajun? Delmonico's is part of the New Orleans Creole tradition of sophisticated restaurants, so here they call it a "Creole Dirty Rice," though the components are essentially the same.

The dirty rice is delicious all by itself, but the crispy pork cheeks are definitely worth the effort. Make a confit of the pork cheeks by cooking them covered with oil in the oven at a low temperature until they are fork-tender. Then sauté the pork in a little butter until they are slightly crispy. "This dish has developed quite a following in New Orleans," says Lagasse, "and is one of our most popular dishes."

Pork Cheeks

2 1/2 pounds pork cheeks, cleaned and trimmed of all tough membranes

8 cloves garlic

6 sprigs thyme

1 1/2 tablespoons kosher salt

1 tablespoon coarsely ground pepper

1 tablespoon coriander seeds

Vegetable oil, as needed

1 cup all-purpose flour, plus more as needed for dusting

2 tablespoons (1/4 stick) unsalted butter

Dirty Rice

1 tablespoon vegetable oil

1 tablespoon unsalted butter

1/2 cup chopped yellow onion

1/2 cup chopped green bell pepper

1/4 pound ground pork

1/4 pound chicken livers, pureed

2 bay leaves

1 tablespoon finely chopped jalapeño

1/2 teaspoon salt

1/4 teaspoon ground coriander

1/4 teaspoon ground cumin

1/4 teaspoon cayenne pepper

2 cups cooked long-grain white rice

1/4 cup beef stock or canned, low-sodium beef broth

Dash of Tabasco, or other Louisiana hot sauce

SERVES 4 TO 6

To Make the Pork Cheeks

1. Preheat the oven to 325°F.

2. Place the pork cheeks, garlic, thyme, salt, black pepper, and coriander seeds in a baking dish just large enough to hold the pork in one layer. Add enough vegetable oil to completely cover the pork. Cover the dish tightly with aluminum foil and bake until the cheeks are fork-tender, 4 to 4 1/2 hours. (The cooking time will depend on the size of the pork cheeks you are able to procure, so check periodically during the cooking.)

3. When the pork cheeks are tender, remove them from the oven and allow them to cool in the oil. Once cool, remove the cheeks from the oil and pat dry with paper towels. (The oil may be strained and used for another purpose.)

4. Dust the cheeks lightly with flour. Heat a medium sauté pan over medium-high heat. When hot, add 2 tablespoons of oil to the pan and, when the oil is hot, add 1 tablespoon of the butter. Sauté the cheeks, in batches if necessary, until golden brown on all sides, 2 to 3 minutes. Remove from the pan and repeat with any remaining cheeks, adding more vegetable oil and remaining butter if necessary.

5. Serve the cheeks hot, with the dirty rice.

To Make the Dirty Rice

1. In a large skillet, heat the oil over medium-high heat. When hot, add the butter, onion, and bell peppers and sauté the vegetables until tender and lightly caramelized, 4 to 6 minutes.

2. Add the pork and cook, using the spoon to break the pork into small pieces, until well browned, 1 to 2 minutes. Add the liver puree, bay leaves, jalapeño, salt, coriander, cumin, and cayenne and cook until the liver is cooked through and the spices are fragrant, 2 to 3 minutes. Add the rice and beef stock and continue to cook, stirring, until well combined and the rice is heated through, 2 to 3 minutes longer. Remove and discard the bay leaves. Taste and adjust the seasoning if necessary, and add hot sauce to taste.

DEER
BOUDIN
ANDOUILLE
HOTDOG
SPICY JALAPEÑO
HOT SAUSAGE
BRATWURST

RIBEYE
HANGERSTEAK
KUROBUTO PORK
BELLY
JAMBALAYA STUFFED
CHICKEN
STUFFED QUAIL

SKIRT STEAK

SALAMI

SPICY FENNEL
GENOA
CHORIZO
SOPRESSATA
WE HAVE BLOOD SAUSAGE!!
✦ WHOLE HOGS AVAILABLE ✦

Grilled Pork Roast and Cajun Chow Chow

DONALD LINK [Herbsaint and Cochon, *New Orleans, Louisiana*]

DONALD LINK OPENED COCHON ("PIG" IN FRENCH) AND COCHON
Butcher in 2006. Cochon is one of the most important restaurants to open post hurricane
Katrina. Cochon Butcher is a light, airy space, part butcher and charcuterie, part sandwich
counter (the best muffaletta in town), and part wine store. The clinical white subway-tiled
walls are livened up with graphic poster art of the cuts of pork and brightly colored chalk
on a blackboard announcing specials. The hip, young crowd also adds color. I find Link
standing by the counter dressed in the chef coat for his restaurant Herbsaint. Link asks
one of his staff members for a sausage. The server's skeleton-tattooed hand reaches in to
get it, next to a crown of ribs.

Within minutes of meeting, Link is feeding me his white boudin sausage with pickles and mustard. The rice and pork liver encased in the sausage skin is peppery and delicious. Link tells me he eats one every day and I can understand why. This food is old-school Cajun, which has recently been having a renaissance in New Orleans. "I eat all around," says Leah Chase. "I'm going to have dinner at Cochon tonight. That's not a new thing to me, because he serves what we used to eat in the country. It's just fun to see all that again." Keeping close to his roots and tapping into childhood memories means there's a deep authenticity to the food he serves and the meat he butchers and cures.

This James Beard award-winning chef invites me to meet him that night at Herbsaint, where he cooks French-inspired cuisine and classic Big Easy dishes like roast pork with crackling, bananas Foster tart, and gumbo. Link passes plates of food through the hatch to the servers in the dining room. The kitchen is very small, and everything is prepared here, including desserts.

Link's grilled, bone-in pork roast is cooked outside. "In South Louisiana, slow-cooking meat outdoors has a long history and is still very alive and well," says Link. "This method works the same with almost any large cut: lamb, beef, turkeys, et cetera. Men in South Louisiana cook just about everything outside and most of them have their own homemade smokers."

In *What Mrs. Fisher Knows About Old Southern Cooking,* there is a simple recipe for "Roast Pork" over a fast fire.

A recipe for "Roast Pork" from What Mrs. Fisher Knows about Old Southern Cooking *by Abby Fisher, published in 1881.*

18   Roast Pork.

To be seasoned with salt and pepper before being cooked, and in cooking baste with the gravy that comes from the meat. Must be cooked with a fast fire. To make the gravy, take one tablespoonful of flour browned in the pan and stir in a little water.

CHOW-CHOW PICKLE

Take a quarter of a peck each, of green tomatoes, pickling-beans, and white onions (scald the onions separately), add one dozen cucumbers, green peppers, and a head of cabbage chopped. Season with ground mustard, celery seed, and salt to taste. Pour over these the best cider vinegar to cover them, and let all boil two hours, and while hot add two tablespoonfuls of sweet oil and the same of white sugar. Bottle and seal up carefully in wide-mouthed glass jars.

A recipe for "Chow-Chow Pickle" from La Cuisine Creole *by Lafcadio Hearn, published in 1885.*

Link is very interested in the little Lafcidio Hearn book *La Cuisine Creole* from 1885, which I have with me. We flick through the recipes; he lights up at the pickle chapter and decides on a Cajun chow-chow pickle recipe to go with his roast pork.

"There is a bit of knife work involved with the chow chow but you can also use a food processor," says Link. "This is a great condiment to have around; it is exceptionally great with pork dishes. At Cochon we serve it with our grilled shrimp. My favorite use, however, is on sandwiches of almost any kind, but especially fatty pork sandwiches like pulled pork, pork belly, or grilled whole pork."

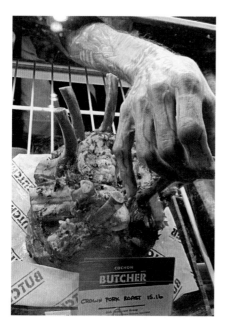

Grilled Pork Roast and Cajun Chow Chow

"All animals are equal, but some animals are more equal than others," wrote George Orwell in *Animal Farm*. The same goes for Donald Link's Pork Roast—definitely "more equal" than your average pig, especially paired with Link's spicy Cajun Chow Chow.

Cajun Chow Chow

1 small head cabbage

1 medium carrot

2 medium red bell peppers

3 large jalapeños

1 small onion

4 green tomatoes

1 cup sugar

1 cup sugar cane vinegar

1 cup apple cider vinegar

1/2 cup red wine vinegar

1 tablespoon salt

1/2 cup whole grain mustard

2 teaspoons cayenne pepper

1 teaspoon celery seed

1 tablespoon mustard seed

1 tablespoon dried oregano

1 teaspoon freshly ground pepper

5 bay leaves

1 tablespoon hot red-pepper flakes

Makes 4 quarts

Grilled Pork Roast

One bone-in pork roast (6 to 8 pounds), center cut, 10 to 12 ribs, Frenched and with chine bones cut

1/2 cup olive oil

1/2 cup kosher salt

1/4 cup fresh cracked black pepper

1/2 cup of good dried thyme (optional)

SERVES 8 TO 10

To Make the Cajun Chow Chow

1. Slice the cabbage in quarters, removing the tough stem and core. Place each quarter flat on a cutting board and cut into long, thin slices. Cut the slices into 1-inch pieces.

2. Grate the carrot.

3. Cut the peppers and onion into thin 1-inch pieces. The tomatoes can be diced small.

4. In a medium saucepan, bring 2 cups of water, the sugar, vinegars, salt, mustard, and all the spices to a boil and then simmer for 10 minutes. Strain this mix into a pot large enough to hold all the vegetables and return to the boil. Add the vegetables and bring to a boil again. Boil for 5 minutes, and turn off the heat.

5. Distribute the chow chow among sterilized canning jars and let cool. Seal with clean lids and store the chow chow until you are ready to use it.

To Grill the Pork Roast

1. Let the pork stand at room temperature for 1 to 2 hours.

2. Heat a coal or full-gas grill to 450°F.

3. Smear the oil, salt, pepper, and thyme all over the pork, getting as much as you can to stick.

4. Grill the pork on the medium-hot grill. Turn the temperature down after it gets really hot, turning the meat every 5 minutes. Continue for 20 minutes, or until golden brown.

5. Remove the pork from the grill and let it stand at room temperature. Reduce the grill temperature to 275°F, either by lowering the gas temperature all the way down or by moving coals to one side of the grill.

6. Place the pork on the higher rack in your grill, if it has one, and lower the lid, leaving a 2-inch gap. Raise the temperature to high.

7. Cook the pork slowly for 1 to 1 1/2 hours. When the internal temperature of the meat is 145°F, remove the roast and let it rest for 30 to 45 minutes.

8. Slice and serve.

Chef Link's Tips

"Have the butcher French the bones and cut the chine bones so the roast can be easily cut into chops after roasting."

"An oven thermometer will work inside the grill as well."

"I always find a cow-bell cheese grater is good for grating carrots."

Desserts

Baked Alaska

WAYLYNN LUCAS [The Bazaar, *Los Angeles, California*]

THE PASTRY CHEF AT THE BAZAAR, WAYLYNN LUCAS, IS THE queen of the playful pink fantasy world that is the Pâtisserie—giant crystal cloches cover cakes almost too perfect to be real; large glass bowls of delicate bonbons, sweet treats, and gold-dusted chocolates shimmer like jewels under lights where monkeys dance around the inside of the shades. In this sophisticated fairy-tale environment I photograph Lucas next to a giant mirror, creating a beautiful twin in matching chef coat, ready to bake a cake, whip up a batch of meringue, freeze coconut custard with liquid nitrogen, handle a blowtorch, and arrange delicate petals to make a magical, tropical baked Alaska.

Harking back to a bygone era of dessert on ocean liners, baked Alaska—cake covered in ice cream, wrapped in meringue and then fired—is said to have been invented by Charles Ranhofer at Delmonico's in New York in 1869, to celebrate America's acquisition of Alaska. Yet, seventy years before this, Thomas Jefferson had experimented with baking ice cream and creating a hot-and-cold dessert. The meringue and cake base insulates the ice cream so it doesn't melt from the heat. They use a lot of modern techniques and tools at The Bazaar, but here Lucas keeps it simple and less of a science experiment—the main gadget being her blowtorch, paired with her imagination.

"Egg whites are mostly water," she says. "So I have used egg white powder and rehydrated it with pineapple juice for the meringue. Torching the pineapple in the meringue gives it a roasted pineapple flavor. I like to make it look like a little pineapple."

Lucas does not have a sweet tooth and likes to keep her desserts light on sugar; she tends to go toward more savory flavors, acidity, and spices.

Baked Alaska

We are big fans of making baked Alaska in our family—the children request it as a special occasion dessert and I readily oblige. The magic of heating the meringue without melting the ice cream never ceases to amaze, but the proof of this pudding is always in the eating. The caramelized pineapple, tres leche cake, and coconut ice cream make it all the more enticing.

Baked Alaska

9 tablespoons (1 stick plus 1 tablespoon) butter

1¼ cups granulated sugar

5 large eggs

2 teaspoons vanilla extract

2 cups all-purpose flour

1 teaspoon baking powder

½ teaspoon salt

1 can (12-ounces) evaporated milk

1 can (14-ounces) sweetened condensed milk

1 cup half-and-half

1 cup pineapple purée

½ cup simple syrup (equal parts water/sugar, brought to a boil then cooled)

5 tablespoons egg-white powder

Pinch of xanthan gum (optional)

Assembly

12 slices ripe banana, cut ¼ inch thick

1 teaspoon granulated sugar

Favorite coconut ice cream

¼ cup shredded coconut

2 tablespoons coconut flakes (optional, for garnish)

Fresh pineapple (optional)

SERVES 4

To Make the Baked Alaska

1. Preheat the oven to 350°F.

2. Place the butter in the mixing bowl of a stand mixer fitted with the paddle attachment and mix until pale and soft. Slowly add the sugar and mix until fluffy. Add the eggs, one at a time, and then add the vanilla. Last, add the flour, baking powder, and salt. Mix until combined, stopping to scrape down the sides and bottom of the bowl to ensure incorporation of all ingredients.

3. Spread the batter evenly in an 11-inch square baking dish, or 9 by 13-inch rectangluar baking dish. Bake for 15 to 18 minutes, until lightly golden brown. Let the cake cool for 30 minutes.

4. With a fork, poke holes all over the cake, then prepare the glaze by combining the milks and half-and-half; mix well. Pour this over the cake, cover it with plastic wrap, and let it sit overnight.

5. For the meringue, combine the pineapple purée, simple syrup, egg-white powder, and xanthan gum and beat on high speed with whisk attachment until stiff peaks form. This may take several minutes. You cannot overmix.

To Assemble and Serve

1. Cut 4 rounds of cake, 3 inches in diameter.

2. Place 3 slices of banana on top of each cake, sprinkle with sugar, and brûlée with a blowtorch until dark golden brown. Sprinkle coconut flakes on top of bananas to help hold ice cream in place.

3. Place a scoop of ice cream the same size as the cake on top. You can set aside in freezer if not going to eat right away.

4. Pipe or spread the meringue, starting at base of cake and working all the way up, to completely cover. Lucas likes to create little peaks to make the baked Alaska look like a pineapple.

5. Brûlée with the blowtorch until golden brown on the edges.

6. Garnish with fresh diced pineapple and toasted coconut flakes. Dig in!!!

Chef Lucas' Tips

"Best to make meringue no more than 20 minutes prior to use, to prevent the meringue from falling. If necessary, you can re-beat slightly."

"Xantham gum can found at specialty stores—it slightly thickens the mixture for a stronger meringue"

Creole Bread Pudding Soufflé with Whiskey Sauce

TORY McPHAIL [Commander's Palace, *New Orleans, Louisiana*]

TORY McPHAIL IS KEEPING EVERYTHING UP-TO-DATE WITH HIS playful modern Creole cooking at Commander's Palace, the grande dame of the New Orleans fine-dining scene. Ever mindful of the rich history of the food served there, McPhail is given full reign to come up with new ways of tasting the past in a way that is palatable for the present. His Foie Gras du Monde is a good example—foie gras served five ways, inspired by the legendary beignets and coffee at Café Du Monde in the French Quarter.

Ella Brennan, the owner and matriarch, lives next door to the restaurant and has run Commander's for the past sixty-five plus years. Ruth Reichl, as editor-in-chief of *Gourmet* magazine, wrote that Brennan "helped define a new kind of American restaurant" and "brought a new pride in Americanism, a dependence on American regional cuisine and a belief in it, which was new—a sense that America should have its own style of restaurant." Her daughter, Ti Adelaide Martin, has inherited much of her mother's elegant wit and wisdom, not to mention her restaurateur smarts, and was a delightful dining companion

during my visit. She introduced me to the pleasure of a Whiskey Smash as we tasted such Commander's classics as turtle soup spiked with sherry, gumbo, Gulf shrimp flambéed with cognac on stone-ground grits, and Creole cheesecake.

Sitting in the sumptuous dining room with its white, starched tablecloths, deferential waiters, and pretty wallpaper of branches and birds surrounding gilt mirrors, you would never know the restaurant was completely rebuilt after hurricane Katrina, only to suffer again when hurricane Rita wreaked yet more havoc later that year. An oasis of civil fine dining, Commander's Palace still holds its own after over 130 years at the top. Its kitchen was the birthplace of "haute Creole cuisine" and has schooled many chefs who have passed through on their way to becoming culinary masters, including Paul Prudhomme and Emeril Lagasse.

"The Queen of Creole desserts, the bread pudding soufflé, is actually not my dish," says McPhail. "It's not Jamie's [Shannon] or Emeril's either. Our great friend Paul Prudhomme came up with it while talking to Ella about how to celebrate Commander's 100th birthday back in 1980. It's all the flavor of New Orleans—bread pudding whipped into a light Creole soufflé, finished tableside with warm whisky cream. It has become one of Commander's most iconic dishes and people travel from all over the world to eat it. I was only seven years old back then, but I've now made well over 30,000 of them."

Bread Pudding

3/4 cup sugar

1 teaspoon ground cinnamon

Pinch of freshly grated nutmeg

3 medium eggs

1 cup heavy cream

1 teaspoon pure vanilla extract

5 cups New Orleans French bread or an equally light and airy French bread, cut into 1-inch cubes

1/3 cup dark raisins

Whiskey Sauce

1 cup heavy cream

1 1/2 teaspoons cornstarch

3 tablespoons sugar

1/4 cup bourbon

Meringue

1 tablespoon of butter for buttering ramekins

9 medium egg whites, at room temperature

3/4 cup sugar

1/4 teaspoon cream of tartar

SERVES 6

To Make the Bread Pudding

1. Preheat the oven to 350°F.

2. Combine the sugar, cinnamon, and nutmeg in a large bowl. Add the eggs and beat until smooth, then work in the heavy cream. Add the vanilla, then the bread cubes, and allow the bread to soak up the custard.

3. Place the raisins in a greased 8 x 8-inch baking pan. Top with the custard mixture, which will prevent the raisins from burning. Bake for 25 to 30 minutes, or until the pudding is golden brown and firm to the touch. When a toothpick inserted in the pudding comes out clean, it is done; the pudding mixture should be nice and moist, not runny or dry. Cool to room temperature.

To Make the Whiskey Sauce

1. Place the cream in a small saucepan over medium heat and bring to a boil. Whisk together the cornstarch and 1 tablespoon of water to make a slurry. Add the slurry to the cream, whisking constantly, and bring back to a boil. Simmer for a few seconds, continuing to whisk and taking care not to burn the mixture on the bottom of the pan. Remove from the heat.

2. Stir in the sugar and the bourbon. The sauce should have a thick consistency. Taste to check if it is sufficiently sweet and has a good bourbon flavor. Cool to room temperature.

To Make the Meringue and Soufflé

1. Preheat the oven to 350°F.

2. Butter six 6-ounce ramekins.

3. In a large bowl or in the bowl of a stand mixer, whip the egg whites and cream of tartar by hand or in the mixer until foamy.

4. Add the sugar gradually and continue whipping until the egg whites are shiny and thick. Test them with a clean spoon: If the whites stand up stiff like shaving cream when you pull out the spoon, the meringue is ready.

5. In a large bowl, break half the bread pudding into pieces. Using your hands or a spoon, gently fold in one-fourth of the meringue, being careful not to lose the air and reduce the volume in the whites. Divide the base mixture equally among the buttered ramekins.

6. Place the remaining bread pudding in the bowl, break it into pieces, and carefully fold in the remaining three-quarters of the meringue. Top off the ramekins with this lighter mixture, to about 1 1/2 inches above each rim. Smooth and shape the tops with a spoon into a dome over the ramekin rim.

7. Bake the soufflés immediately for approximately 20 minutes, or until golden brown.

8. Serve the soufflés immediately. At the table, poke a hole in the top of each soufflé with a spoon, and pour in the room-temperature whiskey sauce.

Brennan's Bananas Foster

LAZONE RANDOLPH [Brennan's, *New Orleans, Louisiana*]

RIPE BANANAS, BROWN SUGAR, RUM, BUTTER, AND CINNAMON— all caramelized together before being set on fire with a flourish and served over cold vanilla ice cream. It's a winning combination of ingredients that has been copied and reinvented many times over. While in New Orleans, I came across numerous iterations of Bananas Foster inspired by the classic flambéed original at Brennan's.

Brennan's lays claim to this dessert, created by Chef Paul Blange back in 1951 and named after Richard Foster, a loyal customer and good friend of Owen Brennan, the founder of the restaurant. However, dig back a little in history, and there are many recipes from the late nineteenth century for the home cook to prepare pan-warmed bananas (or their close relative, plantains). These recipes invariably called for little more than butter and perhaps a sprinkling of sugar—a far cry from Brennan's transcendent banana dessert.

Watching Chef Lazone Randolph cook up Bananas Foster tableside in the restaurant's dining room is pure theater, as the flames leap up to the ceiling and diners gasp in awe. Add to Randolph's own lofty height a towering pristine toque, and it's not just the flames that seem to graze the giant chandeliers.

He started in the kitchen working under Chef Blange in the early '60s, honing his skills and working his way up to take the reins after his mentor passed away. Like many chefs, he's a man of few words in the dining room. Happy to perform the flambé ritual that he's done countless times before, he hides behind the spectacle. After posing for a few photographs and greeting a table of regulars he hurries back to his comfort zone of the large kitchen to oversee the Sunday brunch rush at this always-packed 550-seat restaurant. The most requested item on the menu: Bananas Foster.

> **FRIED BANANAS.**
>
> Strip the skin from four bananas, and cut them in half-inch slices. The yellowish kind, called plantains, not quite ripe, are the best for this dish. Have ready over the fire a frying-pan containing about half an inch of fat, smoking hot; put the bananas into the hot fat, brown them quickly, dust them with salt and pepper, and serve them hot. If fried bananas are required for dessert, sugar should be substituted for salt and pepper.

A recipe for "Fried Bananas" from Miss Corson's ractical American Cookery and Household Management *by Juliet Corson, published in 1886.*

---

4 tablespoons (½ stick) butter

1 cup brown sugar

½ teaspoon cinnamon

¼ cup banana liqueur

4 bananas, cut in half lengthwise, then halved

¼ cup white rum

4 scoops vanilla ice cream

SERVES 4

1. Combine the butter, sugar, and cinnamon in a flambé pan or skillet. Place the pan over low heat and cook, stirring, until the sugar dissolves.

2. Stir in the banana liqueur, then place the bananas in the pan. When the banana sections soften and begin to brown, carefully add the rum.

3. Continue to cook the sauce until the rum is hot, then tip the pan slightly to ignite the rum. When the flames subside, lift the bananas out of the pan and place 4 pieces over each portion of ice cream.

4. Generously spoon the warm sauce over the top of the ice cream and serve immediately.

Banana Crackle Pudding

SHERRY YARD [Spago, *Beverly Hills, California*]

QUITE LITERALLY THE PASTRY CHEF TO THE STARS, SHERRY Yard creates fabulous desserts every year for the Academy Awards Governors Ball—including 5,500 mini chocolate gold Oscars. She cooks for celebrities on a day-to-day basis at Spago, but life in the kitchen is really anything but glamorous. However gorgeous the sweets are, it's hard work. That's not to say Yard doesn't love what she does—it's written all over her smiling face—she's always so bubbly and vivacious, pretty in pink in her signature chef's coat. Yard has worked with Wolfgang Puck for many years—they are a team, joking with each other as old friends do. According to him, she's the boss.

Yard has chosen to do a gourmet version of the Southern classic Banana Pudding. The richness of the crème fraîche with the slices of banana and the pastry cream, laced with Grand Marnier, all add up to one rather yummy dessert.

I grew up on a dairy farm in Devon, England, and my father would pour the milk from the cows into a large separating machine and out of the bottom would come the cream, which was collected in large tubs and refrigerated. Once cold, it would become so thick you could stand a spoon up in it. We would often have bananas smothered in cream and sprinkled with a little sugar after supper. Another favorite dessert was trifle, popular in America in the nineteenth century, which also resembles the banana pudding with the layers of cake, custard, and whipped cream topping. Banana pudding is a version of English trifle and early American cookbooks contain recipes for both.

> **BANANA PUDDING.**
> Cut sponge cake in slices, and, in a glass dish, put alternately a layer of cake and a layer of bananas sliced. Make a soft custard, flavor with a little wine, and pour over it. Beat the whites of the eggs to a stiff froth and heap over the whole.
> Peaches cut up, left a few hours in sugar and then scalded, and added when cold to thick boiled custard, made rather sweet, are a delicious dessert.

A recipe for "Banana Pudding" from the White House Cook Book *by Fanny Lemira Gillette, published in 1887.*

Bananas first began being imported into America from the West Indies in the late nineteenth century and this exotic delicacy, always eaten with a knife and fork, was all the rage in the fashionable houses of New Orleans, New York, and Boston. At the 1876 Philadelphia Centennial Exposition, bananas sold for ten cents a piece—which translates as extremely expensive in today's market. In *How We Cook in Los Angeles* (1894), they are listed by Mrs. Paxton on her breakfast menu, sliced up in a "Heavenly Hash" (think layers of fruit with sugar to make a salad), fried up like early bananas Foster, and used to make "Banana Jelly." In the *White House Cook Book* (1887), there is not only a picture of the President's wife, but a recipe for banana pudding that uses bananas, broken-up cake, custard, cream, and wine!

Banana Crackle Pudding

"This is one of the best Americana recipes I ever have made," says Sherry Yard of her take on an old Southern favorite, banana pudding. Yard layers bananas, crème fraîche, cream, Valrhona chocolate pearls, and caramel crackle to create her modern ode to a classic dessert—"it kicks it into another universe," she says. One bite and you'll know just what she means.

Bananas and Marinade

1 cup freshly squeezed orange juice

2 tablespoons freshly squeezed lemon juice

2 tablespoons Tia Maria

2 tablespoons light brown sugar

2 tablespoons granulated sugar

1/2 vanilla bean, split and scraped

6 bananas, sliced into 1/2-inch coins

Pastry Cream

2 cups whole milk

1/2 cup granulated sugar

1/2 vanilla bean, split and scraped

1/8 teaspoon orange zest, finely chopped (optional)

4 large egg yolks, separated directly into the bowl of a stand mixer

3 tablespoons all-purpose flour

1 tablespoon cold unsalted butter, straight from refrigerator

Crème Baumanière

1 1/2 cup pastry cream

1 tablespoon Grand Marnier

2/3 cup heavy cream

To Marinate the Bananas

1. In a medium bowl, whisk together the orange juice, lemon juice, Tia Maria, light brown sugar, sugar, and vanilla seeds.

2. Toss the banana slices in the marinade and set aside for 15 minutes.

To Make the Pastry Cream

1. In a small heavy-bottomed saucepan, add the milk, one-third of the sugar, the vanilla seeds and pod, and the orange zest. Place the saucepan over medium heat and bring the mixture to a simmer. Remove from the heat and let infuse for 10 minutes.

2. Meanwhile, in the bowl of a stand mixer fitted with the paddle attachment, whip together the egg yolks and one-third of the sugar for 4 minutes on high speed, or until light colored and fluffy. Scrape down the sides of the bowl.

3. Sift together the flour and the remaining sugar. On low speed, stream the sifted flour into the yolk mixture. Paddle for 1 minute. Scrape down the sides of the bowl.

4. Place the saucepan of milk back over medium heat and bring to a boil. Remove from the heat.

5. With the mixer on low speed, temper the yolks with one-fourth of the boiling milk. Scrape down the sides of the bowl.

6. Remove the bowl from the mixer and whisk the yolk mixture back into the remaining milk in the saucepan.

7. Place the saucepan over medium-low heat and whisk the mixture gently and continuously; it will bubble and boil. Continue to cook 2 to 3 minutes until thickened and the starchy flour taste is cooked out.

8. Whisk in the butter. Cool the pastry cream over a bowl of ice until it reaches 40°F. Wrap with plastic wrap pressed directly on top of the cream to prevent a skin from forming, and refrigerate.

To Make the Crème Baumanière

1. Place the pastry cream in a medium bowl and whisk in the Grand Marnier until smooth. Set aside.

2. Whip the heavy cream to very stiff peaks.

3. Fold half of the whipped cream into the pastry cream to lighten it.

4. Fold in the remaining whipped cream. Refrigerate the cream until ready to use. (The cream will keep for 4 hours.)

Assembly

Marinated banana slices

1 cup crème fraîche, whipped soft

Crème Baumanière

1/4 cup Valrhona crunchy chocolate pearls (les perles craquantes)

32 wafer cookies

1/2 cup sugar

8 chocolate caramel candies, for garnish

SERVES 8

Chef Yard's Tip

"If needed, you can sub out the crème fraîche for cream and the pearls for chocolate sprinkles."

To Assemble and Serve

1. Fill eight pretty glasses (about 8 ounces each), starting from the bottom and working your way up to the top, building the following layers:

> 1 tablespoon soft whipped crème fraîche
> 2 tablespoons crème Baumanière
> 5 banana slices
> 1 tablespoon banana marinade
> 2 vanilla wafers, broken up into 1/2-inch pieces
> 2 tablespoons crème Baumanière
> 5 banana slices
> 1 tablespoon banana marinade
> 2 vanilla wafers, broken up into 1/2-inch pieces
> 1 teaspoon Valrhona chocolate croquantes pearls
> 1 tablespoon soft whipped crème fraîche

2. Cover the individual glasses with plastic wrap and refrigerate until ready to serve. The desserts can be made 4 hours in advance.

3. When ready to serve, make a caramel for the topping. In a small sauté pan over medium-high heat, sprinkle a thin layer of granulated sugar. Continue to cook until the sugar is dissolved and caramelizes to a deep amber color. Carefully pour some of the hot sugar directly into the center of a glass. With your free hand, turn the glass to cover the entire surface of the cream with the caramel. Repeat for all the filled glasses. Garnish each with a chocolate caramel candy and serve.

Sushi Rice Pudding with Golden Raisins

STEPHEN DURFEE [Culinary Institute of America-Greystone, *St. Helena, California*]

GREYSTONE IS ONE OF THE MOST BEAUTIFUL CAMPUSES FOR culinary education in the world. This West Coast outpost of the Culinary Institute of America in picturesque Napa Valley is where Stephen Durfee teaches plated desserts to the pastry stars of the future.

Before Durfee took up his post at the CIA in 2000, he was part of Thomas Keller's opening team at the French Laundry. In his five-plus years there, he worked his way through the garde manger and fish stations before finding his niche, when he assumed the responsibility for the pastry department. During this time he won the 1998 James Beard Award for Pastry Chef of the Year and was named one of the "10 Best Pastry Chefs in America" in 1999 by *Pastry Art & Design* and *Chocolatier* magazines. Durfee has traveled and worked in France, where he apprenticed at restaurants in Paris and Chambéry.

I ask Durfee to make me the best rice pudding ever made, referencing recipes from the nineteenth century that I supply. In *The New-England Cookery* (1808)—the full title reads: *The New-England Cookery, or the art of dressing all kinds of flesh, fish, and vegetables, and the best modes of making pastes, puffs, pies, tarts, puddings, custards and preserves, and all kinds of cakes, from the imperial plumb to the plain cake. Particularly adapted to this part of our country*—Lucy Emerson includes six recipes for rice puddings. At this time, custard-based puddings were cooked in a piecrust (pumpkin pie was called pumpkin pudding). She suggests *butter or puff paste* for No. 1 and No. 2—today we would call this a rice pie.

Durfee skips the crust and focuses on the pudding. "This was an interesting exercise," he says. "Without question, the best choice is to cook rice in water and then blend it with a custard. Otherwise, the results are so inconsistent." For me the most interesting twist in his recipe is the use of short-grain rice. "The turning point came with choosing sushi rice," he says. "The logical next step is to use rice flour to thicken the custard. I can't wait for you to try it!"

A Rice Pudding.

One quarter of a pound rice, a stick of cinnamon, to a quart of milk (stired often to keep from burning) and boil quick, cool and add half a nutmeg, 4 spoons rose-water, 8 eggs ; butter or puff paste a dish and pour the above composition into it, and bake one and an half hour.

No. 2. Boil 6 ounces rice in a quart milk, on a slow fire 'till tender, stir in one pound butter, interim beet 14 eggs, add to the pudding when cold with sugar, salt, rose-water and spices to your taste, adding raisins or currents, baked as No. 1.

No. 3. Eight spoons rice boiled in two quarts milk, when cooled add 8 eggs, 6 ounces butter, wine, sugar and spices, bake 2 hours.

Three recipes for rice pudding from The New-England Cookery *compiled by Lucy Emerson, published in 1808.*

This recipe is quick and easy to make. The main thing to keep in mind is patience—don't rush the heating of the milk or it will scald, and when you temper the hot milk into the egg mixture, do it very slowly: you don't want scrambled eggs. I am pretty sure Durfee's thick, creamy, custard-based rice pudding, topped with golden raisins steeped in cognac, is hands down the best rice pudding that America has ever seen—or tasted.

½ cup short-grain rice,
    such as California Sushi Rice,
    Arborio rice, or Carnaroli
    rice

⅛ teaspoon salt

2 cups whole milk

1 extra-large egg

1 tablespoon sweet rice flour

4 tablespoons granulated sugar

1 bay leaf

½ vanilla bean, split scraped,
    pod and seeds reserved

½ cup golden raisins

¼ cup cognac (optional)

SERVES 4

1. Combine rice, salt, and 1 cup water and bring to a boil. Lower the heat to barely simmering, cover the pan, and cook the rice for 18 minutes. Turn off the heat, keep the pan covered, and allow the rice to steam for an additional 5 minutes. Transfer the cooked rice to a bowl. Cover with plastic wrap to seal in the heat.

2. In a small bowl, combine ¼ cup of the milk with the egg and the rice flour. Be certain to whisk out any lumps. Blend in 2 tablespoons of the sugar and set aside.

3. Pour the remaining 1 ¾ cups milk into a saucepan and sprinkle in the remaining 2 tablespoons of sugar. Add the bay leaf and the scraped vanilla bean pod and seeds. Bring the mixture slowly to the boil.

4. Temper the egg/rice-flour mixture with the boiling milk, then return all to the saucepan. Whisking constantly, slowly bring this mixture back to a bubbling boil, being careful not to scorch it. The mixture will thicken up to a nice sauce consistency. Pour this mixture over the cooked rice and stir to ensure an even blending.

5. In a small saucepan, heat the raisins and the cognac for 2 minutes. Transfer to a small bowl and set aside to steep. If you don't wish to steep the raisins in cognac, stir the raisins directly into the pudding.

6. Remove the bay leaf and vanilla bean pod. Transfer the pudding to serving glasses, press plastic wrap directly onto the surface of the pudding, and refrigerate several hours or overnight. Remove the plastic covers, place a spoonful of raisins on top of each pudding, and serve.

Tiramisu—A Modern Coffee Charlotte Russe

LYDIA SHIRE [Scampo, *Boston, Massachusetts*]

LYDIA SHIRE IS A WOMAN OF MANY FIRSTS—FIRST FEMALE CHEF at the Bostonian, first female to open a Four Seasons restaurant, and first woman to own the Boston male-dominated establishment Locke-Ober (where women weren't allowed to dine in the main dining room for over a century). Her restaurant Scampo is housed in an old clink (jail) on the first floor of the stunning Liberty Hotel. The red brick walls are lined with graphic posters containing various crime references. At one end of the room is a wood-burning oven and large open kitchen, and outside is a patio for warmer months. Her menu at Scampo is traditional Italian but with influences from around the world. My favorite is her Elephant Ear Walking—a large piece of very thin flat bread that's in the shape of a wave, topped with cheese and tomatoes. Shire is a whimsical chef, full of little quirks and foibles—her nickname and the way she signs off is Lyd-the-kid.

When I interview Shire, she is tired and fending off a cold. She has just spent a week on the West Coast helping her longtime friend Wolfgang Puck cook the Academy Awards Governors Dinner. "I made one thousand Dover sole," she says. I ask about the logistics of feeding such a large number of people and what a thousand Dover sole look like. "It's about seven rolling racks filled with sheet pans of fish," she says. "It's a lot." What she needs is a pick-me-up, which is exactly what *tiramisu* means in Italian.

Everyone knows and loves tiramisu—or almost everyone. I think of the scene in the movie *Sleepless in Seattle* from 1993, when Sam (Tom Hanks) asks his friend Jay (Rob Reiner) for advice on dating. Sam: "What is tiramisu?" Jay: "You'll find out." Sam: "Well, what is it?" Jay: "You'll see!" Sam: "Some woman is gonna want me to do it to her and I'm not gonna know what it is!" The joke is referencing the rapid rise in popularity of tiramisu as a dessert in the late '80s and early '90s. Just like fashion, food comes and goes in cycles—recipes are reinvented, copied, and adapted. Ten years on and tiramisu is much more widely known but people today have never heard of Charlotte Russe. This cousin of tiramisu is made of ladyfingers lining a mold filled with Bavarian cream, and rarely appears on modern menus. Popular in the nineteenth century, Charlotte Russe was a dish originally made by the first celebrity chef Marie Antoine Carême, for his employer, the czar of Russia. It is said to be named after the czar's sister-in-law, Queen Charlotte, wife of King George III of England.

"A Bavarian cream contains a bit of gelatin," says Shire. "However, in a tiramisu the mascarpone is rich and heavy enough when folded in, so you won't need gelatin." This light whipped-cream dessert laced with sponge fingers soaked in Tia Maria is the perfect pick-me-up.

Charlotte Russe (Cream).

1 pint rich cream.   ½ cup sugar.
1 teaspoonful vanilla.   Sponge cake.

Mix the cream, vanilla, and sugar. Place the bowl in ice water, and when chilled whip to a stiff froth, and skim off the froth into a sieve. Drain, and whip again that which has drained through. When nearly all whipped, line a glass dish with lady fingers or sponge cake, fill with the cream, put cubes of *wine jelly* or any bright jelly on the cream, and keep on ice till ready to serve.

A recipe for "Charlotte Russe (cream)" from Mrs. Lincoln's Boston Cook Book *by Mrs. Mary J. Lincoln, published in 1884.*

1½ cups (10 ounces) mascarpone cheese

1 cup heavy cream, chilled

½ cup egg yolks

Scant ½ cup sugar

Scant ½ cup Tia Maria liqueur, plus extra for serving

32 ladyfingers, crisp Italian type (*savoiardi*)

1½ cups strong cold coffee, preferably espresso

Unsweetened cocoa powder for dusting

SERVES 6

1. In a mixing bowl (either for a stand mixer or handheld mixer), combine the mascarpone cheese and heavy cream. Cover and refrigerate.

2. Over simmering water (in a bowl large enough to accommodate the addition of the mascarpone-and-cream mixture later on), whisk the yolks, sugar, and Tia Maria, whipping constantly until mixture lightens in color and whisk leaves tracks when lifted out.

3. Remove the bowl from the heat and set it over another, larger, bowl of ice water, stirring occasionally until completely cool.

4. Meanwhile, dip the ladyfingers in the cold coffee for 4 to 5 seconds, taking care that they do not become too soggy.

5. Place the dipped ladyfingers standing up around the inside of a large bowl, or cups if making individual portions.

6. Whip the mascarpone and cream to medium-stiff peaks (a little stiffer than sour cream). Fold this into the cooled egg yolk/Tia Maria/sugar mixture until no white streaks remain.

7. Fill the ladyfinger-lined bowl or cups with the cream (optional: top with more soaked ladyfingers).

8. Chill the tiramisu for several hours or overnight (if assembled in a larger bowl) before cutting.

9. Sift cocoa over the top of your cake for additional flavor and decoration.

Chef Shire's Tips

"Ladyfingers must be put into the bowl immediately after dipping in coffee or they will break."

"In my perfect world, when serving the tiramisu, I pour extra Tia Maria in or around the cake. I love Tia Maria!"

Milk Chocolate Panna Cotta

MICHAEL MINA [Michael Mina, *San Francisco, California*]

I FIRST ATE AT MICHAEL MINA ABOUT FIVE YEARS AGO. I FLEW UP to San Francisco from Los Angeles for the night to join my best friend Amelia and her husband who were visiting from England. The creative menu, excellent service, and stunning room blew us all away. Plate after beautiful plate of ingredients, each "done three ways," was served—every dish more tempting than the last. I remember feeling so full after dinner that it hurt; my eyes were definitely bigger than my belly. Michael Mina has recently relocated his eponymous restaurant to the space that was previously the restaurant, Aqua, where he began his illustrious career in San Francisco over twenty years ago.

Born in Cairo, Egypt and raised in Ellensburg, Washington, Mina fell in love with cooking at the age of fifteen, working as the garde manger in a local restaurant. Formal training followed at the Culinary Institute of America in Hyde Park with weekends spent honing his talent in Charlie Palmer's kitchen at the upscale Aureole in New York City. With his bold restaurant concepts, this Michelin-star chef has certainly built upon San Francisco's reputation as a world-class dining destination. In 2002 he partnered with Andre Agassi to found Mina Group, which has since opened eighteen restaurants, scattered across America.

Mina gives us his recipe for chocolate panna cotta, perhaps the most effortless dessert to make ever, proving that even the fanciest of chefs can turn their attention to something supereasy. I was struck by how similar the recipe for panna cotta (which means cooked milk in Italian) is to early American recipes for blancmange, a milk dessert that is thickened with gelatin so it sets. The recipe is a cross between a chocolate pudding and a milky Jell-O.

I love the breezy, chatty voice of Marion Harland in *Breakfast, Luncheon and Tea* (1875), in which she includes an early recipe for "Chocolate Blanc-Mange" in her chapter "Fancy Dishes for Desserts." Nineteenth-century cookbooks are full of recipes for jellies, blancmanges, custards, and creams. These wobbly creations are a lost art of wonderful translucent colors and subtle flavors, most often set in whimsical molds and then turned out. In *The Ladies Receipt-Book* by Eliza Leslie (1847), there is a long recipe for "Chocolate Blanc-Mange" that calls for "four calves' feet, or eight or ten pigs' feet." She goes on to say that you can substitute "Russian isinglass." And people think molecular gastronomy is something new? Thank goodness for modern packets of dried gelatin.

I love whipping up a batch of chocolate mousse based on an Elizabeth David recipe but this eggless custard, panna cotta, gives a similar chocolate fix and is foolproof. You can get fancy and serve it in pretty glasses or keep the presentation simple and turn out the dessert onto a plate, once it's set up. Either way, enjoy the wobble.

CHOCOLATE BLANC-MANGE. ✛

1 quart of milk.
½ package gelatine, dissolved in 1 cup cold water.
1 cup sugar.
3 great spoonfuls grated chocolate.
Vanilla to taste.

Heat the milk; stir in sugar and soaked gelatine. Strain; add chocolate; boil ten minutes, stirring all the time. When nearly cold, beat for five minutes—hard with your "Dover" egg-beater, or until it begins to stiffen. Flavor; whip up once, and put into a wet mould. It will be firm in six or eight hours.

A recipe for "Chocolate Blanc-Mange" from Breakfast, Luncheon and Tea *by Marion Harland, published in 1875.*

½ **pound milk chocolate**

½ **cup whole milk**

½ **teaspoon gelatin powder**

1½ **cups cream**

½ **teaspoon salt**

Fleur de sel, for garnish (optional)

SERVES 4

1. Gently melt the chocolate in a bowl set over a saucepan of barely simmering water; the bottom of the bowl should not touch the water.

2. Pour the milk into a pot and sprinkle the gelatin over the cold milk. Cook on low heat for 5 minutes.

3. Add the salt and pour the mixture over the melted chocolate in the bowl. Mix with a silicone spatula until smooth.

4. Add the cold cream and mix until completely incorporated.

5. Fill four 6-ounce glasses two-thirds full with the panna cotta mixture.

6. Refrigerate until set, about 4 hours.

7. Just before serving, top with a little fleur de sel.

Flourless Molten Chocolate Cake

DOUGLAS TAYLOR [B&B, *Las Vegas, Nevada*]

SIN CITY, FAMOUS FOR ITS EXCESSIVE CONSUMERISM, GAMBLING, and light pollution, is now home to Mario Batali and Joe Bastianich's farmers' market, Molto Vegas. The market was Executive Pastry Chef Douglas Taylor's doing when he persuaded his bosses, Batali and Bastianich, that Vegas' top restaurants needed a source of local produce. "Amazing thing in the middle of an artificial-looking world to have a green market," says Batali. "People think I'm putting on a circus show but it's real. I have to loan the farmers money to get the produce here. It's the idea of being part of a community, of interacting with farmers and having them interact with us." This is what Batali feels sustainability really is, a word he dismisses as overused. "It's a pop term that means jack to me!" he says.

As well as the market, Taylor has another project that fascinates me—growing fruit on trees inside bottles that are then used to make grappa. "My idea is to help farmers save their first stone fruit crops from the high winds that rip through the desert in March and April," says Taylor. "I have almost 200 bottles at the orchard on apricot, peach, plum, nectarine, pear, apple, persimmon, and pomegranate branches. My goal is to produce a crop income for the farmers." Taylor's day job is making all the delicious desserts at B&B where he shows off a bottle for decorative purposes behind the bar—the fruit floating inside the bottle is intriguing.

Baking with chocolate begins to creep into cookbooks in the nineteenth century. However, chocolate was mainly considered a drink, and in the second half of the century, a candy. It's not until post World War II that there's an explosion in all things chocolate—cookies, cakes, milkshakes, and fudge. With Chef Albert Kumin's Chocolate Velvet Cake from the Four Seasons, New York in 1959, and then Jean-Georges Vongerichten's claim to molten chocolate cake in 1987 (a result of undercooking his chocolate cake), chefs have certainly paved the way, as chocolate cakes grace dessert menus across America.

The farmers' market's seasonal offerings pair perfectly with Taylor's flourless molten chocolate cake. "In spring I pair it with fresh strawberries; in summer wild boysenberries are the best; in fall I have to have wild huckleberries with this cake; in winter, blood oranges or salted caramel."

"I gave this recipe to a friend of mine about seven years ago," says Taylor. "After he made it for his girlfriend, she married him!"

½ **pound 70% chocolate,**
preferably Amano

2 sticks unsalted butter

1 ³/4 cups confectioners' sugar

½ **teaspoon salt**

4 whole large eggs

4 large egg yolks

MAKES 8 CAKES

1. Preheat the oven to 400°F.

2. Melt the butter in a bowl placed over a saucepan of simmering water; the bottom of the bowl should not touch the water. Add the chocolate to the butter and whisk until the chocolate is completely melted and hot.

3. Whisk in the sugar and salt until completely dissolved.

4. Remove the bowl from the saucepan and whisk in all the eggs until the batter is fully incorporated.

5. Spray eight 8-ounce ramekins with nonstick cooking spray and fill to three-quarters with the batter.

6. Bake the cakes for 10 to 13 minutes.

Chef Taylor's Tips

"The batter will keep up to 4 days in the refrigerator. You can prepare the batter and fill the ramekins, refrigerate, and then bake them up later."

"The key to this recipe is the baking time—don't let them overbake or you'll get chocolate cake with no molten center."

Doughnuts with Spiked Milkshakes

MARIAH SWAN [Grace and BLD, *Los Angeles, California*]

WHEN MARIAH SWAN, PASTRY CHEF AT BOTH OF NEAL FRASER'S restaurants BLD and Grace, came up with the idea of adding alcohol to milkshakes, the cocktails she created became instant modern classics. I'm not sure if Swan knew that she was referencing the nineteenth-century origins of the milkshake, but long before this icy blended drink was a favorite at diners and drive-throughs across America, it was served as a cocktail made with eggs, milk, and whiskey.

Swan pairs her grown-up milkshakes with another beloved American sweet—doughnuts. Washington Irving, in his *History of New York* (1809), refers to "balls of sweetened dough, fried in hog's fat, and called doughnuts or olykoeks." In many of the eighteenth-century recipe books, these sugary treats are called "fried cakes" or "dough nuts," and were as popular back then as they are today.

Serve a tower of Swan's homemade doughnuts with an ice-cold, spiked milkshake—this is one childhood treat that is for adults only.

Doughnuts

Doughnut Dough

1 tablespoon plus 2 teaspoons active dry yeast

7 tablespoons sugar

1 1/2 teaspoons salt

1/3 cup nonfat dry milk powder

2 large eggs

7 tablespoons (7/8 stick) unsalted butter, softened

Canola oil for frying

To Make the Doughnut Dough

1. Pour 3/4 cup warm water into the bottom of the bowl of a stand mixer. Sprinkle the yeast on top and allow it to dissolve for 5 minutes. Whisk and let bloom until bubbly.

2. Meanwhile, combine the sugar, salt, milk powder, and flour in a small bowl.

3. Once the yeast is bubbly, whisk in the eggs. Place the dry ingredients on top of the egg mixture. Place the bowl on the mixer fitted with the dough hook and mix on low speed until a ball of dough begins to form. Turn the mixer to medium speed and mix until the dough is smooth and elastic. Add the butter and mix until it is completely emulsified into the dough; the dough should feel supple and not greasy.

4. Place the dough in a greased medium bowl, cover with plastic wrap, and place in a warm, draft-free area. Allow the dough to rise until doubled in volume, 1 1/2 to 2 hours. After the dough has risen, gently deflate it and rewrap in plastic wrap. At this point, you may refrigerate the dough overnight or allow it to double once more for immediate use. If you chill the dough, you must allow it to come to room temperature before working with it on the following day.

5. Once the dough has gone through two rises, turn it out onto a well-floured work surface. Lightly dust the top of the dough with more flour and roll out to a 1/4-inch thickness. Using a floured cutter, cut the dough into 2-inch to 3-inch circles with holes, and let rise again for 30 minutes before frying.

6. Fill a large, heavy-bottomed pot with canola oil to a depth of 4 to 5 inches and heat to 350°F. Gently drop the doughnuts into the oil. Using a spoon, carefully baste the tops of the doughnuts with the hot oil. Once the tops puff, turn the doughnuts. Repeat the basting process and fry until the bottoms of the doughnuts are golden brown. Turn the doughnuts one more time and fry the opposite side until golden brown. Carefully remove the doughnuts from the oil, using a slotted spoon or skimmer, and place on paper towels to drain excess oil.

Brown Butter Glaze

³/₄ cup confectioners' sugar, sifted

¹/₄ cup buttermilk

4 tablespoons (⁷/₈ stick) unsalted butter, melted and browned

Salt and Pepper Glaze

2 cups granulated sugar

1 cup heavy cream

Salt

Pinch of kosher salt

¹/₂ pinch freshly ground pepper

MAKES SIXTEEN 2¹/₂- TO 3-INCH DOUGHNUTS

To Make the Brown Butter Glaze

1. Create a well in the center of the sugar. Pour the buttermilk into the center of the well and whisk the ingredients together, starting from the center and working out, bringing in more sugar as you go.

2. Once the ingredients are mixed and smooth, whisk in the brown butter.

3. Dip the warm doughnuts into the glaze and rest on a metal rack.

To Make the Salt and Pepper Glaze

1. Place the sugar in a medium, heavy-bottomed saucepan. Add ¹/₂ cup water and gently mix to combine. If any sugar sticks to the sides of the saucepan, wash it off with a little more water. The sides of the pan should be completely clean.

2. Place the saucepan over high heat and bring the mixture to a boil. As the sugar cooks, you may see crystals begin to form on the sides of the pan; wash them down with a pastry brush dipped in ice water. Once the sugar comes to a rolling boil, do not walk away from the pan. Cook the sugar until you begin to see it change color. As the sugar starts to caramelize, you may gently swirl the pan to ensure even cooking. Continue to cook the sugar until it turns a medium amber color.

3. Remove the pan of caramel from the heat and slowly pour in a little of the cream; take care, it will bubble up and steam. Whisk in the cream and return the caramel to low heat. Continue to whisk in the remaining cream until the sauce is emulsified.

4. Remove the pan from the heat and dip a spoon into the caramel. Drizzle a little of the caramel onto a plate and taste to check consistency. If it is too thick, add a little more cream to the caramel. Continue to adjust the consistency until the sauce is no longer sticky. As you adjust the consistency, add a little salt as well until the flavor is balanced.

5. Dip the warm doughnuts into the glaze, sprinkle with salt and pepper, and rest on a metal rack.

Spiked Milkshakes

Mint Chip Bailey's Milkshake

1 pint premium mint chip ice cream, such as Häagen-Dazs

¹/₄ cup whole milk

2 shots Baileys Irish Cream

Whipped heavy cream

Chocolate Oatmeal Stout with Jack Daniels Whiskey

1 pint premium chocolate ice cream

¹/₂ cup chilled oatmeal stout, such as Barney Flats Oatmeal Stout

2 shots Jack Daniels

Whipped heavy cream

To Make the Mint Chip or Chocolate Oatmeal Milkshakes

1. Place all the ingredients for either of the milkshakes into a blender and blend on low speed until smooth.

2. Serve in two chilled glasses topped with the whipped cream.

Chocolate-Oatmeal-Walnut Freezer Cookies

Elisabeth Prueitt [Tartine, *San Francisco, California*]

I WAS EARLY FOR MY INTERVIEW WITH CRAIG STOLL AT DELFINA because Charles Phan had kindly driven me up to the Mission District from the Slanted Door, so I went next door to Tartine and enjoyed a café latte. Despite the nip in the air I sat at one of the outside tables—inside was full and the line stretched out the door. This apparently is normal business for this little corner café. People come for the award-winning breads made by Prueitt's husband, renowned baker Chad Robertson, and to marvel at and indulge in Prueitt's desserts. The two met at the Culinary Institute of America when they were fortuitously paired together in a class because their last names fell in alphabetical order. Upon graduation they traveled to France to learn all they could about baking before returning to open Bay Village Bakery in Point Reyes Station, California. After six years of countryside living, the two moved to San Francisco and opened Tartine in 2002. Flour-dusted loaves of artisan bread in all shapes and sizes are stacked behind a glass case full of tried-and-true pastries and delights for the sweet tooth—some given a twist, like Prueitt's chocolate-chip cookie: every perfect bite comes with chocolate chunks, nuts, and the texture of oats.

Chocolate-chip cookies were invented in 1937 by Ruth Graves Wakefield, who, together with her husband, owned the Toll House Inn in Massachusetts. The story goes that she didn't have bakers' chocolate for a colonial recipe for "Butter Drop Do" cookies, so she substituted by cutting up a bar of chocolate given to her by Andrew Nestlé. The chocolate chips didn't melt completely and a classic was born. Nestlé agreed to give Wakefield a lifetime's supply of chocolate in return for permission to print her recipe for Toll House cookies on the wrapper of the chocolate bar. In 1939, Nestlé introduced precut semi-sweet chocolate chips to make baking up a batch even easier for home cooks, and Betty Crocker featured the chocolate-chip cookies and Wakefield on her radio show "Famous Foods From Famous Eating Places."

Keeping cookie dough in the freezer means that you can whip up a batch of freshly baked cookies at a moment's notice—perfect around the holidays or if an unexpected guest pops in for a cup of tea.

> ### Butter drop do.
> No. 3. Rub one quarter of a pound butter, one pound fugar, fprinkled with mace, into one pound and a quarter flour, add four eggs, one glafs rofe water, bake as No. 1.

A recipe for "Butter Drop Do" from American Cookery *by Amelia Simmons, published in 1798.*

One of my favorite films is *Clueless*, and frozen cookie dough always reminds me of the scene where Cher prepares for Christian's imminent arrival for their movie-watching date. "Whenever a boy comes you should always have something baking," she says as she throws the whole uncut log of cookie dough into the oven—to be forgotten until Christian smells it burning and they race down to the kitchen to discover the charred remains.

Prueitt makes up batches of her thin Chocolate-Oatmeal-Walnut Cookies for Tartine in giant five-inch rounds and, as she has given us here, a delicate petit-four size. Nothing beats eating them warm, straight out of the oven.

12 ounces bittersweet chocolate

2 cups all-purpose flour

1 teaspoon baking powder

1 teaspoon baking soda

2 cups old-fashioned rolled oats

1 cup (2 sticks) unsalted butter, room temperature

1 3/4 cups sugar

4 teaspoons blackstrap or other dark molasses

2 large eggs

2 tablespoons whole milk

1 tablespoon vanilla extract

1 teaspoon salt

1 cup walnuts, coarsely chopped

MAKES FORTY-EIGHT 1¹/₂-INCH COOKIES OR TWENTY-FOUR 3-INCH COOKIES

1. Coarsely chop the chocolate into ¹/₄- to ¹/₂-inch pieces; a serrated knife works well for this task. Chill in the freezer until needed.

2. In a mixing bowl, stir together the flour, baking powder, baking soda, and oats. Set aside. Using a stand mixer fitted with the paddle attachment, beat the butter on medium-high speed until light and creamy. Slowly add the sugar and mix on medium speed until light in color and fluffy. Stop the mixer and scrape down the sides of the bowl with a silicone or plastic spatula as needed.

3. Add the molasses and beat until well combined. Add the eggs one a time, beating well before adding the next.

4. Beat in the milk, vanilla, and salt, and then stop the mixer again and scrape down the sides of the bowl.

5. Add the flour mixture and beat on low speed until well incorporated. Stop the mixer, scrape down the sides of the bowl, and fold in the chocolate chunks and the walnuts with the spatula.

6. Shape the dough into 2 logs about 1¹/₂ inches in diameter. (If you wish to make larger, 3-inch cookies increase the diameter of the logs and increase the baking time to 10 to 12 minutes.) Wrap the logs in parchment paper, wax paper, or plastic wrap, and place in the freezer for at least 4 hours and up to overnight.

7. When the dough has frozen and you are ready to bake the cookies, preheat the oven to 350°F. Line a sheet pan with parchment paper or a nonstick silicone mat.

8. Remove the dough from the freezer, unwrap, slice into ¹/₄-inch-thick rounds, or use wetted fingers to make little balls of dough, and arrange on the lined sheet pan. Bake until the edges of the cookies are lightly browned but the centers remain pale, 4 to 7 minutes. Transfer the cookies to a wire rack and let cool.

Chef Prueitt's Tips

"If you wish to make 3- or 5-inch cookies, you can skip freezing the dough in logs and simply scoop the dough onto a prepared baking sheet with a spoon or an ice-cream scoop. Dip your fingers into some water and press out each scoop into a thin, flat 3-inch or 5 inch circle. Bake as for the 1¹/₂-inch cookies but increase the baking time to 10 to 12 minutes. Experiment to find the size cookie that suits you."

"Freezing the dough in a log and then slicing it up into rounds not only makes for easy preparation, but all the cookies will be exactly the same diameter."

"The cookies will keep in an airtight container at room temperature for up to 2 weeks."

Chocolate Espresso Ice Cream Sandwich

LAURA MATIS [Osteria Stellina, *Point Reyes Station, California*]

A portion of Thomas Jefferson's handwritten recipe for "Vanilla Ice Cream," from the 1780s.

THERE'S ALWAYS ROOM FOR ICE CREAM, AS THEY SAY, AND IN the case of Laura Matis' ice cream sandwiches they are reason enough for Michael Bauer to write "don't miss desserts" in his three-and-half star review of Osteria Stellina for the *San Francisco Chronicle*. He obviously enjoyed "the sweet note" of Matis' Gingersnap-Meyer Lemon Ice Cream Sandwich, which she makes with local lemons. The flavors change seasonally; there's a strawberry ice cream sandwich with shortbread cookies during the summer months, when fresh local fruit is sparse, Matis turns to coffee ice cream sandwiched between chewy chocolate cookies. Regardless of the flavor or time of year, the ice cream sandwich is always the most popular item on the dessert menu. The restaurant's house-made ice cream was inspired by the extra-creamy organic milk from the Strauss Family Creamery, a short drive away on the beautiful shores of Tomales Bay.

Ice cream has a surprisingly long history in America considering that modern freezing methods only came about in the early twentieth century. The first ice cream parlor opened in New York in 1776—at that time, ice would have been harvested from the mountains and rivers during the winter and stored in icehouses underground. In the 1780s, Thomas Jefferson handwrote his recipe for ice cream, which calls for the ice cream mixture to be transferred into a canister known as a Sabottiere, and then submerged in a bucket filled with ice and salt, and manually rotated. On the back of the ice cream recipe is his recipe for Savoy cookies to accompany the ice cream—an unwitting precursor to the commercial ice cream sandwich, which would not appear until the late 1890s, quickly becoming popular with street vendors in New York City.

Chewy Chocolate Cookies

1 cup plus 1 tablespoon
all-purpose flour

¼ cup plus 2 tablespoons
cocoa powder

½ teaspoon baking soda

Pinch of salt

10 tablespoons (1¼ sticks)
unsalted butter

1 cup bakers' sugar

1 large egg

1 teaspoon vanilla extract

1 cup turbinado or raw brown
sugar, for rolling cookie
dough

Espresso Ice Cream

2 cups heavy cream

1 cup whole milk

¾ cup granulated sugar

½ cup coffee beans

1 vanilla bean, cut lengthwise
and scraped

6 large egg yolks

2 ounces brewed espresso

Assembly

1 recipe Espresso Ice Cream

1 cup sliced almonds, toasted

**MAKES 6 ICE CREAM
SANDWICHES**

To Make the Cookies

1. Sift the flour, cocoa powder, baking soda, and salt into a bowl.

2. In a stand mixer fitted with the paddle attachment, beat the butter and bakers' sugar on medium speed until pale and fluffy, about 2 minutes.

3. Add the egg and vanilla and beat until just combined.

4. Reduce the speed to low, gradually add the flour-cocoa mixture, and mix until combined.

5. Form the dough into a disk, wrap in plastic wrap, and refrigerate for at least 1 hour.

6. Preheat the oven to 350°F.

7. Line a baking sheet with parchment paper. Divide the dough into 1½-ounce balls (12 total) and roll in the turbinado sugar. Place on the lined baking sheet and flatten just a little. Refrigerate for 5 minutes.

8. Bake in the preheated oven for 7 minutes, rotate the pan, and bake for another 2 minutes.

9. Transfer the cookies to a wire rack and let cool completely.

To Make the Ice Cream

1. Pour the cream and milk into a small saucepan over medium heat. Add half of the sugar, the coffee beans, and the vanilla seeds and pod. Bring the mixture just to a simmer, stirring occasionally, and remove from the heat.

2. In a medium mixing bowl, whisk together the egg yolks and the remaining half of the sugar.

3. Temper the egg-sugar mixture with the warm cream mixture by slowly adding it in small amounts as you whisk, until a third has been added. Pour in the remainder and return the entire mixture to the saucepan. Cook over low heat, stirring constantly, until the custard thickens enough to coat the back of a spoon, and has reached 180°F.

4. Strain the custard through a fine-mesh sieve to remove the coffee beans and vanilla pod.

5. Stir in the brewed espresso and place the custard in an ice bath until it reaches room temperature, then refrigerate for at least 1 hour.

6. Pour the chilled custard into an ice cream maker and process according to the manufacturer's directions.

To Assemble

1. Line a baking sheet with parchment paper.

2. Divide the ice cream into 6 large balls and place on the lined baking sheet, about 3 inches apart. Top the scoops with another sheet of parchment paper and gently flatten into disks, about 2 inches wide and 1 inch thick. Freeze until ready to serve.

3. Place each ice cream disk between two cookies to form a sandwich and roll in the toasted sliced almonds.

Linzer S'mores with Hazelnut Ganache and Homemade Marshmallows

CHARLIE PALMER [Aureole, *New York, New York*]

A recipe for "Pineapple Marshmallows" from Good Things to Eat *by Rufus Estes, published in 1911.*

TAPPING INTO A MUCH OLDER COOKIE SAND-wich tradition than s'mores, Charlie Palmer gives us one fancy take on the Girl Scout classic of two graham crackers, a piece of chocolate, and a toasted marshmallow or two. Palmer's Linzer S'mores are filled with homemade marshmallows and lashings of hazelnut ganache.

Linzer cookies, or sablés, have the same components as a Linzertorte—a tart with a rich buttery crust that includes almonds, lemon zest, and cinnamon, and a filling of black currant jam. The dough used for the crust is also made into cookies and sandwiched around the preserves with a small cut-out in the top, exposing the dark purple filling.

Franz Hölzlhuber claimed to have brought Linzertortes to America in 1856. When a promised position as the conductor of an orchestra in Milwaukee didn't work out, he got a job with a baker and introduced this Austrian dessert. Using this centuries-old cookie sandwich as inspiration, Palmer then adds a thick chocolate ganache and marshmallows.

Marshmallows have been made for thousands of years and both the Romans and the Egyptians ate this confection, originally made as a medicine from the sap of the root of the marsh mallow plant. The French, as is their way, transformed it into a candy not unlike what we enjoy today. Recipes for marshmallow confections appear in early American cookbooks, with instructions for cleaning the root. In *Good Things to Eat* (1911) by Rufus Estes (one of the few early African-American cookbook writers), there's a delicious-sounding recipe for "Pineapple Marshmallows," which is suggested as a good confection for Thanksgiving. Homemade marshmallows are supereasy to cook up at home and an easy way to impress your friends.

Palmer told me he was once going to be a pastry chef, and at one point early in his career he had two different kitchen jobs, making desserts by day and working at another restaurant at night. Given the way he's transformed a marshmallow sandwich treat into something any Girl Scout would be proud of, this big guy is obviously talented on the sweeter side of the kitchen.

PINEAPPLE MARSHMALLOWS—This is a good confection for Thanksgiving. Soak four ounces gum arabic in one cupful pineapple juice until dissolved. Put into a granite saucepan with a half pound of powdered sugar, and set in a larger pan of hot water over the fire. Stir until the mixture is white and thickened. Test by dropping a little in cold water. If it "balls," take from the fire and whip in the stiffly whipped whites of three eggs. Flavor with a teaspoonful vanilla or orange juice, then turn into a square pan that has been dusted with cornstarch. The mixture should be about an inch in thickness. Stand in a cold place for twelve hours, then cut into inch squares and roll in a mixture of cornstarch and powdered sugar.

Marshmallows

3 envelopes (³/₄ ounce) Knox powdered gelatin

1¹/₂ cups light corn syrup

1¹/₂ cups granulated sugar

2 cups confectioners' sugar

¹/₂ cup cornstarch

Nonstick cooking spray

Makes one 18 x 13-inch half sheet pan of marshmallows

Almond Linzer Cookies

¹/₂ cup almonds, toasted and then pulsed in food processor to a coarse powder

³/₄ pound (2¹/₂ sticks) unsalted butter

1 cup granulated sugar

Finely grated zest of 1 orange

1¹/₂ large eggs, lightly beaten

¹/₂ teaspoon vanilla extract

2¹/₃ cups all-purpose flour

1¹/₈ teaspoons baking powder

1 tablespoon ground cinnamon

Confectioners' sugar, for dusting

Chocolate-Hazelnut Ganache

4¹/₂ ounces dark chocolate couverture

14 ounces milk chocolate couverture

1 cup heavy cream

1¹/₂ teaspoons hazelnut-flavored liqueur

Pinch of fleur de sel

¹/₂ cup crème fraîche

MAKES 2 DOZEN S'MORES

To Make the Marshmallows

1. In a small bowl, sprinkle the gelatin over ¹/₂ cup of cold water and allow to bloom.

2. Place half the corn syrup, the granulated sugar, and ¹/₂ cup of water in a saucepot and cook until it registers 260°F on a candy thermometer. Whisk the bloomed gelatin into the hot corn syrup.

3. In the bowl of a stand mixer fitted with the wire whip attachment, whisk the remaining corn syrup on high speed, gradually pouring in the hot syrup-gelatin mixture. Continue to whisk on high speed until the mixture turns white, doubles in volume, and has the consistency of marshmallow.

4. In the meantime, sift the confectioners' sugar and cornstarch onto a parchment paper–lined half sheet pan. Set aside a spoonful for dusting your knife.

5. Using a bowl scraper, remove the marshmallow mixture from the bowl and spread onto the prepared half sheet pan. Spray a piece of plastic wrap slightly larger than the half sheet pan with nonstick cooking spray and cover the marshmallow for 20 minutes until set.

6. To cut the marshmallow, dust a knife with the confectioners' sugar-cornstarch mixture and slice into large, square pieces. Cover with plastic wrap until ready to use.

To Make the Almond Linzer Cookies

1. Preheat the oven to 320°F.

2. In the bowl of a stand mixer fitted with the paddle attachment, cream the butter until smooth. Sift the granulated sugar and gradually add to the butter. Add the orange zest. Add the eggs and vanilla. Sift together the flour, baking powder, and cinnamon. Add by thirds until incorporated. Add the ground almonds and mix in.

3. Roll out the dough between 2 sheets of parchment paper. Chill for 30 minutes.

4. Cut the chilled dough into cookies.

5. Bake for 10 to 12 minutes until golden brown.

To Make the Chocolate-Hazelnut Ganache

1. Melt the milk and bittersweet chocolates in a very clean, dry, stainless steel bowl.

2. In a small saucepan, scald the heavy cream mixed with the liqueur. Remove the pan from the heat and cover the heavy cream mixture with plastic wrap for 30 minutes to intensify the flavor.

3. Strain the cream through a chinois. Set the bowl with the chocolate on a damp towel. Gradually whisk in half of the cream mixture; the chocolate mixture will begin to separate and will look granular. This is okay; it is a necessary part of the process when incorporating liquid into chocolate. Whisk in the remaining cream; the chocolate mixture will start to emulsify and become stiff. Keep whisking until the chocolate looks smooth and has a creamy texture.

4. Whisk in the crème fraîche for a glossy finish. Pour the ganache into a pastry bag.

To Assemble

Place half the linzer cookies onto a flat surface and pipe the warm ganache on top. Set a marshmallow on top of the ganache and lightly burn with a blowtorch. Place a second cookie on top of each and finish with a sprinkling of confectioners' sugar.

Red Velvet Cupcakes

DAVID GUAS [Bayou Bakery, *Arlington, Virginia*]

SERVING DOWN-HOME SOUTHERN FARE AT THE HIP, RUSTIC Bayou Bakery, David Guas leaves plenty of room on the menu for his award-winning signature desserts. There also are Cuban influences in the pressed sandwiches, reflecting Guas's heritage (his father was born in Havana). His Louisiana country cooking shines in house-made boudin and andouille sausages, savory breakfast biscuits, pimiento cheese, hogshead cheese, and jars of bread-and-butter pickles for purchase at the register. Hot beignets and chicory-coffee pralines are good to go, along with Guas's more-elaborate cakes, pies, puddings, and his gourmet New Orleans snowballs. As the *Washington Post's* restaurant critic wrote, "I have yet to find a single dessert I can say no to."

Red velvet cake is similar to another American favorite chocolate cake—devil's food cake—and at the turn of the twentieth century, the two names may have been used interchangeably in cookbooks. The Waldorf Astoria lays claim to baking the first red velvet cake, and the recipe was the source of an urban legend, like the Nordstorm cookie myth. Both cakes are light, moist, and chocolaty—red velvet cake usually has cream-cheese frosting, like Guas's recipe, and devil's food cake has a rich chocolate frosting. In the second edition of the *Neighborhood Cook Book* by the Council of Jewish Women, 1914, there are recipes for "Devil Layer Cake" and "Devil's Cake." It's not until later that large quantities of red food coloring were added to the light chocolate cake to give it that distinctive color.

"Let them eat cake." So said Marie Antoinette, as a bad harvest and harsh winter led to bread riots and peasant revolts. Leap forward two centuries and find one indulgence that continues to grow in popularity as many others decline: cupcakes. These little cakes are the perfect, affordable treat, guaranteed to brighten even the gloomiest of days.

This hunting, fishing, Harley-riding pastry chef from the South makes the daintiest of red velvet cupcakes, using natural food coloring made from the extract of beets instead of the usual chemical dye. The resulting beautiful red, exquisite-tasting cupcakes are topped with whipped cream cheese frosting.

Devil Layer Cake

Dark Part: One cup brown sugar, one-half cup milk, one cup chocolate, yolk of one egg. Boil slowly until thick, then let cool, stirring all the time.

Cake Part: One cup brown sugar, one-half cup butter, two eggs, two cups flour, one teaspoon soda which is dissolved in a little warm water, one-half cup milk. Cream the sugar and butter; add yolks of eggs, milk, flour, and then whites. Beat together, and stir in dark part. Last, add soda.

Filling: One cup granulated sugar, one-half cup water. Boil until it threads. Add one-half pound marshmallows. When dissolved, beat into stiffened white of egg, until smooth.

Devil's Cake

Piece of butter size of an egg, yolks of three eggs, one cup brown sugar, four tablespoons chocolate, one-half cup milk. Mix well; then add two teaspoons of Crescent baking powder, with one and one-half cups flour; add the whites of three eggs, and bake in three layers.

Recipes for "Devil Layer Cake" and "Devil's Cake" from the Neighborhood Cook Book *by The Council of Jewish Women, published in 1914.*

Cupcakes

12 tablespoons (1 1/2 sticks) unsalted butter, softened at room temperature

2 cups granulated sugar

2 teaspoons vanilla extract

2 tablespoons red color (India Tree), Natural Vegetable Colorants

3 large eggs

2 1/4 cups all-purpose flour

2 tablespoons unsweetened cocoa powder

3/4 teaspoon baking powder

1/2 teaspoon baking soda

1 1/2 teaspoons kosher salt

1 1/2 cups buttermilk

Whipped Cream Cheese Frosting

1/2 pound cream cheese, softened

8 tablespoons (1 stick) unsalted butter, softened

2 cups confectioners' sugar, sifted

1 teaspoon vanilla extract

MAKES 24 CUPCAKES

To Make the Cupcakes

1. Heat the oven to 325°F.

2. In the bowl of a stand mixer, fitted with the paddle attachment, cream the butter, suga, vanilla, and the coloring for 2 minutes on medium to high speed. Lower the speed and add the eggs, one at a time. Sift together the flour, cocoa, baking powder, and baking soda onto a piece of parchment paper. Add the salt after sifting, and reserve. Add the dry ingredients to the wet in thirds, alternating with the buttermilk and finishing with the dry. Line a cupcake pan with cupcake liners and spoon in the batter—filling each liner about 2/3 full. Bake for 8 minutes, rotate the pan, and bake for an additional 8 minutes. Remove the cupcakes and allow them to cool for 5 to 10 minutes in the pan before removing them. Then cool the cupcakes an additional 20 to 30 minutes before frosting.

To Make the Frosting

In the bowl of a stand mixer, fitted with the paddle attachment, mix the cream cheese and butter for 3 minutes. Stop and add the confectioners' sugar. Mix on low speed until all the sugar is well incorporated. Increase the speed to medium high and beat for 2 minutes more. Pipe the frosting onto the cooled cupcakes.

Chef Guas' Tips

"Note that you will need two of the vials of coloring for this recipe."

"If you can't find natural food dye you can substitute with regular food dye."

Torta Caprese Brownies

BROOKS HEADLEY [Del Posto, *New York, New York*]

BROOKS HEADLEY WORRIED THAT HE WASN'T QUALIFIED TO take the post of pastry chef at Del Posto with upwards of 400 covers on a Saturday night, because, at the time, he was working in a 30-seat restaurant, and before that he was a drummer in a punk rock band. When the job was advertised he took a chance to fulfill his dream to work for one of his heroes, Mario Batali, and Del Posto's chef de cuisine, Mark Ladner. Together Ladner and Headley have worked to raise the profile of the food at Del Posto to the dizzying heights of four stars in the *New York Times*—becoming the first Italian restaurant to ever receive this rating.

Headley started his cooking career when he was twenty-seven—fairly late, as he concedes. "I literally fell into the world of desserts when I landed a job at the top Italian restaurant in Washington, D.C. in 1999—I have no formal training, but I did work under Nancy Silverton at Campanile—that was my education. When I started it wasn't glamorous like it is now. *Kitchen Confidential* was a turning point. When that book came out suddenly everyone was interested in the kitchen."

Headley still loves to drum—even at work. He claims he annoys his staff with his constant tapping on whatever is at hand—marble, bowls, cutting boards, mixers, and whisks. Asked about what he does in his spare time, Headley says, "I like to sit and read books about food, Kitchen Arts & Letters on Ninety-third Street in New York City is my temple and I always advise my cooks to hang out there and study on their days off."

He also likes to watch the early cooking shows. *Molto Mario* is his favorite, and not because it happens to star his boss—"It was genius," Headley says. "Because of that show I wanted to work for Mario Batali. That style of food, very direct Italian, no bullshit. I'm not the pastry chef who's interested in making perfect curlicue chocolate garnishes—I like my chocolate sculptures to be totally free-form." Ladner and Headley have been making videos of their techniques together in the kitchen at Del Posto and posting them on the Internet. The video for the chocolate free-form dessert uses Headley's music as the score.

While visiting Headley in Del Posto's kitchen, he produces a tray of freshly baked mini brownies. The lines of little cakes remind me of the Manhattan streets from above, and together we play with the little cubes of brownies to create a New York skyline on a cake stand. Then he gives them his signature dusting of confectioners' sugar. "I love putting confectioners' sugar on stuff. Not many modern pastry chefs at this level of three and four stars like it, it's considered grandmotherly and homey, but I think it's totally classy and underrated."

Brownies, either fudgy or cakey, first appeared in America in 1893 when Bertha Palmer requested that the chef of the Palmer House Hotel create a dessert for the ladies attending the Chicago Columbian Exposition that was "smaller than a piece of cake and easily eaten from boxed lunches." In 1896, Fannie Farmer includes a recipe called "Brownies" in her cookbook but it calls for molasses, not chocolate. It's not until the 1906 edition that two squares of baker's chocolate appear in the recipe's ingredient list.

7/8 **pound 66% chopped chocolate (preferably Tcho or Amedei)**

1 **pound lightly toasted walnuts**

1 **cup plus 1 1/2 tablespoons sugar**

2 1/2 **teaspoons salt**

2 **sticks plus 5 tablespoons unsalted butter, melted and cooled**

8 **large eggs, separated**

Confectioners' sugar, for dusting

MAKES APPROXIMATELY 150 MINI, BITE-SIZE BROWNIES

1. Preheat the oven to 325°F. Line an 11 x 17-inch sheet pan with parchment paper.

2. Using a food processor, grind the chocolate and walnuts together to make a crumbly texture. Don't go overboard, or you will melt the chocolate. Add 2/3 cup plus 1 1/2 tablespoon of the granulated sugar and salt and grind until you have a gritty mix.

3. Place the chocolate mixture in a large bowl and add the melted butter and the egg yolks.

4. In a stand mixer fitted with the wire whisk, whip the egg whites with the sugar until thick and foamy; a soft meringue.

5. Gently combine the egg whites with the chocolate mixture.

6. Spread out the batter in the prepared sheet pan and bake for about 25 minutes, or until a toothpick inserted in the center comes out clean. Be careful not to overbake—you want the cake to be firm, the edges dark, and the center slightly underdone so that the cake remains moist as it cools.

7. Cool completely and cut into little squares. Don't forget to dust with confectioners' sugar!

Chef Headley's Tip

"Get the best-quality chocolate you can get your hands on. I like this artisan fair-trade chocolate from San Francisco called Tcho."

Spicy Ginger Whoopie Pies

April Bloomfield [Spotted Pig, *New York, New York*]

"COME TO THE PIG" SAYS THE TEXT MESSAGE FROM APRIL Bloomfield, so off I trot. Having enjoyed her food many times, I am excited to finally meet this fellow Brit, who has made it big in New York. The thrice-fried fries and the lamb burger topped with blue cheese at the Breslin probably set me back a few years if cholesterol has anything to do with longevity, but it was worth every bite. With her strawberry blonde hair pulled back off her face in a ponytail, and wearing clogs, black kitchen pants, and a black Spotted Pig T-shirt, she looks every bit the serious chef that she is. She doesn't enjoy schmoozing her guests—she leaves that to her business partner Ken Friedman and focuses on the cooking at three of New York's hottest restaurants, the Spotted Pig—the city's first gastropub—the Breslin, and most recently the reopened, relocated John Dory.

Bloomfield is best known for cooking up hearty British and Italian food at the Spotted Pig, which the *New Yorker* described as "a Chasen's on the Hudson, by way of the Thames . . . a place where normal people go to feel like celebrities and celebrities go to feel like normal people." Her celebrity status as a chef, with all the press and accolades she's garnered, does not sit easily on her shoulders, and she is definitely in the category of normal people. She is surprisingly shy but really into the idea of cooking from the past.

"I totally want to do this, but if you've got all these chefs already, are you sure you want me as well?" she asks. This humility is genuine. "You know I did cook an old recipe once, given to me by the late Rose Gray. She asked me to make it at the River Café [in London]. It was a marble cake made with potato, almonds, and chocolate. I made it like ten times and it just didn't work. She then tells me it was from a book from the 1600s or something! I realized I'd been hugely overwhipping the eggs with my modern electric whisk."

Bloomfield decides she wants to make whoopie pies—a piece of Americana. Part cookie, part pie, part cake, this sweet, cream-filled treat is usually made with fluffy white marshmallow filling sandwiched between two light chocolate cakes. Their origin, like so much of American food, is passionately debated by those who care. Those arguing that the origin is Pennsylvania, point to the Amish of Lancaster County and claim they would make little cakes using leftover batter and put them in their children's lunch boxes—when the kids found their pies, they'd cry "Whoopie!"

The pie was probably taken to Maine at the beginning of the twentieth century where it is now the official state treat. The New England pies are supersized—about the dimensions of a hamburger—and are surely made to share over a tall glass of chilled milk.

Bloomfield's whoopie pies are made of spicy ginger cakes and a creamy vanilla bean filling. Her recipe is almost identical to a recipe for "Drop Ginger Cakes" from the *Presbyterian Cook Book* (1873). It's hard not to imagine Mrs. William Craighead taking two of her drop ginger cakes and smothering one with a vanilla frosting before topping with another. The first recorded recipe for "Amish Whoopie Pie" appeared in the *Yummy Book* put out by the makers of Marshmallow Fluff in the 1930s. Bloomfield's pies certainly fill the yumminess quotient—and they are easy to make. The spices and fresh ginger in the cakes give them a definite bite that cuts the sugariness and fills the house with a warm sweet smell when baking. The hardest part of the recipe is resisting the temptation to jump right in before they cool completely. After sandwiching them together with lots of filling, this little piggie went "whoopie, whoopie, whoopie" all the way home!

DROP GINGER CAKES.
Mrs. William Craighead.

One pint of molasses; one teacupful of sugar; one cupful of butter; four eggs; two tablespoonsful of ginger; same of ground cinnamon; one teaspoonful of salt; one tablespoonful of soda in a half teacupful of hot water; flour enough to make a stiff batter. Drop on tins and bake.

Mrs. William Craighead's recipe for "Drop Ginger Cakes" from the Presbyterian Cook Book *compiled by The Ladies of the First Presbyterian Church, Dayton, Ohio, published in 1873.*

Cakes

4 tablespoons (1/2 stick) unsalted butter

1/2 cup packed light brown sugar

1/2 teaspoon baking soda

1 1/2 teaspoons baking powder

1/4 teaspoon salt

1 1/2 teaspoons ground ginger

3/4 teaspoon ground cinnamon

1/4 teaspoon ground cloves

3/5 of a lightly beaten large egg (about 2 tablespoons plus 1 teaspoon)

1/8 cup grated fresh ginger

2 3/4 cups all-purpose flour

1/2 cup molasses

Cream Filling

4 1/2 large egg whites (about 1/2 cup plus 1 tablespoon)

2 1/4 cups granulated sugar

1 1/2 cups (3 sticks) unsalted butter

1 vanilla bean, cut lengthwise and scraped, pod discarded

MAKES 8 WHOOPIE PIES

To Make the Cakes

1. Preheat the oven to 325°F.

2. In the bowl of a stand mixer fitted with the paddle attachment, beat together the butter, brown sugar, baking soda, baking powder, salt, ginger, cinnamon, and cloves.

3. Add the egg and fresh ginger.

4. Add the flour. Stream in the molasses and 3/4 cup hot water.

5. On a large baking sheet lined with parchment paper, spoon 2 tablespoons of batter into mounds, evenly spaced about 2 inches apart.

6. Bake the cakes for 10 to 15 minutes, or until a toothpick inserted into the middle comes out clean.

7. Let cool on the baking sheet before removing.

To Make the Cream Filling

1. Preheat the egg whites and granulated sugar in a bowl set over a saucepan of simmering water until sugar dissolves.

2. In the bowl of a stand mixer fitted with the wire whip attachment, mix on high speed until light, fluffy, and glossy.

3. Add the butter and whip until the cream comes together.

4. Add scraped vanilla seeds.

To Assemble

When the cakes are completely cool, sandwich two equally sized domes together with a generous amount of vanilla bean filling. Repeat 7 more times.

Key Lime Tart

FRANÇOIS PAYARD [FPB, *New York, New York*]

A THIRD-GENERATION PASTRY CHEF FROM NICE, FRANCE, François Payard has sugar in his blood. Payard trained in Paris before moving to America in 1990 to work first at Le Bernardin and then Daniel. Within five years, his beautiful creations, delicate flavors, and chocolate work caught the attention of his peers and he was crowned Pastry Chef of the Year by the James Beard Foundation. Sitting in the patisserie as a child watching his grandfather at work, he had dreamed of one day opening his own restaurant. In 1997 he opened Payard on Lexington Avenue.

When I first moved to the States, I lived in New York in a brownstone on the Upper East Side. There were many things I loved about my new home and my life as a newlywed, but very occasionally, I missed England. Prevented by U.S. immigration from leaving the country until my green card came through, I had two cures for this homesickness—I would hop on the subway down to Greenwich Village for hot Ribena and beans on toast with HP sauce at Tea & Sympathy, or I would walk up Lexington Avenue to have tea at Payard. The restaurant wasn't English—it was as French as you could find outside of Paris, and it was this authentic European sensibility that was precisely what I needed. A good cup of tea, a pastel-colored melt-in-your-mouth macaron, and I'd be ready to go back. I'd walk home loving the hustle and bustle of Manhattan, carrying a Payard bag containing a slice of Key lime pie to take home to my new husband (it's his favorite).

The Key lime pie originated in the Florida Keys about a hundred years ago and has since become a regional icon, topped with meringue, whipped cream, or nothing, as is the case with Payard's tart. A traditional Key lime pie contains sweetened condensed milk; Payard's does not (Key lime pie purists will be puckering up their lips in horror.) Drinking milk before Louis Pasteur discovered pasteurization was risky anywhere in America. Condensed milk, invented and launched on the market by Gail Borden in the late 1850s, offered a safer alternative. In the Florida Keys, where citrus was prevalent, dairy cows were not. Refrigeration was limited, as was transportation, and so Floridians, like much of America, relied upon canned milk.

There are many stories and theories about who invented the pie—some say it was fishermen, who would take condensed milk and limes to sea, others believe it was the

Floridian millionaire William Curry's cook, Aunt Sally. The oldest published recipes for Key lime pie date back to the 1930s, though a predecessor can be found in *What Mrs. Fisher Knows about Old Southern Cooking* (1881). The recipe for "Cocoanut Pie" calls for the rind and juice of lemons to be mixed with butter, sugar, eggs, and "one-half tea-cup of sweet milk."

In the kitchen behind FPB, Payard's new, more-casual bakery-café on West Houston Street, I watch the master *pâtissiér* brush the apricot glaze on the top of his tart and add the lime garnish. He is a man of few words, and those he speaks are in perfect English with a thick French accent. He tells me that if you can't find Key limes, a mix of half regular (Persian) lime and half lemon juice can be substituted to get the correct balance of sharpness and color (Key limes have yellow juice, Persian limes green). He uses a large knife to cut a tiny slice and hands it to me to taste. Payard is not afraid of making his tart *tart*. The rich, buttery crust complements the acidity of the creamy filling. "When people want Key lime, they don't want to eat a bowl of sugar. With this tart, you taste the Key lime, perfectly balanced between the sweet and sour."

> 51   Cocoanut Pie.
>
> One cocoanut fresh, draw off the milk, then place the nut in a hot oven and let it stay long enough for the shell to pull off; then grate with the nut juice one tea-cup of powdered white sugar, one tablespoonful of butter and lard rubbed together until creamed, then take the yelks of four eggs and beat into sugar and butter until perfectly light; grate the rind of one lemon into it, and squeeze the juice of the lemon into the creamed butter and sugar; beat the white of four eggs light, and add also to creamed butter and sugar, and stir them well, add also one-half tea-cup of sweet milk. Will make three pies. Use a half pound of flour for the pastry, one tablespoonful each of butter and lard—you only want crust at the bottom of plate, and bake in quick oven. Mix flour as directed in No. 49.

A recipe for "Cocoanut Pie" from What Mrs. Fisher Knows about Old Southern Cooking *by Abby Fisher, published in 1881.*

Key Lime Tart

Pastry chefs have a tendency to overcomplicate things, but this minimal Key lime tart from François Payard proves that simplicity is often best. "When I first started making it," says Payard, "both customers and staff agreed that it was better than the labor-intensive tart we were serving in the shop at the time. The rich, buttery *pâté sucrée* complements the acidity of the creamy yellow filling."

Sweet Tart Dough

1 cup plus 1 tablespoon confectioners' sugar

1 3/4 cups all-purpose flour

Pinch of salt

9 tablespoons unsalted butter (1 stick plus 1 tablespoon), softened, plus more for buttering foil

1 large egg

Makes two 9 1/2-inch tart shells

Tart Filling

2 teaspoons finely grated Key lime zest

3/4 cup Key lime juice (about 6 Key limes)

3 large eggs

1/2 cup plus 1 tablespoon

3 tablespoons unsalted butter, cut into 1/2-inch pieces

One 9 1/2-inch tart shell made from Sweet Tart Dough, prebaked

2 or 3 Key limes, for garnish

1/3 cup apricot preserves

MAKES ONE 9-INCH TART

To Make the Sweet Tart Dough

1. Sift together the confectioners' sugar, flour, and salt into a bowl.

2. Place the butter in a food processor and process until smooth, about 15 seconds. Scatter the flour mixture over the butter; add the egg, and process just until the dough forms a mass; do not overmix. Turn the dough out onto the counter and divide it in half. Shape each half into a disc, wrap in plastic wrap, and refrigerate for at least 2 hours and up to 24 hours. Dough may be frozen for up to one month if well wrapped.

3. Let the dough stand at room temperature for 30 minutes to soften. Lightly butter two 9 1/2-inch fluted tart pans with removable bottoms.

4. Dust a work surface lightly with flour. Dust one of the discs lightly with flour and, using a floured rolling pin, roll it out into a rough 12-inch circle. Lift the dough often, making sure that the work surface and dough are lightly floured at all times. Roll the dough up onto the rolling pin and gently unroll it over one of the prepared tart pans. Press the dough into the pan and roll the pin over the top of the pan to remove the excess dough. Repeat with the remaining dough and tart pan. Prick the bottom of the tart shells all over with a fork. Chill the tart shells for 20 minutes. (The tart shells can be refrigerated for up to 24 hours.)

5. Heat the oven to 325°F.

6. Lightly butter two pieces of aluminum foil large enough to generously line each tart pan. Line the tart shells with the foil, buttered side down, and fill with dried beans, rice, or pie weights.

7. Bake the tart shells for 15 minutes. Remove the foil and weights and continue baking for 5 minutes, until just set; the tart shells should have little or no color. Cool completely on a wire rack.

To Make the Tart

1. Preheat the oven to 325°F.

2. Fill a medium saucepan one-third full with water and bring to a simmer. Put the zest and Key lime juice in a medium bowl and whisk in the eggs. Add the sugar and butter. Place the bowl over the simmering water—the water must not touch the bottom of the bowl—whisking constantly, until the butter is completely melted and the mixture is smooth. Remove the bowl from the pan of hot water and allow the mixture to cool for 15 minutes.

3. Place the prebaked tart shell on a sheet pan. Pour the filling into the shell and bake the tart for 8 to 10 minutes, or until the center is just set. Cool the tart completely on a wire rack.

4. Cut a crosswise slice from the center of a key lime and place it in the center of the tart. Slice the remaining key lime halves lengthwise in half and then cut the sections into half-moons. Arrange the slices around the edge of the tart with the cut sides out.

5. Place the preserves in a small heatproof glass measure and microwave on high power for 30 to 45 seconds, until bubbling. Strain the hot preserves through a fine-mesh sieve into a small bowl. Using a pastry brush, lightly brush the top of the tart with the warm apricot glaze.

Chef Payard's Tips

"Apricot glaze adds sheen and a subtle flavor to many French tarts and cakes. It also helps keep them moist."

"The tart shell can be made the day before, and so can the filling, but they should be stored separately. This recipe for the rich, sweet short dough known as pâté sucree makes enough pastry for two tart shells. You can freeze half for another time, or you can roll out and shape both shells and freeze one of them, well wrapped, ready to use."

"If you can't find Key limes, substitute lime and lemon juice in a 50:50 ratio, same for the zest."

Not Your Same Old Pumpkin Pie

RICHARD RUSKELL [Montage Hotel, *Beverly Hills, California*]

I FIRST MET PASTRY CHEF RICHARD RUSKELL WHEN WE JUDGED the Beverly Hills Farmers' Market annual pie contest together. I was relieved to be sitting beside such an expert of crust and pie filling, as slice after slice was set in front of us to taste. I seem to remember a lot of huckleberries, a nod to the market perhaps, followed by a sugar coma. As the eager eyes of contestants zeroed in on our every gesture, we tasted, poker-faced, then recorded our scores. As one pie arrived, Ruskell whispered to me, "Store-bought crust—too perfect." I was shocked to find that he was right, and neither of us had to try more than one bite; it certainly wasn't going to win.

Sadly, my desire for pie has been forever diminished by this overload. Ruskell's, however, seems stronger than ever. "I want to make a pie," he says, when I ask him what recipe he'd like to contribute.

Ruskell is given the task to take that all-American favorite, pumpkin pie, and make it into something new. Everyone knows and loves traditional pumpkin pie, but Ruskell has raised this classic to whole new level. His beautiful pie has a dark gingersnap crust, golden streusel topping and a rich, creamy pumpkin filling. As an added bonus, you also get a killer recipe for molasses spice cookies to use for the crust, or to eat on their own.

In old American cookbooks, custard-based pies, including pumpkin pies, are called puddings. Amelia Simmons, in *American Cookery* (the first cookbook of American authorship to be printed in the United States) has a recipe for "Pompkin Pudding"—a traditional American Pumpkin Pie.

In her book *Seventy-Five Receipts for Pastry, Cakes and Sweetmeats* (1827), Eliza Leslie shares recipes, or "receipts" as they were called then, that are "drawn up in a style so plain and minute, as to be perfectly intelligible to servants, and persons of the most moderate capacity." She goes on to bemoan the fact that European recipes often fail due to their complicated nature and lack of "explicitness" in quantities of ingredients. She states: "The receipts in this little book are in every sense of the word American…prepared *precisely* according to these directions will not fail to be excellent." Her recipe calls for half a pound of stewed pumpkin, three eggs, a quarter pint of fresh butter or cream, a quarter of a pound of powdered white sugar, half a glass of wine or brandy, half a glass of rosewater, and a teaspoon of mixed spices—nutmeg, mace, and cinnamon. This early ancestor of the pumpkin pie has all the components that we put in our pies today, apart from the rosewater.

PUMPKIN PUDDING.

Half a pound of stewed pumpkin.
Three eggs.
Quarter of a pound of fresh butter, or a pint of cream.
Quarter of a pound of powdered white sugar.
Half a glass of wine and brandy mixed.
Half a glass of rose-water.
One tea-spoonful of mixed spice, nutmeg, mace and cinnamon.

———

Stew some pumpkin with as little water as possible. Drain it in a colander, and press it till dry. When cold, weigh half a pound, and pass it through a sieve. Prepare the spice. Stir together the sugar, and butter, or cream, till they are perfectly light. Add to them, gradually, the spice and liquor.

Beat three eggs very light, and stir them into the butter and sugar alternately with the pumpkin.

Cover a soup-plate with puff-paste, and put in the mixture. Bake it in a moderate oven about half an hour.

Grate sugar over it when cool.

Instead of the butter, you may boil a pint of milk or cream, and when cold, stir into it, in turn, the sugar, eggs, and pumpkin.

A recipe for "Pumpkin Pudding" from Seventy-Five Receipts for Pastry, Cakes, and Sweetmeats *by Miss Leslie of Philadelphia, published in 1827.*

Not Your Same Old Pumpkin Pie

Richard Ruskell transforms a traditional pumpkin pie into a modern creation with just a few additions. His pie is not overly sweet, the texture of the filling is light, and not cloying, and the molasses spice cookies in the crust give it that extra zip.

Molasses Spice Cookie Crust

2 1/4 cups plus 1 tablespoon all-purpose flour

2 teaspoons ground ginger

1 teaspoon baking soda

3/4 teaspoon ground cinnamon

1/2 teaspoon ground cloves

1/4 teaspoon plus a pinch of salt

1 1/2 sticks plus 5 tablespoons unsalted, softened butter

1 cup light brown sugar

1 large egg

1/4 cup molasses

2 tablespoons granulated sugar

1/4 cup packed dark brown sugar

Streusel Topping

2 tablespoons all-purpose flour

2 tablespoons light brown sugar

2 tablespoons rolled oats (not quick or instant oats)

2 tablespoons cold butter

Pie Filling

3/4 cup heavy cream

1 cup granulated sugar

2 tablespoons dark rum

2 tablespoons (1/4 stick) unsalted butter

1 cup canned pumpkin purée

1 1/4 teaspoons ground cinnamon

3/4 teaspoon ground ginger

Pinch of ground nutmeg

Pinch of salt

2 teaspoons pure vanilla extract

2 large eggs

MAKES ONE 10-INCH PIE

To Make the Crust

1. Preheat oven to 350°F.

2. To make the cookies for the crumbs, stir together 2 1/4 cups flour, the ginger, baking soda, cinnamon, cloves, and 1/4 teaspoon salt. Set aside.

3. In the bowl of a stand mixer fitted with the paddle attachment cream 1 1/2 sticks of the softened butter and the light brown sugar until light and fluffy. Beat in the egg, then stir in 1 tablespoon of water and the molasses.

4. Gradually add the reserved dry ingredients to the molasses mixture.

5. Shape the dough into round balls; then roll them in the granulated sugar. Place the balls 2 inches apart on a parchment paper-lined sheet pan, and flatten slightly.

6. Bake for 8 to 10 minutes in the oven. (For gingersnap cookies, take from the oven and allow the cookies to cool on the sheet pan for 5 minutes before removing. Store in an airtight container.) To use the cookies for the crust, turn the temperature down to 300°F and bake for an additional 5 minutes.

7. Allow the cookies to cool completely and put in a food processor. Process until you have a fairly fine powder.

8. Center a rack in the oven and preheat the oven to 350°F.

9. Melt the remaining 5 tablespoons of butter. In a large bowl, mix together 2 cups of the gingersnap crumbs, dark brown sugar, the remaining tablespoon of flour, and a pinch of salt. Add the melted butter and stir until mixture is moist and well combined. The crumbs should hold together when pinched with your fingers. If the crumbs do not hold together, add up to 1 tablespoon of cold water, a teaspoon at a time, and stir to combine.

10. Press the crumb mixture into a French flan ring, a pie pan, or a spring-form pan, evenly covering the bottom and sides. Place the shell on a sheet pan and bake until crust is fragrant and set, about 10 minutes. Transfer the shell to a wire rack and let cool completely.

To Make the Streusel Topping

With a fork or your fingers mix together the flour, brown sugar, rolled oats, and cold butter until crumbly. Refrigerate until ready to use.

To Make the Filling

1. To make the caramel, pour the heavy cream into a microwave-safe measuring cup and heat until very hot. Sprinkle 1/2 cup of the sugar evenly over the bottom of an 8- to 12-quart pot. Place over medium-high heat and cook until the sugar begins to melt and caramelize. Stir it so it melts evenly and cook until it turns a deep mahogany color. When it darkens dramatically and starts to foam, add the hot heavy cream, little by little. Continue until all the cream has been added and

the caramel stops bubbling. The caramelized sugar may clump; turn the heat to medium and cook until the sugar melts and you have a nice caramel sauce. Add the rum and butter, and cook just until the caramel is smooth. Pour the caramel into a heatproof pitcher or bowl and cool it for about 15 minutes.

2. In a large bowl, combine the pumpkin and remaining $1/2$ cup sugar and hand whisk until smooth. Add the cinnamon, ginger, nutmeg, pinch of salt, vanilla extract, and eggs, and whisk until smooth. Mix in the caramel and pour into the shell.

3. Bake the pie for 10 minutes. Scatter chunks of streusel over the top and continue baking for another 35 to 40 minutes, or until the filling is puffed and set. A thin knife inserted into the center of the pie will come out clean.

4. Transfer the pie to a rack and cool to room temperature. Serve with freshly whipped cream, if desired.

Chef Ruskell's Tips

"I tend not to use pie plates, because invariably you never get a great slice of pie from the first piece. In the restaurant business you can't afford to waste that one piece. I use a French flan ring—it can be lifted off the baking sheet with ease."

"I highly recommend using the often dreaded canned purée to anything else. The pumpkins used in canned purée are grown only for the purposes of baking. It will produce consistent results and great texture."

"Don't be afraid to get a real dark caramel color when you cook the sugar. It will result in a really earthy and delicious flavor."

Deep Dish Bourbon Pecan Pie with Butterscotch Sauce

ALEX SEIDEL [Fruition, *Denver, Colorado*]

AT FRUITION, CHEF-OWNER ALEX SEIDEL SERVES ELEVATED comfort food using fresh local ingredients—many grown at his latest venture, his farm. He has brought this philosophy to many items on his menu—including desserts. "Pecan pie is the most well-known nut dessert in the South," Seidel says. "We have taken this traditional pie and transformed it into an elegant dish."

Pecan trees are indigenous to southern America, dating back to prehistoric times. *Pecan* means "hard nut" in Algonquian and has been the state tree of Texas since 1919. Before then, however, pecan trees were cut down in large numbers to make way for the cash crop—cotton. It wasn't until the early twentieth century that the potential value of the nut was recognized. It's now the biggest commercially grown nut in Texas.

Finding early pecan pie recipes proved near impossible. That's not to say people weren't mixing pecans with sugar, eggs, and vanilla to pour into a piecrust before the

1900s—but why didn't they write the recipes down? Most pecan pie recipes in the twentieth century date from the 1930s and all call for Karo corn syrup. Perhaps Karo's claim that a salesman's wife invented pecan pie as a "new use for corn syrup" in the 1930s is true. Just as Santa's suit is red because of a Coca-Cola advertising campaign, Karo may be responsible for an American classic, not to mention a holiday staple.

The sauce that Seidel makes to go on his pie is addictive. Like the pie, it contains bourbon. I like make an ice cream sundae with small pieces of leftover cold pie, vanilla ice cream, some pecan nuts, and lots of butterscotch drizzled on top.

Filling

½ pound pecan halves

3 large eggs, at room temperature

¾ cup light brown sugar

½ cup light corn syrup

½ tablespoons dark molasses

¼ teaspoon salt

1 teaspoon vanilla paste or extract

2 tablespoons bourbon

4 tablespoons (½ stick) unsalted butter, melted

Piecrust

1 chilled pie shell (recipe page 312)

Butterscotch Sauce

½ pound (2 sticks) unsalted butter

½ cup water

¼ cup light corn syrup

2 cups granulated sugar

1 cup heavy cream

2 teaspoons vanilla paste

½ teaspoon salt

½ cup bourbon

MAKES ONE 10-INCH DEEP DISH PIE

To Make the Filling

1. Preheat the oven to 325°F.

2. Toast the pecans in the oven until they have a little color and are not raw, reserving some whole pecan halves for the top.

3. In a medium mixing bowl, whisk together the eggs and brown sugar.

4. Whisk in the corn syrup, molasses, salt, vanilla paste, and bourbon.

5. Whisk in the warm melted butter slowly and emulsify.

6. Fold in the toasted pecans. Set the filling aside.

To Make the Pie

1. Preheat the oven to 350°F.

2. Pour the pie filling into the chilled pie shell and arrange the whole pecans on top.

3. Bake in the oven for 50 minutes until the filling is set but has a little movement when the pie is jiggled. Check the pie after 40 minutes; if the crust is baking too fast, loosely cover it with a piece of aluminum foil to protect the edges.

4. Cool the pie at room temperature on a wire rack.

5. Serve the pie warm with the warm butterscotch sauce and vanilla ice cream,

To Make the Butterscotch Sauce

1. In a nonreactive or stainless steel heavy-bottomed saucepot, heat the melted butter with ¼ cup water and the corn syrup.

2. Add the granulated sugar and cook until the sugar dissolves and the mixture turns a light brown caramel color and forms a soft ball, 240°F on a candy thermometer.

3. Add the cream, vanilla paste, salt, and bourbon. Stir well and cook for another 10 minutes to make a smooth sauce.

Chef Seidel's Tips

"The filling is very easy to put together and requires no cooking before baking the pie except toasting the nuts and melting the butter. It should be made first and refrigerated so you are ready to make the pie as soon as the dough comes out of the freezer."

"In the restaurant we use a half hotel pan to make the pie. For the home cook, I recommend using a 10-inch deep dish pie plate because pecan pies have a tendency to overflow in a regular 9-inch pie plate."

Apple Chess Pie

EVAN KLEIMAN [Angeli Caffé, *Los Angeles, California*]

TRADITIONAL, COMFORTING, AND ICONIC, IT'S AS AMERICAN AS
apple pie! Who better to give us this recipe than Evan Kleiman, host of KCRW's weekly *Good Food* radio show, and creator of the annual Good Food Pie Contest? The contest grew out of Kleiman's self-imposed Pie-A-Day challenge, in which she experimented, practiced, and perfected her pie-making proficiency every day from summer through Thanksgiving. As chef-owner of Angeli Caffé since 1984, author of six cookbooks, and founder of the Slow Food chapter in Los Angeles, Kleiman is a culinary multitasker to the nth degree. Any free time Kleiman does have (usually during the early hours) is spent doing what she calls "pie tinkering," rolling out dough and researching what to fill it with.

"I wanted to make an apple pie that was old-fashioned and comforting," says Kleiman, "but something beyond my default classic apple pie. So I started thinking about combining sweet, tender apples with a custard. But I didn't want to use a milk- or cream-based custard so I turned to the old super-homey classic, the Chess Pie, which is basically a sugar-butter custard."

Chess pies are part of a rich sweet Southern baking tradition. Recipes call for a pie crust filled with a mixture of eggs, butter, and sugar. No one is certain where the name comes from although it doesn't seem to have anything to do with the game, perhaps an old English derivation of the word cheese, the phrase "just pie," from the English place-name Chester, or perhaps a piece of furniture called a pie chest common in the early South.

In this single crust pie the apples are put into Kleiman's flexible 3-2-1 Ratio Pie Dough (3 parts flour, 2 parts fat, and 1 part liquid), covered tightly with aluminum foil, and baked with just a hint of sugar and no thickener until they soften. A chess pie filling is then poured over the apples, binding all the free juices into a delicate, buttery custard with the slight lift of lemon and an earthy touch of corn.

> *Chess Pie.* — Beat the *yolks* of *three eggs* until light and thick; add *half a cup* of fine *granulated sugar*, and beat again; add *one third* of a *cup* of *butter* rubbed to a cream, and *half a teaspoonful* of *vanilla*. Bake on a plate lined and bordered with puff paste. When done, cover with the *whites* of *three eggs* beaten stiff, and mixed with *half a cup* of *powdered sugar* and *one teaspoonful* of *lemon juice.* Brown slightly, and cut while hot, but serve cold.

A recipe for "Chess Pie" from Mrs. Lincoln's Boston Cook Book *by Mrs. Mary J. Lincoln, published in 1884.*

Apple Chess Pie

Evan Kleiman's apple pie has it all—the sweetness of the fruit cooked in sugar, the creaminess of the custard with just a hint of cinnamon, and the crunchiness of a perfect flaky crust. There's something about baking this pie that is deeply satisfying. Nothing can be hurried; it has a slower rhythm that simply makes one feel good.

3-2-1 Ratio Pie Dough

2 cups all-purpose flour

1 pinch of salt

1 cup fat, such as unsalted butter, lard, vegetable shortening, or solidified coconut oil

1/4 teaspoon freshly squeezed lemon juice

1/2 cup cold water

Makes two 8- to 9-inch pie crusts or one 8- to 9-inch double pie crust

Pie Filling

5 to 6 sweet juicy apples, such as Golden Delicious or Fuji, peeled, cored, and sliced into 3/8-inch slices (not too thick)

1 tablespoon all-purpose flour

2 tablespoons brown sugar

Pinch of salt

3 large eggs

1/2 cup granulated sugar

8 tablespoons (1 stick) melted, unsalted butter

2 tablespoons freshly squeezed lemon juice

1 tablespoon fine corn flour

Pinch of ground cinnamon

MAKES ONE 8- TO 9-INCH PIE

To Make the Pie Dough

1. Mix the flour and salt together in bowl. Work the fat into the flour, using your fingertips or a pastry blender. Cut the fat in until most of the dough looks like crumbs the size of peas but some of the fat is still in bigger clumps about the size of shelled almonds.

2. Add the lemon juice to the 1/2 cup water. Add the lemon-water mixture to the dough one tablespoon at a time, using a fork to mix. When the dough holds together, you have added enough water. Give a couple of quick gentle kneads to hold the dough together. Divide the dough into two equal-size disks, wrap each disk with plastic wrap, and set them in the refrigerator to rest, preferably for at least 1 hour.

3. Before you start rolling out the dough, be sure you've cleared off your work surface; you will need room to move. To roll a single piecrust, remove one of the disks of dough from the refrigerator, reserving the second disk for another use. Place dough on the work surface that has been lightly dusted with flour. Dust your rolling pin, too, but not too much. Gently rap the dough disk several times across the surface with the rolling pin to make it thinner and easier to roll out. Flip the thick dough disk over, lightly dust it with flour again, and, again, rap the dough with the pin, this time in the opposite direction. Now you're ready to roll.

4. As you roll, remember not to press down directly on the dough. Think of rolling the dough away from you. Always start rolling from the middle of the dough outward, giving the dough a little quarter-turn after each couple of passes. Then flip the dough over and once again roll from the middle outwards, giving the dough a quarter-turn each time. Lightly dust the pin, the counter, and the dough with additional flour as needed. When the dough circle is a couple of inches larger than your pie pan, you're ready to move the dough from the counter to the pan.

5. Gently fold the dough in half, and in one movement lift it off the rolling surface and into the pie pan. Unfold the dough circle and gently ease it into the pie pan; do not stretch the dough. When it heats up in baking, it will bounce back. If there is excess dough hanging over the lip of the pie pan, simply fold the dough under so that the rim of the pan supports it. You can then either crimp the edge with the tines of a fork or flute the edge with your fingers.

5. Refrigerate or freeze piecrust for 1 hour.

To Make the Pie

1. Preheat the oven to 375°F.

2. Remove the piecrust from refrigerator or freezer. Mix the sliced apples with the brown sugar and arrange them in the cold crust. Cover the pie, including the fluted edge, tightly with aluminum foil. Place in oven and bake for 30 to 40 minutes, or until the apples are just tender when pierced with a knife.

3. While the pie is baking, make the chess pie custard. Whisk the eggs, sugar, melted butter, lemon juice, corn flour, and cinnamon together until well blended.

4. When the apples are done, remove the foil. Don't be scared by the amount of juice you may see, the custard will bind the juice. Pour the custard over the apples using a knife to help the custard fill the gaps.

5. Return the pie to the oven, uncovered. Bake until the custard is set, the top is dotted with deep golden brown spots, and the crust is done, 15 to 20 minutes. Serve warm or chilled.

Index

Acknowledgments

A BOOK SUCH AS THIS INEVITABLY MEANS THAT enormous debts of gratitude—far greater than space allows—are owed for support, advice, encouragement and expertise. At the risk of leaving someone out I want to say a special thank you to the following people for their invaluable contributions:

My loving husband, Didier. You are the inspiration for everything I do and I am more than grateful that you brought me to America, your loving support made this happen. Minty and Rémy, my two little Americans, for your patience, sophisticated palates and never-ending enthusiasm. Jean-Jacques Rachou, I will treasure the times we spent together in my kitchen cooking these recipes. You are a legendary chef and a genius at the stove and I am lucky to have you as my father-in-law. Mummy, Daddy, and my entire family, those near and far, for all the wonderful food memories we have shared over the years. You are all a part of this book. In loving memory of my late grandmother, Doreen Lean, whose style and grace I miss and try to emulate every day.

Joe Bastianich, you opened so many doors for me across the country, vouched for me and helped me reach the stars. I value our friendship immensely. Anneli McLachlan, for your sage advice, keen eye for detail, quick wit and wicked sense of humor. Julie Kremkus for your photography lessons and design suggestions, this book looks the way it does in large part because of you. Geraldine McGinty and John Greally for the exceptionally stylish NYC board and lodging—hope I never overstay my welcome. Margot Tenenbaum, Ali Tenenbaum, Pamela Levine, Cindy Capobianco, and Pam Berger for filling in the gaps at our breakfast meetings in paradise. The Mother Forkers, I love you all for the laughter, *in vino veritas* and the dinners—I guess I'll be cooking omelets! Caroline and Roland Orzabal, there will always be a Rosé Corner. Julia Short and Ian Ford-Batey for the word wizardry. Miles and Charlotte Millar for the weekly dose of sanity on the court. My colleagues from the online food community for your help with everything from cameras to food styling, recipe testing to photos, you all inspire me daily: Matt Armendariz, Elise Bauer, Brooke Burton, Diane Cu, Lucy Dahl, Gaby Dalkin, Jaden Hair, Adam Pearson, Todd Porter, Michael Procopio, Jo Stougaard, Marla Meredith, Susan Salzman, Amy Scattergood, Carrie Vitt, and Bumble Ward. Deborah Trainer (pies brought us together and continue to deepen our friendship), Ellen Rose, Joan McNamara, and all the Spoons, you all make me want to be a better cook. Anne Willan for talking old recipes over tea and "chocolate sausage" in your pretty kitchen. Karen Beverlin my produce guru, for your encyclopedic knowledge. Lisa Lucas for your legal expertise and diligent guidance. Aeron Wilson at STA Travel for arranging my extensive and impossible itinerary. Shane McCoy Fermelia, you found *How to Cook in Los Angeles* (1894) in the Doheny Library—little did we know back then that it would lead to this.

My publisher Lena Tabori for believing in me and to everyone at Welcome Books, in particular Gregory Wakabayashi for your stunning design and my editor Katrina Fried (who never sleeps), my great-uncle, the film director David Lean talked about editing his best shots for the benefit of the movie, so thank you for working around the clock editing 'my best shots'.

All the chef's assistants, wives, GMs, photographers, and PR people who made things happen behind the scenes and who efficiently helped me meet with 100 plus chefs around the country and then followed up with recipes, answers, and good cheer.

Lastly, and most importantly, the talented chefs across America who welcomed me into your kitchens, shared food and techniques and then trusted me with your recipes. You all embraced this book with such generosity of spirit, particularly those of you who developed recipes from the early cookbooks—thank you for making this book so much better than I ever dreamed of and for making America taste so delicious!

With love and heartfelt gratitude to all of you.

—Lucy Lean